CRAVEN COUNTY COURT OF PLEAS AND QUARTER SESSIONS

MARCH 1792 TO MARCH 1795

TRANSCRIBED BY VICTOR T. JONES, JR.

MAPLE BRANCH PUBLISHING
ERNUL, NC
2017

INTRODUCTION

The Court of Pleas and Quarter Sessions in North Carolina was more than just a place for litigants to sue each other for wrongs done or for criminals to stand trial for murder, assault, theft, or other crimes against the state. Indeed, the court transacted all sorts of business for the county. The justices heard petitions to build roads, bridges, ferries, and mills, and appointed overseers to make sure the roads and bridges were kept passable. They appointed guardians and apprenticeships to children who were orphans. They appointed Executors and Administrators to estates of the deceased. They manumitted slaves upon petition of their master. They approved tavern keepers and set prices for fares at those taverns and inns. They set the annual tax rate and appointed collectors to collect the tax. They also appointed many of the county officers, including the Sheriff (until elected by the popular vote in the mid-1800s). Those and many other acts can be found in the minutes of the court.

This transcription contains the minutes of Craven County Court of Pleas and Quarter Sessions from March 1792 until March 1795. I have used the microfilmed version of the court records, as the originals are in the State Archives in Raleigh. From 1978 to 2006, Weynette Parks Haun transcribed available Craven County Court records from 1712 to 1791. Her nine volumes are the building blocks to this volume, which continues where she stopped due to her death.

While transcribing, handwriting is sometimes hard to interpret, words like Daniel and David look similar and may be transcribed one way one time and the other the next. I have tried to be consistent in interpreting names. Ink blots, poor microfilming, or other problems may make some words illegible. If I could determine what the word should have been, I have entered that word in brackets [ ] or underlined portions of words with missing letters (i.e. _no. or S__te). If the word was stricken in the original, it is stricken in the transcript. Words that were troublesome, I spelled as I saw it and placed a question mark in brackets [?] to indicate that is my best guess at the word.

While the index contains an every name index by last name, it also includes the names of women by their first name. So, women are indexed twice: once by their last name and once by their first; however, they are interfiled in the main index and not separated into their own index. Some place names are also included, check under Branch, Creek, Road, River, and County for those entries.

Victor T. Jones, Jr.
February 16, 2017

1792
[page] 17   March 1792
At a County Court of Pleas & Quarter Sessions begun and held for the County of Craven at the Court House in Newbern, on the second Monday of March being the 12th day of the Month in the 16th year of our Independence A.Dom. 1792.

Present the Worshipfull, Joseph Leech, John Tillman, Levi Dawson, Jno. F. Smith} Esquires.

The Court being opened in due form _no. Bryan Esqr. Sheriff of Craven County returned the Venire for Jurors duly summoned to attend this Court in these Words "Executed in part."

Ordered that George Ellis be appointed Administrator ___ the Estate of Richard Ellis Esqr. upon his Qualifying _nd entering into Bond of £5000- with John Devereux __d Richd. D. Spaight Esqr his Securities. Whereupon the said George Ellis Qualified & rendered an Inventory of said Estate & Entered into Bond accordingly.

The last Will & Testament of Joseph James decd. _as proved by the Oath of Joseph James one of ___ Subscribing Witnesses thereto and at the same ___e Mary James the Executrix therein Named _ppeared in Court & Qualified as such and _lso rendered An Inventory of said Estate.

18   March 1792

1

Ordered that John Carpenter be appointed administrator of the Estate of George Carpenter decd. upon his entering into Bond in the Sum of £500- with Isaac Hollis & Levi Dawson Esqr his Security. Letters issd.

John C. Bryan Esqr. is appointed ~~Constable~~ Sheriff of Craven County for the present year upon his entering into Bond with John Tillman & Levi Dawson Esqr. his security. Whereupon the said Jno C. Bryan appeared in Court & Qualified & entered into Bond agreeable to Law.

Ordered that the Defaulting Jurors be fined Nisi in the sum of forty shillings each. Afterwards the fines cancelled.

Read the Petition of Levi Dawson & Aaron Ernull praying leave to Build a Public Water Grist Mill on Little Swifts Creek, where they own Land on Both sides. Ordered that the prayer of said Petition be granted.

An Acct. Sales of the Estate of Wm Wood Decd was returned by the Sheriff & filed.

An Inventory of the Estate of Saml Sparrow decd was returned by the Admr & filed.

Ordered that the Petition fil'd in this Court by Abner Nash for a Filial portion be heard on Friday next.

19—Sarah Sparrow Appeared in Court and Resigned the Administration of the Estate of Saml. Sparrow decd Whereupon the Court appointed Samuel Sparrow son of said decd Administrator Debonis Non c/. __ said Estate upon his Qualifying and entering into bond of £1000- with Charles Williams & Henry Tillman Esqr his Security.

Ordered that Richard Nixon & William Slade be appointed Administrators of the Estate of Silas Sears Stevenson decd upon their Qualifying & entering into Bond of £5000- with William B. Fonvielle & William Henry their Securities.

Ordered that Stephen Whitehead Dun be bound to Jno. Whitehead to learn the Coopers Trade aged 8 years the 29th Jany last. (Indentures Signed)

Ordered that Sarah Sparrow be appointed Guardian _f Joseph & Elizabeth Sparrow, Orphans of Samuel Sparrow decd upon her entering into Bond in the sum of £200 for each Child with Benj. Brinson & Samuel Sparrow her Securities.

Read a Commission from His Excellency Alexr. Martin __qr. appointing William Tisdale, William McClure, William __enry, Southey Rew, Charles McLin, John Sears, John Dawson Esqr Justices of the Peace for __aven County. Whereupon Wm. Henry Esqr appeared in Court & Qualified agreeable to Law.

20 — The last Will & Testament of Barre Neale de__ was proved in Open Court by the Oath of Jess_ Bryan one of the Subscribing Witnesses thereto agreeable to Law. & Mathew Neale Qualified as Exe__ thereto. Ordered that Letters Testamentary Issue.

Acct. Sales of the Estate of Samuel Sparrow decd. was returned by the Sheriff & filed.

A Settlement of the Accounts of William Surles Administrator of the Estate of John Griffin decd. was returned by the Auditors appointed to Settle the same which was approved of by the Court & ordered to be filed.

Abraham Warren is henceforth discharged from attending as a Juror & Working on the Roads by reason of his Infirmities. Isd.

William Holland is appointed Guardian of William Roe & Thomas Roe Orphans of Thos. Roe decd upon his entering into Bond of £250 each with Levi Fulsher & Mathew Stevens his Securities.

Ordered that John Knox & James Davis Jurors at this Term be find ~~ten~~ twenty shillings each. Fined for their non attendance & neglect of this Court (fine Remitted.)

Adjourned till 3oClock this afternoon.

50/ paid
Mrs. Heath renewed her Tavern License.

21 — Met Pursuant to adjournment. Present the Worshipfull John Tillman, Levi Dawson, Richd Nixon, John Allen, Henry Tillman} Esquires

Then were the following Gentlemen Sworn on the Grand Jury, To Wit:
Frederick Foy (foreman) John Arthur William Whitford 4. Joseph Willis 5. Lewis Bryan 6. Joseph Palmer 7. John Nelson 8. Jonathan Perkins 9. Abraham Warren 10. Francis McIlwean 11. John Gatlin 12. Zachah. Dubberly 13. Lewis Jones John Barrington Constable

_he last Will & Testament of Alexander ~~Bigg~~ Biggam decd. was proved in Open Court by the Oaths of Leonard Cutting & David Prindle two of the Subscribing Witnesses thereto and Ordered to be Recorded.

_n Inventory of the Estate of William Rountree decd. was returned on Oath by Jno. Sears Executor.

John Sears Esquire appeared in Court and Qualified by taking the Oath of Allegiance & also the Oath of a Justice of the peace as prescribed by Law.

Adjourned till tomorrow m___ 10 oClock.

22 — Tuesday March 13, 1792

Met Pursuant to Adjournment. Present the Worshipfull John Tillman, John Allen, Henry Tillman, Wm. Henry} Esquires.

Read the Petition of Aaron Ernul praying leave to Build a public Water Grist Mill on the North side of Neuse River on a Branch of Little Swifts Creek called James Swamp, he being the proprietor of the Lands on Both side said Stream. Ordered that the pray__ of said Petition be granted. Dr. Is.

An Account Sales of the Estate of Ann Lambert decd was returned & filed.

The last Will & Testament of Duryvault De St Ledger was proved by the Oath of James Little a subscribing Witness thereto and at the same time Francis X. Martin one of the Executors therein named Appeared in Court & Qualified agreeable to Law. __n Charged.

The last Will & Testament of Briscoe Davis Decd was proved in Open Court by the oath of Moses Spivey a subscribing Witness thereto and at the same time Lawson Davis one of the Exrs therein named appeared & Qualified agreeable to Law & also rendered an Inventory of said Estate.

23 — Ordered that Thomas Turner have letters of administration upon the Estate of Wright Stanly decd upon his entering into Bond of £10000, with Jno C. Bryan and John Tillman Esqr his Securities. The Widow of said decd having resigned her right of administration to said Turner.

__n on the demise of Joseph Allen vs. __chd Fen & Thomas Fish} Ejct.
The following Jury empanelled & sworn, viz:
1. Walter Jones 2. James Gatlin 3. William Moore 4. William Cox 5. Britain King} Jury of Vissi 6. Jno. Knox 7. James Davis 8. John Clark 9. James Wilson 10. Ignatitus Wadsworth 11. William Dunn 12. Jno Green} Original Panel.
Juror withdrawn. Cause contd. for Trial next Term

__port Inventory of the Estate of Thos. Gaston __cd was returned by the Admr on Oath.

__dered that Lawson Davis Exr of Briscoe Davis decd sell at Public Vendue the Perishable property of said decd agreeable to Law.

24 — No. 8 Richard D. Spaight vs. Sarah Burney Exx Wm. Burne decd. discon tort} Debt. The following Jurors empanelled & sworn, viz.
1. John Knox 2. James Davis (J.P. Ives) 3. John Clark 4. James Wilson 5. Joseph Allen 6. William Dunn 7. Ignatius Wadsworth 8. Jacob Johnston Jun. 9. Herman Gaskins 10. Isaac Kemp 11. John Green (Th. Fish) 12. Britain King Find for the Plaintiff £20.13.8 & Costs.

The last Will & Testament of Thomas Phillips decd. was proved in Open Court by the Oath of George Oxley one of the Subscribing Witnesses thereto & ordered to be Recorded and at the same time James Philips one of the Executors therein named appeared & Qualified agreeable to Law Ordered that Letters Testamentary Issue accordingly.

Farnifold Green Guardn of Ann Greaves vs. William Davis Exr James Davis} Debt
The same Jury as in the last Cause except ~~Thomas~~ Jno. P. Ives & Thomas Fish in the room of James Davis and John Green empanelled & Sworn find the Writing obligatory is the Act & Deed of the Defen__ and assess £22.4- Dam. & 6d Costs. Appeal prayed & Granted Nathan Smith & James Davis Security.

25 — Ordered that James Gatlin & Charles W. Means [?] be apponted to Audit the Account of Nathaniel Street Admr of Arthur Arnold decd & Report thereon to this term.

_o. 12. _m. McClure assignee Thos. Kelly vs. Hardy Hewkins} Case. The following Jury empanelled & sworn, viz.
1. Jno Knox   2. Jno. West   3. Jno Clark   4. James Wilson
5. Joseph Allen 6. William Dun 7. Ignatius Wadsworth
8. Jacob Johnston Junr. 9. Herman Gaskins 10. Isaac Kemp
11. Thos. Fish   12. Britain King
find the Defendd. did assume & assess £47..4 & 6d Costs.

_o. 13 Nathan Smith vs. Joseph Leech} Case. The same Jury as in last cause empanelled & sworn find the Defendt. did assume & Assess £28..5 Dam & 6d Costs.

Read the Petition of John West and Joseph Phipps _raying leave to Build a public Water Grist Mill __ Poplar Branch in Craven County seting forth __y are proprietors of the Land on the south side of _aid Stream and that John Spyers & John Bryan __e the Owners of Land on the other side of said Stream __dered that Notice Issue to John Bryan & John Spyers to appear before the next Court &c.

26 – Ordered that Thomas Hall aged fourteen years be bound apprentice to Isaac Barrington to learn the Coopers Trade.

Ordered that Robert Hall aged twelve years be bound to Amos Cutrell to learn the Coopers Trade.

Ordered that Robert Heartly aged eighteen years the 7th January last be bound to Amos Cutrel to learn the Wheelrights Trade.

Ordered that Isaac Barrington be appointed Guardian of Thomas Hall a minor upon their entering into Bond of £50 with Levi Dawson his security.

Ordered that Amos Cutrel be appointed Guardian of Robert Hall a minor upon their entering into Bond of £50 with Levi Dawson his security.

Ordered that Isaac Barrington, Amos Cutrel & Charles Williams be appointed to settle the Accounts of Levi Dawson & Thomas Hall Executors of Thomas Hall Sen decd. and Report thereon to the next Court.

No. 14 Leonard Cutting vs. Trustees of Newbern Accademy} Case. The same Jury as in the last Cause except Thomas Yo__ in the room of John West empanelled & sworn find Defendants did assume & assess £373.4.3 ½ & 6d Costs.

27 — William McClure Esqr. appeared in Court & Qualified _s a Justice of the peace by taking the Oaths prescribed _y Law.

Ordered that Isaac Reed a Wounded Soldier at the Battle of Alamance be allowed the sum of Twenty Pounds to be paid him out of the County Tax.

Insolvents allowed Jacob Johnston Junr. for the Year 1790 in District No 2. 1510 Acres of Land and 11 Poles.

__dered that Levi Dawson, Samuel Smyth, Moses Ernul & James Gatlin, be appointed _or any three of them) to settle & Divide the Estate of Thomas Gaskins decd and make a Return to the next Court.

____ last Will & Testament of Hezekiah McCotter _as proved in Open Court by the Oath of Elijah __al and at the same time Archibald McCotter _ualified as an Executor to the same. John _illman Esqr also Qualified as an Executor to the same.

Adjourned till tomorrow Morning 9 oClock.

___nesday March 14th 1792. Met Pursuant to adjournment. Present the Worshipfull John Tillman, James Gatlin, Francis Lowthorp, William Henry} Esqr.

28 — Joseph Allen & Ignatius Wadsworth are fined twenty shillings each for Neglect attending this Court as Jurors this morning. Wadsworth's fine remitted also Joseph Allen's.

Ordered that James Probart be bound apprentice to John Dewey to learn the House Carpenters Trade. Aged 13 years 28 Feby last. Dr. Indr. made out.

William P. Moore vs. William McClure Exr. of John Green jr decd.} Case. Plene adminis trabit
The following Jury empanelled & Sworn viz:
1. John ~~Clark~~ Knox 2. Thomas York 3. John Clark 4. James Wilson 5. William Dun 6. Jacob Johnston Jun. 7. Ignatius Wadsworth 8. Robert Hunt 9. Thomas Parsons 10. Thomas Curtis 11. Mathew Neale 12. William Good
Find the Defendants Testator did Assume & assess Two hundred & fifty five pounds Dam & 6d Costs and that the Executor has fully administered and hath no assetts in his Hands.

No. 21. George McFarlane vs. Benjamin Shepard} Case. The same Jury as in the last cause empanelled & Sworn find no Cause of action.

29 — An Account of Sale of the Estate of Thomas Gaskins _ecd. was returned by the Sheriff & filed.

The Referees appointed to settle the accounts of Nathaniel Streets Admr. of Arthur Arnold decd. ~~was~~ made a Report thereon which was approved of by the Court & ordered with the Accounts to be filed.

__22. Abner Neale vs. __seph Clark} Trespass. The same Jury as in the last Cause except Joseph Allen in the room of John Clark, empanelled & Sworn find the Defendant Guilty & assess twenty shillings Damage & 6d Costs.

__arles McLinn Esqr. appeared in Court and Qualified as _ Justice of the Peace, by taking the Oath of Allegiance __d the Oath of a Justice as prescribed by Law also __ Oath of Allegiance to the United States and __k his seat upon the Bench.

__dered that Asa Bryan aged Nineteen years __ 9th day of April next be bound to Thomas _liver to learn to House Carpenters Trade.

Richard Hunley renewed his Tavern license. _aid.

30 — Ordered Susannah Pearce be appointed Guardian of Mary and Ephraim Pearce minors — orphans of Ephraim Pearce decd. upon her entering into bond of £500 with James Gatlin & Thomas Willis her securities.

On the Petition of Philip Knowis for a mill on Broad Creek. Levi Dawson, Charles Williams, James Gatlin and William Speight were appointed to Value & appraise one Acre of Land upon each side of said Stream — returnd that they have Valued the same at Twenty shilling ℘ acre Whereupon Benjamin Williams Esqr. paid the said sum of twenty shillings in Open Court to the Clerk agreeable to Law.

Read the Petition of Frederik Lane praying leave to reBuild a Water Grist Mill across flat Swamp where Ephraim Lane the father of said Frederick formerly built a Mill — setting forth that he owned the Land upon the one side of said Stream Which was Objected to by James McCafferty. Ordered that a Sci Fa: Issue &c. (Issued Dr.)

Adjourned till 4 oClock.

Met pursuant to Adjournment. Present the Worshipful John Tillman, James Gatlin, Jno. F. Smith, Francis Lowthorp} Esquires.

31 – Ordered that Richard D. Spaight, John Haywood and William Shepard be appointed to audit the Accounts of John Green Executor of Richard Cogdell decd. and make report to this Term.

__ motion of Wm. Surles – Ordered that a Citation Issue to John Bedscot Senr. Guardian of the Orphans of David Purify that _e appear before the next Court and Settle his Accounts of said Guardianship. (Issued)

__hn Bryant produced his petition for building a water grist mill __ poplar Branch which was read and continued til next term.

__aac Covington of age to choose a Guardian appeared __ Court and make Choice of John Fell for his Guardian _hich choice was approved of by the Court upon __ said John Fell entering into Bond of £1500--_ith Thomas Speight & Henry Tillman his Secry. (Bond taken.)

A Settlement and Division of John Ives' Estate was returned by the Referees and ordered to be filed.

__lliam McClure Exr. __o Green Jun. decd. vs. ___coit Hilbert} Case. The following Jury empanelled & Sworn, viz:
1. John Knox   2. John Clark   3. Thomas York 4. James Wilson 5. William Dunn 6. Jacob Johnston Jun. 7. Ignatius Wadsworth 8. Robert Hunt 9. Thomas Parsons 10. Thomas Curtis 11. Mathew Neale 12. William Good
____ the Defendant did assume & assess £27..12 & 6d Costs.

32 – No. 29. Thomas Haslin Exr. of Bartho. Rooke vs. Mary Heath Exx. of William Heath} Debt. The same Jury as in the last Cause empanelled & Sworn find ~~no Cause of Action~~ the Bond has been paid.

Isaac Covington aged ~~aged~~ Seventeen years is bound to John Fell to learn the Coopers Trade. Indenr. made out}

Then were the following Gentlemen appointed to Attend as Jurors at the next Term vizt.
1. George Ellis 2. John Kennedy 3. Stephen Tinker 4. Joseph Oliver 5. Thomas Oliver 6. Robert Hunt 7. William Hawley 8. James McCafferty 9. William Good 10. John Devereux 11. James Stewart 12. James Coor 13. Enoch Alexander 14. Constantin Whitfield 15. John Holloway 16. John Green Senr. 17. John Cox 18. Joseph Masters 19. Philip Neale 20. George Lovick 21. William Lovick 22. John Moore 23. David Lewis 24. John Smith 25. William Searls 26. William Gaskins 27. Joseph Gaskins 28. Thomas Speight 29. Benjamin Brinson 30. William Dixon 31. Richard Hickman 32. Joseph Clark 33. Benjamin Foscue 34. Joseph Franklin 35. Evan Swann 36. William Anthony 37. James Little. (Venire Issued)

Adjourned till Tomorrow Morng. 9 oClock.

33 — Thursday, March 15th, 1792. Met Pursuant to Adjournment. Present the Worshipful John Allen, John F. Smith, William Henry} Esquires.

__hn Ince vs. __ph Crispin} Case. The following Jury empanelled & Sworn viz:
No. 1. John Knox 2. Thomas York 3. John Clark 4. William Dunn 5. Jacob Johnston, Jun. 6. Ignatius Wadsworth 7. Joseph Allen 8. John Gatlin 9. William Shine 10. Joseph West 11. John Sheffield 12. Robert Hunt One of the Jurors failing to Answer, Mistrial.

__dered that William Fulsher aged fifteen years the _8th September last be bound to Archibald McCallap __learn the Taylors Trade for five years only.

__dered that James McCallap aged fourteen years __ bound to Archd. McCallap to learn the Taylors Trade.

___ persons appointed to lay off the Right of Dower __ Elizabeth West Widow of James West decd. in said __d Estate Have Reported their proceedings thereon _hich is Ordered to be Recorded.

34 – No. 35. Thomas Haslin Exr. Barth. Rooke vs. David Witherspoon Adm. Debonis Non of the Estate of Abner Nash} On argument of a plea in Abatement to the Disability of the plaintiff the Court overruled the plea aforesaid, with Whitch Determination the Defendants being dissatisfied craved an Appeal and filed his Reasons &c Which was granted upon his Entering into Bond of £100 with William Slade ~~John~~ and Thomas Hall Esqr. his Securities for prosecuting said appeal. Bond signed & Reasons filed.

No. 37 John C. Bryan vs. George Emmerson} Default & Enqy.
The following Jury empanelled & Sworn
No. 1 James Wilson 2. Joseph Carraway 3. Thomas Oliver 4. William Good 5. Joseph Gaskins 6. Joseph Crespin 7. Thomas Parsons 8. James Sandy 9. Joseph Oliver 10. John Biggs   11. Joseph Franklin 12. Isaac Hollis
find the Defendant Guilty & assess 1d Dam & 6d Costs.

No. 40. James McKinlay & Benja. Williams vs. Robert Hunt}
Case. Contd.
~~The same Jury as in the last cause empanelled & Sworn.~~

14

No. 44. Nathan Smith vs. } Case. The same Jury as in last Cause empanelled & Sworn find the Defend. Did assume & assess £245..4..8 Dam. & 6d Costs.

35 — Ordered, that a Citation Issue to Jonathan Perkins, Edmund Perkins & Joseph West Guardians of the Orphans of James Perkins decd. that they appear before the next Court and Settle their Accounts of said Guardianship.

No. 45. Petery Henrion vs. ~~Lewis Hero~~ Charles McLin Admr. Thomas McLin, who was bail for Lewis Hero} Sci Facias to Issue to Nicholas A. Bray.

No. 46. William Good Exr. William Wood decd. vs. Wm. Tooley & Charles Sanders} Debt. The following Jury empanelled & Sworn, viz.
1. John Knox   2. Thomas York 3. John Clark   4. Wm. Dun 5. Jacob Johnston Jun 6. Ignatius Wadsworth 7. Joseph Allen 8. John Sheffield 9. William Shine 10. Joseph Shute 11. George Lovick 12. Jeremiah Parsons find the Writing Obligatory in the Act & Deed of the Defendant and Assess £2.9.9. Dam & 6d. Costs.

John Bedscot has permission to Keep a public House at Clarks ferry he entering into Bond with Thomas Oliver & John Sheffield his Security. __ paid.

36 — No. 65. Fredk. Foy admr. John Foy vs. William Good Exr. William Wood} Sci Fa to venire Isud. The same Jury as in No. 46 empanelled & Sworn find the Money has been paid.

No. 69. Nathan Smith vs. Rachel Hackburn} Sci Fa to venire Judgement. The same Jury as in the last Cause except Robert Hunt in the room of John Knox empanelled & Sworn find there is a Record of Judgment obtained by the Plaintiff against the Defendt. for the sum of £12.16.6 & £ [blank] - costs.

Joseph Gaskins vs. Stephen Hill} Replevin. The same Jury as in the last Cause empanelled & Sworn. Verdict for the Avonant. £10 Dam & 6d Costs.

Ordered that a Citation Issue to John Koone to appear tomorrow Morning & shew Cause why an Orphan Lad named Zadok Rumley should not be taken from him and bound out to some other. Isd.

Adjourned till tomorrow Morng. 9 oClock.

37 – _riday March 10, 1792. Met Pursuant to adjournment.
Present the Worshipful
John Tillman, Jacob Johnston, Henry Tillman, John Sears}

An Inventory and Account of Sales of the Estate of Alexander McAuslan decd. was returned & filed.

An Inventory and Account of Sales of the Estate of Dennis Heron was returnd & filed.

Read the Petition of Benjamin Williams Esqr. praying leave to build a Public Water Grist Mill upon the south side of Upper Broad Creek where he is the Proprietor of the Land on one side and that the Heirs of Simon Edwards are the owners of Land on the Opposite side of said Stream. Ordered that James Gatlin Esqr. Joseph West, Daniel West & William Speight be appointed to lay of and Value one acre of Land, upon both sides of said Stream and make a return thereof to the next Court agreeable to Law & that a Citation Issue to John Isler Executor or Admr. of the Estate of Simon Edwards decd. that he appear at the next Court to shew Cause &ccc. &c. (Summons Issued)

John Koon appeared according to summons to answer the Complaint of Neglecting the tuition of his apprentice Zadock Rumly. The Court having heard the Allegations of the parties, Ordered the Complaint be dismissed.

[Blank Page]

[Blank Page]

38 — The last Will & Testament of Charles Marshall Decd. was proved in Open Court by the Oath of Thomas Worth, one of the subscribing Witnesses there__ & at the same time William Phipps the Executor there__ Named appeared in Court & Qualified agreeable to Law Ordered that Letters Testamentary Issue accordingly.

Dr. 50/ George Talcot renewed his Tavern License.

No. 30. Francis Delamar & Wife vs. Executors John Nelson decd.} Petition. On hearing the Petition and Answer the Court Decreed that the sum of £51.16.0 is due to the plantiffs [sic].

On the Petition of Benjamin Griffin praying to have the Courses of a Tract of Land granted to John Taylor the 18 Novr. in the year 1738 altered agreeable to Act of Assembly. Ordered that John Taylor who owns Land adjoining thereto be notified to attend at the Next Court & shew Cause &c. (Dr. Issued)

No. 56. Abner Nash vs. David Witherspoon Admr. De bonis non of the Estate Abner Nash decd.} Petition for Legacy. Continued for further Argument.

39 — Ordered that John Collins aged twelve years be bound to the Marquis De Bretigny to learn the Trade of a Baker.

Adjourned 'till tomorrow Morng. 8 oClock.

Saturday, March 17th, 1792. Met Pursuant to adjournment. Present the Worshipful John Tillman, Jacob Johnston, James Gatlin, Francis Lowthorp, Hardy Gatlin

Ordered that William Phipps be appointed Guardian of Elizabeth, Seaney, Suckey, & Hollen Marshall, Orphans of Charles Marshall decd. upon his entering into Bond of £500 for each, with James Gatlin & Hardy Gatlin his Securities.

Christiana Powdrill [Pondrill?] renewed her Tavern License __ entering into Bond with F. Lowthorp Esqr. her Security.

It being Represented to this Court that Colo. Benjamin Williams has a Negro Infected with small pox. Ordered that the Commissioner of the Town of Newbern be empowered to remove said Negroe or any other person Infected with said Disorder to some remote and convenient place in order to prevent the Spreading of said Disorder.

40 — Present, John Tillman, James Gatlin, Joseph Johnston Junr., John Allen, John F. Smith, Francis Lowthorp, Henry Tillman, William McClure, John Sears, Hardy Gatlin, Richd. D. Spaight} Esquires.

The Court proceeded to appoint an Inspector at Swifts Creek Bridge, When Jacob Johnston Senr. was appointed upon his Qualifying and entering into Bond with Jacob Johnston junr. & Jno. C. Bryan his Securities (Bond taken)

Ordered that Samuel Chapman, F. Lowthrop & James Ellis Assessors of [--?--] property for the year 1791 be allowed 40/ each. (all issued)

Leonard Cutting vs. Trustees of Newbern Academy.} The Defendants being dissatisfied with the Judgment of the Court in the above cause have prayed for an appeal which is granted upon their filing Reasons & entering into Bond with John F. Smith & John Allen Isaac Guion their Securities.

Ordered that George Ellis Admr. of Richard Ellis Decd. sell at public vendue the perishable part of said Estate agreeable to Law.

41 — State vs. Mathew Clift} Indt. Petit Larceny} The following Jury empanelled & Sworn.   1. John Clark   2. James Wilson   3. Jacob Johnston jr. 4. Joseph Allen 5. Ignatius Wadsworth 6. William Dun 7. George Lovick 8. James Clark   9. Benja. Lancaster 10. William Buxton
11. Levin Dickenson W.I. 12. William Hawley find the Defendant not Guilty.

Read the Petition of John Smallwood, setting forth that he is proprietor of Land on the East side of Duck Creek near the Mouth which place is very convenient for Building a Public Water Grist Mill, and that Joseph Leech Esqr. owns the Land on the opposite side of the Stream. Ordered that the Petition be filed, and a Citation Issue to Joseph Leech, Esqr. to appear at the next court & shew Cause &c.

State vs. Stephen Williams} Indt. Assault & Battery. The same Jury as in the last Cause except William Johnston in the room of Levin Dickinson empanelled Sworn find the Defendant Guilty of an assault.

42—State vs. Stephen Williams} Indt. Assault & Battery. Levin Dickenson pres.
The same Jury as in the last Cause empanelled & Sworn find the defendant not Guilty.

Ordered that James Gatlin, John Harris and Levi Dawson be appointed to Divide the Lands of Thomas Gaskins decd. between William Gaskins, Herman Gaskins, Fisher Gaskins & Levi Gaskins, Heirs of said Decd. Isd.

Ordered that Mary Boon aged twelve Years be bound to William Hawley untill she arrive to the age of eighteen years. Inds. made out.

Whereas the Bonds for the Guardianship of Wm. Slade & Wm. Mitchell for the Heirs of Yelverton Probart when not signed at September December Term. Ordered that the said William Slade & William Mitchell enter into Bond of Six Hundred Pounds for each Orphan with John C. Bryan & William Johnston their Securities.

Ordered that Francis X. Martin Executor of Duryva__ De St. Ledger sell at public vendue the perishable part of said Deced. Estate agreeable to Law.

Ordered that Thomas Turner Admr. of Wright Stanly Decd. sell at public vendue the perishable part of said Decd. Esta. agreeable to Law.

43 – Ordered that Richard Nixon & William Slade admr. of the _state of Silas S. Stevenson [?] decd. sell at public Vendue the perishable part of said Decd. agreeable to Law.
J. Tillman
Richd. Dobbs Spaight
H. Tillman
F. Lowthorp
[End of March 1792 Term]
[June 1792]
44 – At a County Court of Pleas and Quarter Sessions begun and held for the County of Craven at the Court in Newbern on the second Monday of June, being the __ day of the Month in the year of our Lord, one thousan_ seven hundred and ninety two and in the 16th year of American Independence.

Present the Worshipfull John Tillman, John F. Smith, William Henry, Henry Tillman} Esquires.

Saml. Chapman C.C.

John C. Bryan Esqr. Sheriff of Craven County returned the Writ of Venire for Jurors to this Term. Executed. Viz.
1. Geo. Ellis   GJ2. __Kennedy   Sea 3. Stephen Tinker
x4. Joseph Oliver   GJ5. Thomas Oliver   GJ6. Robert Hunt

GJ7. Wm. Hawley   8. James McCafferty, Newbern GJ9. Wm.
Good absent 10. Jno. Devereux 11. James Stewart   x12. James
Coor GJ13. Enoch Alexander x14. Constantin Whitfield x15.
Jno Holloway GJ16. John Green senr. x17. John Cox   x18.
Joseph Masters 19. Philip Neale x GJ20. Geo. Lovick GJ21.
Wm. Lovick 22. John Moore GJ23. David Lewis   24. Jno.
Smith excused 25. William Surles x
26. William Gaskins x   GJ27. Joseph Gaskin   28. Thos.
Speight GJ29. Benja. Brinson   30. William Dixon   31.
Richard Hickman 32 Joseph Clark excused 33. Benja. Foscue
x   34. Joseph Franklin 35. Evan Swann   36. William
Anthony   GJ37. James Little

Pd. 10/ Enoch Alexander renewed his Tavern License.
10/ pd. William Gibbs renewed his Tavern License.
10/ pd. James McCafferty renewed his Tavern License.

45 — Read the Petition of Henry Tillman & Charles [--?--]
praying leave to Build a public Water Grist Mill upon Goose
Creek near the lower Bridge where they own Lands upon both
sides. Ordered that the prayer of said Petition be granted.

Thomas Marshall has permission to keep Tavern for one year
upon his entering into Bond of £100 with P. Henrion his
security. Issd.

Thomas Haslen Exr. of Bartho. Rooke vs. Thomas Turner Exr.
of Jno W. Stanly decd.} Plea in abatement that Barta. Rooke
appointed other Executors in his last Will To wit John Haslen
J.L.C. Van Baerle & Thos. Cumming who ought to be named
in the said Writ. On argument ordered that the suit be
dismissed.

Adjourned till 9 oClock tomorrow morning.

June 12, 1792. Met pursuant to adjournment. Present the Worshipful John Tillman, Joshua Fulsher, Isaac Bryan, Francs. Lowthorp, Jno. F. Smith, Thos. A Green, Wm. Henrey} Esqs.

An Inventory of the Estate of Hezekiah McCotter decd. was returned by Jno. Tillman Esqr.

Ordered that Letters of Administration be granted to William McClure upon the Estate of Edward Potter decd. upon his entering into Bond of £100 with Geo. Ellis & Francis Lowthorp Securities. The Widow of said decd. having resigned her right.

46 – Then were the following grand Jurors Sworn To wit:
1. William Good, foreman 2. Benja. Brinson 3. John Kennedy
4. William Hawley 5. John Green   6. George Lovick 7. David Lewis 8. Thomas Oliver 9. William Lovick 10. Joseph Gaskins 11. Enoch Alexander
12. Robert Hunt 13. James Little John Barrington, Cons__

Ordered that Mrs. Patsey Gainer have Letters of Administration upon the Estate of her Decd. Husband Wm Gainer up__ her Qualifying and entering into Bond of £1000 with Stephen West and John West her Securities (Bond Taken)

An Account Sales of the Estate of Richard Ellis decd. was returned by the Sheriff & filed.

An Account Sales of the Estate of William Wallace decd. was returned by the Sheriff & filed.

An Inventory of the Estate of Barre Neale decd. was returned on Oath by the Executor & filed.

No. 3 James McMains vs. Mary Stevens} Case. The following Jury empanelled & Sworn. 1. James Coor   2. Thos. Speight 3. Geo. Ellis 4. Jas. McCafferty 5. James Stewart 6. William Anthony 7. John Moore 8. Evan Swann 9. James McCafferty (Swifts Creek) 10. James Wilson 11. Moses Griffin 12. Jeremiah Parsons find for the Plaintiff and assess his Damages at £30 & 6d Costs.

47 — Mons. [blank] Fabre has permission to keep a Public House of intertainment in Newbern for one year upon his entering into Bond of £100 with Isaac Guion his security.

Ordered that William Good, William Lawrence & Richd. Hunley be appointed to audit the Accounts of John Clarke Guardian of John Outerbridge and report thereon at this or the next Term.

Then was the following Gentlemen appointed to attend as Jurors at the next Superior Court, To wit,

1. John F. Smith 2. Stephen W. Dunn 3. William Henry 4. William Cox 5. Francis Lowthorp 6. Thomas A. Green 7. Jesse Bryan   8. George Ellis 9. Richard Hunley

Then were the Ordinary Keepers rated as follows, To wit,
Breakfast.... „2- Dinner... „2.8 Supper... „2-
Lodging... „ „ 8 Do. If two in a Bed... „ „ 6
West India Rum ℘Gill or good Brandy... „1-
Continental Rum or Taffea ℘half Pint... „1-
Toddy made of good W.I. Rum or Brandy with loaf Sugar
Quart} „6-   Madeira, Port, Lisbon or Claret Wines ℘Quart
in Bottle} „10-   Fial or Mountain Wines ℘bottle in
Quart... „6- Cyder ℘Quart... „1-
Ale or Porter ℘Bottle or Quart... „3-
Corn ℘Quart... „ „ 4

Stablage of a Horse every 24 Hours with good Hay or Corn Blades} „ 2,8 Pasturage ℗ day or Night... „ „ 6

48 — Then were the following Gentlemen appointed to receive lists of Taxables in Craven County for the year 1792. Viz.
John Sears Esqr.   Capt. Phillips District
Isaac Bryan Esqr.   Capt. Cox's do.
William Henry Esqr.   Capt. Thomas A. Green's do.
John Fonvielle Esqr.   Capt. Lewis' do.
William McClure Esqr. Newbern district
Adam Tooley Esqr.   Capt. Dunn's do.
~~John Carney~~ Southy Rew Esqr. Capt. Masters do.
John Allen Esqr.   Capt. Jones do.
Hardy Gatlin Esqr.   Capt. Bryans do.
James Gatlin Esqr.   Capt. Ernulls do.
Henry Tillman Esqr.   Capt. Tillmans do.
Levi Dawson Esqr.   ~~Joseph David~~ Danl. Wests do.
Joshua Fulsher Esqr.   Capt. Wests do.
Joshua Fulsher Esqr.   Capt. Delamars do.

Edmund Perkins Guardian of the Orphans of James Perkins decd. appeared according to Summons and rendered an account of his Guardianship which was approved of by the Court and ordered to be Recorded.

Ordered that David Witherspoon Esqr. keep a Public Ferry at his Plantation upon Trent where he now lives and that he provide sufficient Boats &c. and take for every Man & Horse one shilling, for every Wheel one shilling, for a single passenger six pence.

Dr. 10/ Joseph Oliver renewed his Tavern License.

David Lewis is appointed patroller in in [sic] his district for the present year.

50—Ordered that [--?--] shillings for 5 days attendance upon this Court at Septem. Term and that the County Treasurer pay the same.

Edward Tinker has permission to keep Tavern for one years. Fr. Lowthorp Security. 10/ __n }year.

Adjourned till tomorrow Morng. 9 oClock.

June 13, 1792. Met Pursuant to adjournment. Present the Worshipful John Carney, William M. Herritage, ~~James Carney~~, ~~Isaac Bryan~~, Isaac Guion} Esquires.

William Tisdale Esqr. appeared in Court and Qualified by taking the Oath of a Justice of Peace for the County of Craven, also the State Oath and the United States and took his seat upon the Bench.

William Blackledge, Esqr. produced a license from the Honle. Judges of the Superior Court empowering him to plead & practice Law in the several County Courts of this State. Whereupon the said William Blackledge Qualified by taking the Oaths appointed by Law and was admitted accordingly.

Southy Rew Esqr. appeared in Court and Qualified by taking the Oath of a Justice of Peace for the County of Craven, also the Oath of Allegiance to the United States & this State and took his seat upon the Bench.

Ordered that Enoch, a Base Born Childe of Lurana Lewis a free Negro Woman, be put under the Care & maintainance of Peter Blosson his reputed Father

50 — till he is Sufficient age to be bound out by the Court. The said Peter Blosson entering into Bond of £50 £100 with Abner Nash & John Harris his Securities (Bond taken.)

On motion of B. Woods on behalf of Thomas McDaniel Ordered that Frederick Clements be cited to appear tomorrow & shew cause why James Ryal who was bound to him by this Court should not be discharged from his said Indentures. Issd.

The last Will & Testament of Alexander Biggam decd. having been proved at the last Term, John Miller one of the Executors therein named appeared in Court and Qualified agreeable to Law. Ordered that Letters Testamentary Issue accordingly.

John Carney, William M. Heritage, Isaac Guion, Francis Lowthorp, Southey Rew, Richard D. Spaight} Esquires upon the Bench.

On motion of William Slade Esqr. Ordered that Letters of Administration be granted to James Carney upon the Estate of Charles McLin decd. upon his Qualifying and entering into Bond of £10,000 with Richard D. Spaight & John C. Bryan Esqrs. Whereupon the said James Carney appeared in Court & Qualified and entered into Bond accordingly. Bond taken.

An Inventory and Account of Sales of the Estate of Wright Stanly decd. was returned & filed.

Ordered that James Carney Admr. Charles McLin decd. have permission to sell the perishable part of said Deceas'ds Estate agreeable to Law. Isd.

51 — Frederick Devoux appeared in Court and took the Oath of Allegiance to the State of No.Carolina.

William Davis vs. Thomas Davis} Atta. Default & Enquiry.
The following Jury empanelled & Sworn. 1. James McCafferty
2. James Stewart 3. James Coor
4. Geo. Ellis 5. John Moore   6. Thos. Spaight 7. William
Anthony 8. James McCafferty 9. William Buxton 10. Jno.
Smallwood 11. Robt. Hatfield 12. Jesse Bryan assess the
Plaintiffs Damages at £93.18.6 & 6d Costs.

Titus Ogden admr. of Thos. Ogden vs. John Starkey }Case. The
same Jury as in the last Cause empanelled & Sworn ~~To Wit~~
find the Defendant did assume & assess £198.0.6 Damage and
6d Costs. Appeal by defendant prayed & allowed upon filing
reasons & entering into ~~Bond of~~ Bond with ~~John~~ William
Bryan & David Witherspoon his secuys. Bond taken.

Then was the Grand Jury discharged. Adjourned until 4
oClock this afternoon.

Met Pursuant to Adjournment. Present the Worshipful
Richard D. Spaight, Isaac Guion, Francis Lowthorp} Esqrs.

No. 11. John Green Exr. of David Barron vs. Ann C.
Biggleston} Indl. Alla. Debt non claim within 7 years. The
following Jury empanelled & Sworn viz.
1. James McCafferty (Newbern) 2. Jas. Stewart   3. Geo. Ellis
4. Jno. Moore   5. Thos. Spight 6. Wm. Anthony 7. James
Coor 8. Jas. McCafferty 9. William Buxton 10. Jno.
Smallwood 11. Frederick Foy 12. Jesse Bryan find there has
been a Demand within seven years and they

52 — then find the Writing Obligatory to be the Act and Deed
of Defendt. Testator and assess £55.6.10 Dam. Judgment for
£84.9.3 Principal together with £56.6.10 Damages.

Francis Lowthorp is appointed Guardian of Benjamin Almand a minor upon his entering into Bond of £200 with Abner Nash & [blank]

Read the Petition of Elizabeth Potter praying to have her right of Dower layed of in the Lands of her Deceased Husband Edward Potter agreeable to Law. Ordered that the Sheriff be directed to Summon ~~twelve men~~ [illegible stricken out] ~~with the parties~~ the Heirs of Edward Potter to [illegible stricken out] appear ~~the presence for some time between them and~~ the next term and ~~lay off and allot to the said~~ shew cause &c why the Widow should not have her thirds in the said Lands & Tenaments agreeable __ the prayer of said Petition [illegible stricken out] (Summons issued)

A further account of Sales of the Estate of Alexander McAuslan decd was returned & filed.

Adjourned till tomorrow morning 9 oClock.

Thursday June 14th 1792. Met Pursuant to adjournment. Present the Worshipful Richard D. Spaight, William M. Herritage, William McClure, Isaac Guion, F. Lowthorp} Esquire

Ordered that Ann Durand have Letters of Administration upon the Estate of Samuel Glover decd. upon her Qualifying & entering into Bond of £50 with Jno. C. Bryan her Security (Bond taken)

53 — Ordered that Jane Worthy have letters of administration upon the Estate of her decd. husband John Worthy upon her entering into Bond of £50 with Jno. C. Bryan her Security (Bond taken)

__15. John Starkey vs. John Charles} Detinue. The following
Jury empanelled & Sworn viz. 1. James McCafferty (Newbern)
2. James Stewart 3. James Coor
4. John Moore 5. Thos. Speight 6. William Anthony 7. James
McCafferty 8. George Ellis 9. William Bryan 10. William
Buxton 11. Jacob Cooke 12. William Davis find the
Defendant does not detain the Negro in Question. Appeal
prayed & allowed upon the Plaintiff's filing reasons &
entering into Bond of £100 with Bazell Smith & William Davis
his securities.

A Division of the Estate of Levin Covington decd. was
returned by the Referees appointed in June Term last to divide
the same which was approved of by the Court & ordered to be
filed. Bond taken.

John Dawson Esqr. appeared in Court and Qualified by taking
the Oath of a Justice of the Peace also the Oath of Allegiance to
this State & that of the United States and took his seat upon
the Bench.

__22. Titus Ogden Admr. Thos. Ogden vs. Robert Hunt} Case.
The same Jury as in the last Cause empanelled & Sworn find
the defendant did assume & assess £32.6.4 & 6d Costs.

_23. James McKinlay & Benja. Williams vs. Robert Hunt} Case.
The same Jury as in the last Cause empanelled & Sworn find
the Defendant did assume and assess the Plffs. Damages at
£424.7.6½ & 6d Costs the defendt. prayed an Appeal to the
next Superior Court which was granted upon his Atto. filing
Reasons & entering into Bond with [blank]
__tiff remits £75.2.0½.

54 — A Settlement of the Account of William Surles, James Rowe, & Ephraim Pearce Guardians of the Orphans of the Orphans of David Purify decd. was returned by the Referees appointed to settle the same (at December Term 17__) which was approved of by the Court & Ordered to be f__

Adjourned till 4oClock this afternoon.

Met Pursuant to Adjournment. Present the Worshipful Wm. M. Herritage, Isaac Guion, Wm. McClure} Esqrs.

Then were the following Gentlemen appointed to attend at the next Court as Jurors vizt.
No. 1. Joseph Oliver 2. John Devereux 3. Joseph Masters Capt. 4. Philip Neale 5. William Surles 6. William Gaskins 7. William Dixon 8. Richard Hickman
9. Benja. Foscue 10. Joseph Allen 11. Thos. Fish 12. Saml. Branton 13. Thos. Phillips 14. Frederick Lane 15. Nathan Tisdale 16. Jesse Bryan 17. John Porter 18. Andw. Richardson 19. Thomas Nelson 20. Francis Carraway 21. Benjamin Williams 22. John Freebody 23. Thos. Curtis 24. Jacob Johnston junr. 25. Sacker Dubberly 26. Thos. G. Fonvielle 27. Jeremiah Parsons 28. Frederick Foy
29. William Shepard 30. Nathan Smith 31. Jonathan Perkins 32. Saml. Lawson 33. Joseph Crispen 34. Roger Jones junr. 35. James Davis 36. James Hollis

Ordered that John Symmes aged Eleven years be bound to Francis X. Martin to learn the Printers Trade. Dr.

55 — No. 91. Joseph West & Wife vs. __ Guardns. of James Perkins decd.} Petition. Judgt. Pro confesso. Decreed that the Guardians of Margerat, James, Hardy, Church, Aggy & Anna Perkins pay to the Complainants the sum of £45 in equal proportions and that the Guardians of Margerat, James, Hardy & Church Perkins pay the Complainants the sum of £7.10 equal shares and the Interest amountint to £15.15 to be paid by the Guardians of all the Orphans & Costs of suit.

Adjourned 'till tomorrow morng. 9 oClock.
June 15, 1792. Met Pursuant to adjournment. Present the Worshipful Isaac Guion, William Henry, Wm. McClure, Jno. F. Smith} Esquires.

Ecekiel Dela Statius renewed his Tavern License.

Abner Nash vs. David Witherspoon Admr. &c Abner Nash decd.} Petition for Legacy. On hearing the Arguments offered to the Court in this Cause Ordered that the Petition be dismissed at the Plantiffs Cost. The Petitioner being dissatisfied with the Judgment of the Court prayed an Appeal to the next Superior Court of Law to be held for the District of Newbern on the 19th Septemr. next which was granted upon his filing reasons and entering into Bond in the sum of £100 — with William Henry & James McCafferty securities (Bond taken).

56 — A Settlement of the Accounts of John Clark Guard__ of John Outerbridge was returned by the Referees appointed to Audit the same which was appro__ of the Court and Ordered to be filed.

Adjourned 'till 4 oClock this Afternoon.

Met Pursuant to adjournment. Present the Worshipfull
William M. Herritage, John F. Smith, William Henry} Esqrs.

Henry Livingston has Permission to keep a Public House of
entertainment in Newbern upon his entering into Bond of
£100 with Wm. Hannis his Security. 10/ pd. Dr.

Ordered that Charles Williams be appointed Guardian of John
Outerbridge a Minor (in the Room of John Clark who has
resigned his Guardianship) upon his entering into Bond of
£500 with John Clark & Edmund Perkins his securities.

No. 88. Reuben Fairfield vs. Geo. Ellis Admr. of Richard Ellis
decd.} Appeal by Defendt. The following Jury empanelled &
Sworn No. 1. Wm. Anthony 2. James Coor
3. John Moore 4. James McCafferty 5. Thomas Cox 6. John
Clark 7. John Smallwood 8. Edmund Perkins 9. Andw.
Richardson 10. Thomas Hyman 11. William Bryan 12. Jas.
McCafferty. One of the Jurors failing to answer, Mistrial [--?--]

57 — Wm. M. Herritage, Wm. Henry, John Sears} Esqrs. upon
the Bench.

No. 31. John Green and Sydney McAuslan vs. Obadiah
Allways} Appeal by Defendant. Dismissed.

James McCafferty vs. Jeremiah Redding} Appeal by Plantiff.
The same Jury as in the last Cause except George Ellis in the
room of James McCafferty (of Newbern) empanelled & Sworn
find the Defendt. did assume & assess the Plantiffs Dams. @
£14.4. & 6d Costs.

John McGraw vs. Joseph West} Appeal by Defendt. The following Jury empanelled & Sworn. 1. Wm. Anthony 2. James Coor 3. John Moore 4. James McCafferty (Newbern) 5. John Clark 6. John Smallwood 7. Edmund Perkins 8. Andw. Richardson 9. Thos. Hyman 10. William Bryan 11. William Buxton 12. Geo. Ellis assess Plffs. Damages @ 17/ & 6d Costs.

John Harvey vs. James McCafferty} Appeal by Defendant. The same Jury as in the last Cause empanelled & Sworn Assess the Plffs. Dam. at £12.6. & 6d Costs.

58 – Ordered that Thomas Hyman be appointed administrator Debonis non upon the Estate of Peter Franklin decd. he entering into Bond of £1500 with ___ McClure & George Ellis his securities.

Ordered that Thomas Hyman be appointed Administrator upon the Estate of Joseph Franklin decd. (the Widow of said decd. having resigned her right to him) upon his entering into Bond of £1600 – with Wm. McClure & George Ellis his Securities.

Ordered that Thomas Hyman Admr. of the Estate of ~~Peter F.~~ Joseph Franklin sell at Public Vendue the perishable part of said Estate agreeable to Law. Isd.

Adjourn'd till tomorrow morng. 9 oClock.

Saturday June 16th 1792. Met Pursuant to adjournment. Present the Worshipfull William M. Herritage, Francis Lowthorp, Wm. McClure } Esqr.

An Inventory of the Estate of Charles Marshall decd. was returned by William Phipps the administer. & filed.

Ordered that Charles Hardy aged fifteen years the 17 day of August next be bound to Thomas Cox to be the House Carpenters Trade. Inds. Isd.

59 — Ordered that James Clark have Letters of Administration upon the Estate of Robert Callihan decd. upon his Qualifying and entering into Bond of £50 with John Allen & Wm. Bryan his securities.

State vs. Peter Burke} Indt. Assault upon [blank] Lane. The following Jury empanelled & sworn, To wit:
1. Wm. Anthony 2. James Coor   3. James McCafferty (Newbern) 4. Benja. Williams 5. James McCafferty (S. Creek) 6. Fredk. Foy 7. James Clark   8. William Burton 9. John S. West 10. Thos. Webber 11. Robert Hunt 12. Benja. Sparrow. find the Defendant ~~Guilty of an assault upon the 28th day of May 1792~~ not Guilty in manner & form as laid in the Indictment.

Peter Gerone has renewed his Tavern license upon his entering into bond of £100 with Wm. Good his security. Isd. 10/-

Ordered that Poll the Daughter of Prudence Brown aged seven years in May last be bound to William Hannis untill she attains the age of Eighteen years. Inds. made out.

Thomas L. Cheek is appointed Guardian of Elizabeth Wrenford agreeable to Act of Assembly to defend the Acct. of William Moore against the Heirs of John Green Jr. decd. also the suit of Mary Wrenford against the Heirs of John Green jr. decd.

State vs. Michl. Venters} Indict. Petit Larceny. The same Jury as in the last Cause empanelled & Sworn find the Defendt. not Guilty.

60 — No. 32. James Coor vs. Samuel Smyth} Case. The same Jury as in the last cause except Wm. Bryan in the room of James Coor empanelled & Sworn — find the defendt. did assume and assess £24.16. Dam & 6d Costs.

~~Orderd that Francis Conner have letters of administration upon the Estate of his decd. mother Elizabeth Ferrell decd. upon his entering into Bond of £200 with James McCafferty~~

Ordered that Abraham Inloes and Francis Lowthorp have Letters of Administration upon the Estate of Anthony Inloes Deceased upon them entering into Bond in the sum of £500 with Abner Nash, William McClure and William Ross their securities. James Ellis Esqr. having also applied for Letters of Administration upon the said Estate being dissatisfied with the determination of the said Court prayed an appeal to the next Superior Court which was granted upon his Atto. Filing reasons and he entering into bond of £[blank] with [blank]

Ordered that Letters Ad Colegeendum Pendent elite issue to Abraham Inloes & Francis Lowthorp and that they have permission to sell the perishable part __ said Estate at Public Vendue for six months Credit.

Is. Guion, J.P.; Jno. F. Smith, J.P.; W. McClure, J.P.

[September 1792]

61 — At a County Court of Pleas & Quarter Sessions begun & held for the County of Craven at the Court House in Newbern on the second Monday of September being the 10th day of the Month in the 17th year of our Independence A.D. 1792. Present the Worshipful John Tillman, Joshua Fulsher, Francis Lowthorp, Wm. Tisdale} Esquires.

John C. Bryan, Esqr. Sheriff of Craven County returned the Writ of Venire for Jurors duly summoned to attend this Court in these Words "Executed."

An Inventory and acct. Sales of the Estate of Silas S. Stevenson was returned on Oath by William Slade one of the Administ. & ordered to be filed.

An Inventory and Account Sales of the Estate of Thos. Collier decd. was returned on Oath by William Slade one of the Admrs. & ordered to be filed.

An Inventory ~~and Account Sales~~ of the Estate of Joseph Franklin decd. was returned by the Admr. on Oath and filed.

An Inventory of the Estate of Peter Franklin decd. was returned by the Admr. & filed.

Then was John Whitford Junr. Peter Reel, Fisher Gaskins & Levi Reel appointed Patrollers in Capt. Ernulls Dist. [??illegible line cut off??]

62 — The last Will & Testament of William Biggs decd. proved by the oath of Benjamin Mahains one of the Subscribing Evidences thereto and at the same time William Biggs one of the Executors therein Names appeared in Court & Qualified agreeable to Law.

Ordered that Peg. Blango aged ten years be bound to David Whitford untill the age of 18 years. Inds. Isd.

The last Will & Testament of James Horsends decd. was proved by the oath of Tamar Harrington one of the subscribing Witnesses thereto and at the same time Joseph Brinson one of the Executors therein named appeared in Court and Qualified agreeable to Law.

Ordered that Thomas Willis be appointed Guardian of Sarah, Edward, Martha, _____, Elizabeth & Thomas Willis Orphans of Joseph Willis decd. upon his entering into Bond of Five hundred pounds with Moses Ernull & James Hollis his Securities. Bond taken.

Ordered that Thomas Hyman be appointed Guardian of John Franklin & Joseph Franklin Orphans of Peter Franklin decd. upon his entering into Bond of £1600 with John Dawson & Jesse Bryan his Securities. (Bond taken)

Ordered that Samuel Hoover be appointed Admin__ to the Estate of Hezekiah Hollis upon his entering into Bond of £300 with Joshua Fulsher & Joseph Brinson his securities. (Bond taken)

63 — Ordered that James W. Stanly have letters of Administration taken upon the Estate of Benjamin Warner decd. upon his entering into Bond of £100 with James Hollis & John Freebody his Securities.

Ordered that Samuel Hover Admr. of Hezekiah Hollis have leave to sell the perishable part of said Estate.

An Account of Sales of the Estate of Jos. Franklin decd. was returned & filed.

Ordered that Joseph Brinson Executor of James Horsends have leave to sell the perishable part of said Estate.

Ordered that Richard Barrington be appointed Guardian of Levi Gaskins & Celia Gaskins upon his Entering into Bond of £500 with William Speight & James Hollis his Securities. (Bond taken)

On Application of Elizabeth Holten Complaining that Harrell Holten her Son bound an Apprentice to Robert Hatfield to learn the Art of a Tanner is ill used & neglected in his Cloathing, diet & instruction. Ordered that the said Robert Hatfield shew Cause tomorrow Morning Wherefore the said Indentures should not be Vacated and the said Holten taken from him.

Ordered that Francis Lowthorp & James Carney be appointed to audit the Accounts of William Slade Administrator of the Estate of Thos. Collier [?] decd.

Adjourned till 4 oClock.

64 — Met Pursuant to adjournment. Present the Worshipful John Tillman, John Carney, Joshua Fulsher, Southy Rew} Esqrs.

The last Will & Testament of Wright Stanly decd. was proved in open court by the Oath of Grisham Hagood one of the Subscribing Witnesses thereto and Ordered to be Recorded.

Mathew Stevens vs. John Whitehead} Upon an Execution issued by Spyers Singleton Esqr. directing Thos. Smith to Levey of the Estate of John Whitehead to satisfy a Judgment Obtained by Mathew Stevens for the sum of £15..17..0. Which said Execution was returned by the said Thomas Smith Constable in these Words "for want of Personal Property have levied this Execution on 280 Acres of Land on South West side of Brices Creek, said to be the property of John Whitehead this 7th Augt. 1792." Ordered that a Write of Vende. Exponas issue accordingly. (Vende. Exponas issued.)

Ordered that Southy Rew, John Carney & Francis Lowthorp be appointed to audit the Accounts of Thomas Collier with the Orphans of George Clark decd. and report thereon to this Court. Issd.

A Settlement of the Account of John Bedscott Guardn. of David, Mary & Edward Purifoy was returned & approved by the Court & ordered to be filed.

65 — Ordered that William Hanson have permission to keep Tavern for One year, he entering into Bond with Abner Nash his Security. Issd.

Adjourned till tomorrow Morning 9 oClock.

Thursday 11th Sept. 1792. Met Pursuant to adjournment. Present the Worshipful John Tillman, John Carney, Francis Lowthorp } Esqrs.

Hardy Gatlin Esqr., Charles Johnston, & William Smith are appointed patrollers in Capt. John Bryan's District.

An Account of Sales of the Estate of Ephraim Pearce decd. was returned by the Administratrix.

Ordered that John Daw have administration upon the Estate of Hugh Tingle upon his entering into Bond of £50 with James Daw & Philip Knowis his Securitys. Ordered that the said John Daw have permission to sell the perishable part of said Estate.

The last Will & Testament of William Jordan decd. was proved in Open Court by the Oath of Joel Patrick Jr. and ordered to be Recorded.

An Inventory of the Estate of William Garner decd. was returned by the Adminr.

Ordered that ~~Frederick Lane~~, Nathan Tisdale, Thos. G. Fonville, ~~Fredk. Foy~~, & ~~Arthur Smyth~~ defaulting Jurors at this Term be fined Five Pounds.

66 – An Instrument of Writing purporting to be the last Will & Testament of Wright Stanly decd. having ___ produced to this Court yesterday and admitted ___ probate & suggested to have been illegally proved. Ordered that the ~~said~~ Order respecting the same which was entered upon the minutes be Rescinded.

3. Wm. M. Herritage vs. Thos. Wilson} Case. The following Jury impannelled & chargd.
1. Joseph Masters 2. Willm. Gaskins 3. Richd. Hickman 4. Benja. Foscue 5. Thos. Fish ~~6. Jesse Bryan~~ 6. Joseph Crispin 7. John Porter 8. Andrew Richardson 9. John Freebody 10. Thos. Curtis 11. Zacher Dubberly 12. Roger Jones Junr. find the defendant did not assume. Appeal prayed by Plffs. granted on filing Reasons & entering into Bond of £100 with Fredk. Lane & Jno. Gooding Secys.

No. 7. Thomas Turner survng. Partner of Jno. W. Stanly decd. vs. John Green admr. of James Green Junr. Decd.} Case. The same Jury as in the last Cause empanelled & Sworn, find the Defendants Intestate did assume & that he assumed Within three years and asses the plaintiffs damage at twenty eight pounds ten shillings & three pence & 6d Costs.

A Settlement of the Accounts of Thomas Nelson Exr. of John Nelson decd. was returned & Ordered to be filed.

Adjourned till 2 oClock.

67 — Met Pursuant to adjournment. Present the Worshipful Joshua Fulsher, Jno. F. Smith, Francis Lowthorp, Hardy Gatlin, William Henry, John Sears } Esqrs.

No. 13. Benja Brady Exr. John Warwick vs. Thomas Hyman admr. Joseph Franklin} Case. The following Jury empanelled & Sworn viz. No. 1 Joseph Oliver
2. Joseph Masters 3. Philip Neale   4. Wm. Surles   5. William Gaskins 6. Richard Hickman 7. Benja. Foscue 8. Thomas Fish 9. Jesse Bryan 10. John Porter 11. Andw. Richardson   12. John Fr___ Plantiff called Non pros.

Daniel West, James West, & John Wise is appointed Patrollers in Capt. Wm. Cox's District from the County line to Moselys Creek. Issd.

Daniel Lane, Thomas Tyre, & Peter Pervatt is appointed Patrollers from Moselys Creek to the half Moon in Capt. Cox's District.

Titus Ogden Survg. Partner of Thos. & Titus Ogden vs. Robert Hunt} Covenant. The same Jury as in the last Cause empanelled & Sworn find the Defendant has not Broke his Covenant appeal prayed and allowed upon filing Reasons & entering into Bond with Jno. C. Bryan & Saml. Chapman his securities.

68 — On Motion of William Slade Esqr. Ordered that John Fonville, John Gooding, & Richard Nixon appointed to Divide the personal Estate of Silas S. Stevenson that remains unsold in the hands of the Administrators between the Heirs of s__ Deceased. 4/ pd.

Adjourned till tomorrow morning.

Wednesday, Septemr. 12th, 1792. Met Pursuant to Adjournment. James Gatlin, Francis Lowthorp, William Henry, Isaac Guion, Hardy Gatlin, Esqrs. }

Ezekiel Delastatius having given in a Billiard Table for the year 1791 which Table was burnt in the late Fire. Whereupon Ordered that one half of the Tax upon said Table should be Remitted.

No. 18. Christopher Mitchell vs. Jeremiah Parsons} Case. The following Jury empanelled & Sworn (to wit). No. 1 Joseph Oliver 2. Joseph Masters 3. Philip Neale
4. William Surles 5. William Gaskins 6. Richard Hickman 7. Benja. Foscue 8. Thomas Fish 9. Jesse Bryan 10. Joseph Allen 11. Frederick Lane 12. John Porter find the Defendant did not assume.

Hardy Gatlin Esqr. returned his list of Taxable propery in Capt. Jno. Bryan's District for the year 1792.

69—Ann Biggleston vs. Edward Tinker} Repn. The following
Jury empanelled & Sworn. No. 1 Andw. Richardson 2. Jno.
Freebody 3. Thos. Curtis
4. Zacker Dubberly 5. Jonathan Perkins 6. Joseph Crispin 7.
Roger Jones Junr. 8. James Hollis 9. Jeremiah Parsons 10.
Lawson Davis 11. Walter Allen 12. Thomas Parsons find for
the Avonant Edward Tinker £24 & 6d Costs.

No. 20 __d Fen, on demise of Barrington & others vs. ___d
Den & Hillary Parsons} Ejct. The same Jury as in No. 18
empanelled & Sworn find the Defendant Guilty and assess 6d
Dam. & 6d Costs. Appeal prayed & allowed the Defndt. Upon
Jeremiah Parsons Atto. For Hillary Parsons, Samuel Smyth &
Levi Dawson entering into Bond of £100 & his Atto. Filing
reasons agreeable to Law.

John F. Smith Esqr. Guardian of William G. Berry a Minor
appeared in Court and prayed to be discharged from his said
Guardianship. Whereupon Ordered that the said Jno. F. Smith
Esqr. be in future discharged therefrom and Francis
Lowthorp, Richard Hunley and John Sears is appointed to
Audit the Accounts of the said Jno. F. Smith Guardian as
aforesaid and that report be made thereon to this Court.

William G. Berry of Age to choose a Guardian appeared and
made Choice of Samuel Chapman for his Guardian Which
was approved of by the Court upon his entering into Bond of
£2000 with Isaac Guion & Francis Lowthorp his Securities.
Ordered that he take into his possession & Care the Estate of
the said William G. Berry and the same Manage for the Benefit
of said Orphan agreeable to Law.

70—Joshua Fulsher Esqr. returned the lists of Taxable p___ in
Capt. Delamar & Capt. Jos. West's Districts for the year.

Moses Lambert, Thomas Clements & Frederick Lewis ___
appointed Patrollers from the half Moon Swamp to Core
Creek.

Ordered that Wallace Stiron & Thomas Nelson be appointed
to Settle the Accounts of Charity James Admx. Of Dernard
James decd. and make return to the next Court.

Ordered that Robert Brothers be released from the payment of
one poll Tax which he is Charged with in the district of Capt.
Delamar for the year 1791 he being over aged.

A Settlement of the Accounts of Thomas Collier with the
Orphans of George Clarke decd. was returned by the Referees
appointed to Audit the same which was approved of by the
Court and Ordered to be Recorded.

Adjourned till ½ past 3 oClock.

Met Pursuant to Adjournment. Present the Worshipful Jno. F.
Smith, Francis Lowthorp, John Sears} Esqrs.

The last will & Testament of Sarah Sanders decd. was proved
in open court by the oath of Francis Lowthorp Esqr. one of the
Subscribing Witnesses thereto and ordered to be Recorded &
at the same time Thomas Thomlinson the Executor therein
named appeared in Court and Qualified as such accordingly.
Whereupon Ordered that Letters Testamentary with the Will
annexed issue.

71—Ordered that Elizabeth Vail have Letters of
Administration upon the Estate of Elizabeth Sarah Vail decd.
upon her entering into Bond of £1000 with Richard D. Spaight
& David Witherspoon Esqrs. her Securities.

Ordered that Joshua Fulsher, John Biggs & Francis Delamar Senr. be appointed to Settle the ~~Estate~~ Accounts between Joseph Franklin & Wife and the Heirs of James Conway decd. and report thereon to the next Court.

Ordered that Joshua Fulsher, John Biggs & Francis Delamar be appointed to settle the Accounts of Joseph Franklin Admr of Peter Franklin decd. & report thereon to the next Court.

Ordered that Joshua Fulsher, John Biggs & Frans. Delamar be appointed to Divide the Estate of Joseph Franklin decd. between the Widow and his Child.

Ordered that Levi Fulsher be appointed Guardian of Robert Williams Franklin (a minor) he entering into Bond of One thousand Pounds with Jesse Bryan & Joseph ~~Covington~~ Masters his Securities.

Richd. D. Spaight vs. Ann Dorsett} Case. The following Jury empanelled & Sworn.
No. 1. Joseph Oliver 2. Joseph Masters 3. Philip Neale   4. William Surles 5. William Gaskins 6. Richd. Hickman 7. Benja. Foscue 8. Thomas Fish 9. Jesse Bryan   10. Joseph Allen 11. Fredk. Lane 12. John Porter find the Defendt. did assume & assess £22 Dam. & 6d Costs.

72 — No. 28. Jno. Green survg. Executor David Barron decd. vs. Winston Caswell Exr. of Richard Caswell decd. & William Henry & Elizabeth his Wife Exrs. Of John Cooke decd. } Debt. The following Jury empanelled & Sworn To Wit.

No. 1. Andrew Richardson 2. John Fen___ 3. Thomas Curtis
4. Zacker Dubberly 5. Joseph Crispin 6. Roger Jones Junr. 7.
James Hollis 8. John Kennedy 9. Daniel Carthy 10. John
Devereux 11. Levin Dickerson 12. Lovick Jones find the
Writing Obligatory is the Act & Deed of the Defendants
Testators and they further find that the Bond hath been paid
all except One hundred & fifty two pounds fifteen shillings &
seven pence half penny which still remains due and assess the
plantiffs Damage to 6d & 6d Costs.

No. 30. Nathan Smith vs. Executor Duryvault St. Leger decd.}
Case. The same Jury as in the last Cause empanelled & Sworn
find the Dedendants Testator did assume and assess £40..18..8
Dam & 6d Costs.

Adjourned till tomorrow morng. 9 oClock.

Thursday 13th Septemr. 1792. Met pursuant to adjournment.
Present the Worshipful John Tillman, James Gatlin, William
M. Herritage, William Henry} Esquires.

73 — James Gatlin Esqr. returned his List of Taxable property
in Capt. Ernul's District for the year 1792.

No. 25. Den & John P. Williams vs. Fen & William M.
Herritage} Eject. The following Jury empanelled & Sworn To
wit. No. 1. Joseph Masters 2. Philip Neale
3. William Surles 4. Wm. Gaskins 5. Richard Hickman 6.
Benja. Foscue 7. Thomas Fish 8. Joseph Allen 9. Frederick
Lane 10. John Porter 11. Zacker Dubberly 12. Jonathan
Perkins find the defendant Guilty and assess 6d Dam. & 6d
Costs.

Ordered that John Thomas, Thomas Burnes, John Cutrell, James Houston & John Smith are appointed Patrollers in Captain Masters District.

Ordered that David West, John Speight, and Benjamin Brinson are appointed Patrollers in Capt. Daniel West's district.

Ordered that Joseph West, John Hover, and Isaac Hollister are appointed Patrollers in Capt. Joseph West's district.

Francis Rountree vs. William Moore} Debt. The same Jury as in the last Cause empanelled & Sworn find the writing Obilgatory is the Act & Deed of the Defendant & assess £5.5 Dam & 6d Costs. Judgment for £55.5 & 6d Costs.

33. James McCaffert Assignee Benja. Williams vs. Abner Nash} Case. The same Jury as in the last Cause empanelled & Sworn find the Defendt. did not assume was an Infant.

74 — No. 34. Cullen Pollock vs. Jno. B. Herritage} Case. The following Jury empanelled & Sworn To wit. No. 1. Nathan Smith 2. John Gatlin 3. Joseph Oliver 4. James Hollis 5. Roger Jones junr. 6. John Freebody 7. Thomas Curtis 8. Jesse Bryan 9. Andw. Richardson 10. Walter Allen 11. Joseph Crispin 12. James McCafferty Newbern find the defendant did assume & assess £24 Dam & 6d Costs.

Ordered that William M. Herritage have permission to Build a Public Water Grist Mill upon the half Moon Swamp at the place where he formerly had an order and where he owns the Land upon both sides of the Stream a Little below Cooper's Old Mill.

No. 35. Moses Griffin vs. John Kennedy} Case. The same Jury as in No. 25. empanelled & Sworn find the defendant did assume & assess £80..9.7 Dam. & 6d Costs. Appeal prayed & allowed the Defendant upon his Entering into Bond with Sam. Smyth & James Ellis his Securities & his Atty. Filing reasons agreeable to Law.

No. 36. Tobias Cobb vs. Henry P. Haines} Case. The same Jury as in No. 34 except Samuel Smyth & William Hill in the room of Jesse Bryan and James McCafferty empanelled & Sworn find the defendant did assume and assess the Plantiff's Damages at £81..0.0 & 6d Costs. Appeal prayed & allowed with Wm. Henry & Jesse Cobb Securities. Appeal dismissed & Ca Sa issued.

Ordered that the former order of this Term appointing Patrollers in Capt. Ernul's District be rescinded and that Moses Ernul, William Willis and David Pearce & Levi Reel be appointed in their room.

75 — No. 37. William Speight Junr. Vs. Charles Churchill} Ord.Atta. The following Jury empanelled & Sworn To wit: No. 1 Joseph Masters 2. Philip Neale 3. William Gaskins 4. Benja. Foscue 5. Joseph Allen 6. John Porter 7. Zacker Dubberly 8. Jonathan Perkins 9. William Surles 10. James Hollis 11. Jesse Bryan 12. Frederick Lane find the Defendant did assume & assess £75 Dam. & 6d Costs. Appeal prayed by the Plff. Atto. & allowed upon filing reasons & entering into Bond of £100 with Levi Dawson & Wm. Speight Senr. his Securities.

Southy Rew Esqr. returned the list of Taxable property in Capt. Master's District for the year 1792.

No. 43. John Kennedy vs. John Smallwood} Case. The following Jury empanelled & Sworn (To Wit). No. 1. Richard Hickman 2. Thomas Fish 3. Andw. Richardson 4. John Freebody 5. Thomas Curtis 6. Joseph Crispen 7. Roger Jones Junr. 8. Nathan Smith 9. William Hill 10. Willm. Ross 11. Thos. Webber 12. Joseph West. find for the Defendant. Appeal prayed by the Plaintiff upon his Atto. filing Reasons and entering into Bond of £100 with Samuel Smyth & James Ellis Securities.

Ordered that James Gatlen, Samuel Smyth and Charles Williams be appointed to Divide the Estate of Joseph Willis decd. between the Widow of said Deceasd. and the Children of said Deceasd.

Adjourned till tomorrow Morng. 9 oClock.

76 — Friday September 14th 1792. Met Pursuant to Adjournment. Present the Worshipfull John Tillman, James Gatlen, Jonas Bryan, John Sears} Esquires.

Ordered that William Good Exr. of William Wood [?] Decd. be exempt from paying for eight polls which was charged upon the Estate of sd. Decd. through mistake in the list for District No. 1 for the 1791. Issd.

Adam Tooley Esqr. returned his list of Taxable property in Capt. Dun's District for the year 1792.

No. 73. Philip & Hannah Roach vs. Martha Sealey} Appeal by Defend. Judgment of the Justice affirmed.

No. 74. Reuben Fairfield vs. Geo. Ellis admr. Richard Ellis decd.} Appeal by Defendt. The following Jury empanelled & sworn viz. No. 1. Joseph Oliver 2. Joseph Masters

3. Philip Neale   4. William Surles 5. William Gaskins 6. Benja. Foscue 7. Jesse Bryan   8. Fredk. Lane   9. John Porter 10. John Freebody 11. Thos. Curtis 12. Zacker Dubberly find the Defendants [illegible] intestate Richard Ellis did assume and assess £7..14 Dam. & 6d Costs.

77 – Joseph Shute vs. Titus Ogden} Appeal by Plaintiff. The following Jury empanelled & Sworn. To Wit. No. 1. Jonathan Perkins 2. Joseph Crispin 3. Roger Jones junr. 4. James Ellis Hollis 5. Nathan Smith 6. Richard Hickman
7. Andrew Richardson 8. John Kennedy F. Gardner 9. Jesse Lester 10. Thomas Hyman 11. Walter Allen 12. William Tyre find the Defendt. did assume & assess £16.0.0 Dam. & 6d Costs. Motion for new Trial. New Trial granted.

No. 110. Stephen West vs. John Faircloth} Appeal by Defendant. The same Jury as in No. 74 empanelled & Sworn. Plaintiff called Non Pros.

Rigdon Smith Assignee Jas. Williams vs. Nathan Smith} Appeal by Defendt. The same Jury as in No. 74 empanelled & Sworn find the Defendant did assume and assess £15 Dam. & 6d Costs. Motion for New Trial. New Trial Granted.

___al Docket. Francis X. Martin vs. Wm. Ross & Levi Dawson} Appeal by Plaintiff. The Same Jury as in No. 95 except Francis Gardner in the room of John Kennedy empanelled & Sworn find the Defendants did assume & assess the Plaintiff's Damages at £20 & 6d Costs.
find the Defendant did assume & the Plffs. Damages al assess £20 Damage & 6d Costs. ~~Motion for New Trial.~~

_4. ___l Docket. James McCafferty vs. John Harvey} Appeal by Defendant. The same Jury as in No. 74 empanelled & Sworn find the Defendant did assume & assess £7.2.0 Dam & 6d Costs.

78 — Isaac Guion vs. Marquis De Bretigny} Danl. Carthy being summoned ___ Court as Garnishee of the Defendant and having delivered into Court a Schedule of the ___ in his hands and being Sworn declares that the Effects ___ed in the said Schedule is all the Property which ___ hath in his hands or that he know of in the hands of any other person or persons whatsoever. Ordered the Schedule be filed.

Wilson Blount vs. Marquis DeBretigny} Danl. Carthy being Sworn declares he has no property in his hands except what he has given in upon the Attachment of Isaac Guion neither doth he know of any other property in the hands of any person whatsoever.

Ordered Thomas King aged fifteen the 4th June next be bound unto Jonathan Fellows to learn the Trade of a Blacksmith. Inds. Exd.

Adjourned till 4oClock this afternoon. Met Pursuant to adjournment. Present the Worshipful John Tillman, John Carney, Francis Lowthorp} Esqrs.

William Henry Esqr. returned the list of Taxable property in Capt. Thomas A. Green's district for the year 1792.

4/ An Inventory of the Estate of Charles McLin decd. was returned by the Administrator & filed.

79 — Ordered that James Gatlin, Samuel Smyth & Moses Ernul be appointed to settle the Accounts of William Surles Administrator of John Griffin decd.

State vs. James Saunders} Indt. For Misdemeanor in Office. The following Jury empanelled & Sworn. To wit. No. 1. Joseph Oliver. 2. Joseph Masters
3. William Gaskins 4. Jesse Bryan 5. Frederick Lane 6. John Porter 7. Thomas Curtis 8. Joseph Crispin 9. Roger Jones junr. 10. James Hollis 11. Richard Hickman 12. Benja. Foscue find the Defendant Guilty.

An Inventory of the Estate of Edward Potter decd. was returned upon Oath by William McClure Admr. and filed.

An account of the Guardianship of Jonathan Perkins with the Orphans of James Perkins decd. which was Committed ___ his Case was returned and approved of by the Court and filed.

_____ Bryan Esqr. returned his list of Taxa___ ___erty in Capt. Cox's district for the year 179_

No. 72. _harles Smallwood vs. Almand Elsbree} Default & Enquiry. The following Jury empanelled & Sworn No. 1. Joseph Masters 2. William Gaskins 3. Jesse Bryan
4. Frederick Lane 5. John Porter 6. Thos. Curtis 7. Joseph Crispin 8. Roger Jones junr. 9. Roger Jones junr. James Hollis 10. Richd. Hickman 11. Benja. Foscue 12. Andrew Richardson assess the plaintif Damages at £23.12.6 & 6d Costs.

80 — Adjourned till tomorrow morning 9 oClock.

Saturday, 15th September 1792. Met Pursuant to adjournment.

Present the Worshipful Levi Dawson, Isaac Bryan, William
Henry}

Ordered that James Carney have Letters of Administration De
Bonis non upon the Estate of Thomas McLin decd. upon his
Qualifying and entering into Bond of £5000 with John Carney
and Richard Hunley his Securities. (Bond taken.)

Ordered that Henry Persse have permission for his Negro
fellow Moses to Carry a Gun upon his Masters Land he
Complying with the Requirements of the Law.

~~Ordered that Moses Chanse have Letters of Administration
upon the Estate of Henry Harrison upon his entering into
Bond of £200 with William Henry & Frederick Lane his
Securities & Qualifying agreeable to Law~~. Rescinded.

__dered that Philip Neale jr. aged fifteen years the 21st day of
__ly last be bound to Edward Carraway to learn the Trade
_____ Ship wright.

__dered that Philip Neale junr. be kept under the Call &
Guardianship of Philip Neale Senr. upon his entering into
Bond of £500 with John Carney & Levi Dawson Esqr. his
Securities.

Ordered that John Carney & Lovick Jones be appointed to
Audit the Account of Philip Neale admr. of Richard Neale
decd. also as Guardian of the Heirs of said deceased.

81 – John Fonvielle Esqr. returned his list of Taxable property
in Capt. D. Lewis' Company for the year 1792.

Ordered that Isaac Guion, Thomas Turner & Samuel Chapman be appointed to Divide the Estate of Sarah Vail decd. between the Heirs of said Decd.

On Motion of Cormick Higgins praying that a former order of this Court for Building a public Water Grist Mill upon Dawsons Creek may be Renewed. Whereupon Ordered that he have his former order be renewed.

William P. Moore has permission to keep Tavern in Newbern he entering into Bond of £100 with William Mitchell his security.

~~Ordered that Moses Chance have Letters of Administration upon the Estates of James Harman, Anthon Graff, George Sailer, Soloman Swindle & Frederick Balston.~~ Rescinded.

Ashly Barnard, Lewis Fonvielle & Michael Higgins are appointed Patrollers from Deep Bottom & Batchelor Creek. And James Gooding, Thomas Wise & Ephraim Swann.

John West, James McCafferty & Joseph Phipps. Stephen Harris, Jacob Johnston Junr. & Rigdon Murphy are appointed Patrollers in Capt. Jones District.

Joseph West Guardians of Agness and Ann Perkins Orphans of James Perkins decd. Returned a Settlement of his Accounts of said Guardianship which was examined by the court and approved of & ordered to be filed.

82 — Then were the following Jurors appointed to attend next ____ Viz.
1. John Bryan (Adams Creek)   2. John S. Nelson 3. Benjamin Mason 4. Charles James 5. John Jones

(Clubfoots Creek) 6. Robert Young 7. Francis Carraway 8. Joseph Nelson 9. James Nelson 10. Amos Squires 11. Thos. Clayton 12. Alexander Carruthers 13. Cason Fulsher 14. Chrisr. Wharton 15. David Wharton 16. John Morris 17. William Tutle 18. William Anthony No. 19. Joseph Clark 20. Edwd. Tinker 21. Joseph Shot__ 22. George Lane 23. Richard Forb__ 24. Thomas Webber 25. Jacob Cooke 26. John Vendrick 27. William Dixon 28. Aaron Ernul 29. Jacob L. Benners 30. William Gas___ 31. Isaac Hollis 32. Jacob R____ 33. Francis _____ 34. Levi Fulsher 35. Fredk. Foy 36. James Hyman. Issued.

Whereas Nero A Negro Man formerly in the Possession of Charles McLin decd. having applied to this Court for his Freedom and praying to be discharged from the Service of the Administrator of Charles McLin, decd. and it appearing to the Satisfaction of the Court that he is entitled to his freedom. Ordered that he be in future Liberated and discharged from any further service. Order issd.

Ordered that Bridget Conner have Letters of Administration upon the Estate of Elizabeth Ferrell decd. upon her Qualifying and entering into Bond of £500 with James McCafferty & Robert Witfield her securities. (Bond taken)

The Court having heard the Complaint of Merrill Holton who is bound to Robert Hatfield and are of Opinion that the same is ill founded & that the Boy continue with his master Robt. Hatfield.

83 – An Inventory and Account of Sales of the Estate of Anthony Inloes decd. was returned & filed.

Elizabeth Peters vs. Thomas Phillips} Petition for Dower. Ordered that a Writ issue to the Sheriff of Craven County to Summon a Jury to lay off the Dower of the Widow of Ethelred Peters decd. in the Lands of said Deceased agreeable to the Petition.

Whereas an Execution issued at the instance of John B. Yates against Samuel Chapman returnable to this Court hath been executed illegally and not returned by the proper Officer. Ordered that the said Execution be set aside and the property taken, restored to the Defendant.

Adjourned till 4 oClock this afternoon. Met Pursuant to Adjournment. Present the Worshipful John Tillman, William Henry, Francis Lowthorp} Esquires.

Ordered that James Carter be appointed Administrator of the Estate of William Shore decd. upon his Qualifying and entering into Bond of £50 with William Henry & Thomas Hyman his Securities (Bond taken)

Ordered that Levi Dawson, Moses Ernull & Charles Williams be appointed to Settle & Divide the Accounts of Fisher Gaskins Administrator of the Estate of Edward Rumley decd. also that they settle the Accounts of Fisher Gaskins Admr. of the Estate of Mary Rumley decd.

84 — The Petition of Joseph Phipps and John S. West ___ Read praying leave to build a public Water Grist Mill upon Poplar Branch. Ordered where they own Land upon one side of the Stream. Ordered that Charles Roach, Joel King, John Allen, Jesse Fillingame & Joseph Hunt & John Fonvielle be appointed to lay off and Value one Acre of Land upon the Appoint both sides of said Stream & report thereon to the next Court.

Ordered that John C. Bryan Esqr. have the Windows and Sashes of the Court House repaired by the sitting of the Superior Court if possible for which he shall be allowed out of the County Tax.

William Slade & William Mitchell Administrators of the Estate of Thomas Collier decd. appeared in Court and Objected to the Settlement of the Accounts of Thomas Collier decd. with the orphans of George Clarke decd. which accounts were returned to this Court.
        J. Tillman, J.P.
        Levi Dawson, J.P.
        F. Lowthorp, J.P.

[December 1792]
85 — At a County Court of Pleas & Quarter Sessions begun and held for the County of Craven at the Court House in Newbern, on the second Monday in December, being the 10th day of the month A.D. 1792.

Present the Worshipful John F. Smith Esqr. Adjourned 'till tomorrow Morning 10 oClock.

Tuesday Decr. 11, 1792. Met Pursuant to adjournment. Present the Worshipful Jno. Tillman, Jno. Fonvielle, Levi Dawson, John Allen, Isaac Bryan, John Daly, Henry Tillman, Wm. M. Herritage, Francis Lowthorp, Wm. Henry, Hardy Gatlin, John Dawson, Henry Tillman, Jacob Johnston, Southy Rew, Spyers Singleton.

John C. Bryan Esqr. Sheriff of Craven County returned the Writ of Venire for Jurors directed to Summoned to attend this Court in these Words "Executed."

Ordered that William Smith & Thomas Smyth have Letters of Administration upon the Estate of Samuel Smyth, decd. upon their entering into Bond of £4000 with Edward Griffith & William Henry Securities. (Bond taken & Letters issd.)

The last Will & Testament of Peter Reel decd. was proved in Open Court by the oath of Jacob Burch on of the subscribing Witnesses thereto and at the same Mary Reel prayed for Letters of Administration with the Will annexed which was granted upon her entering into bond of £100 with Jno Gatlin & Thos. Webber Securities.

86 — Ordered that Mary Green have Letters of Admin. upon the Estate of William Green decd upon his Entering into Bond of £100 with Jno. Fonvielle & William Hannis Secy. & returned an Inventory of said Estate.

Ordered that Letters of Administration be granted to ~~William Blount~~ John Heath upon the Estate of Wm. B. Heath upon his entering into Bond of £200 with John Cox & David Bryan his Securities.

Ordered that Wallace Styron, Philip Neale & Joseph Masters & Wm. Johnston be appointed to Settle and Divide the Estate of Beverly Rew decd. agreeable to his last Will & Testament — and that they or any three of them make return of their proceeding to the next Court [note in margin illegible]

Ordered that William M. Herritage, John Holloway, and James Whitfield be appointed to Divide the Estate of John Stevenson decd. amongst the Heirs and make Return to the next Court. (rescinded)

An Account Sales of the Estate of Charles Marshall decd was returned & filed.

John C. Bryan Esqr. Sheriff of Craven County resigned his appointment & Commission as Sheriff which was received by the Court.

The last Will & Testament of Richard Carlton decd. was proved by the Oath of David Bryan one of the Subscribing Witnesses thereto and at the Same time Mary Carlton & John Cox the Executrix & Exec___ therein Named Qualified agreeable to Law. Ordered that Letters Testamentary issue accordingly.

87 — Ordered that John Fonvielle, John Daly, & Frans. Lowthorp Esqr be appointed to Settle and Divide the Estate of John Stevenson decd. wth the late Guardians, William M. Herritage and the Admrs. Of Silas S. Stevenson decd who was Guardian of the said Orphans.

Ordered that Sampson Morris be appointed Guardian of Macey Stevenson a Minor upon his entering into Bond of £1000 — with Wm. M. Herritage & Malachi Russell his Securities.

Then were the following Gentlemen Sworn as Grand Jurors. Viz.
1. Aaron Ernul (Foreman) 2. Robert Young 3. Jno. Jones 4. Thos. Clayton 5. Alexander Carruthers 6. Joseph Clark 7. George Lane 8. John Vendrick 9. Richard Forbes 10. Jacob Rhem 11. Levi Fulsher 12. Fredk. Foy   13. Joseph Shute. John Barrington Constable

William Henry Esqr. is appointed Sheriff for the County of Craven upon his Qualifying and entering into Bond of £5000 with _____ [blank] his Securities. ~~Whereupon the said William Henry appd. in Court & Qualified and entered into Bond accordingly~~.

Ordered that Thomas Willis have Letters of Administration upon the Estate of James Ives (the Widow of the decd. having resigned) upon his entering into Bond of £200 — with Charles Williams & ~~S__ Lee   Aaron Ernul~~ Jas. Gatlin his Securities & Qualifying agreeable to Law. (Bond taken)

88 — The last Will & Testament of George Paul decd. was proved by the Oath of Thomas Gooding one of the Subscribing Witnesses thereto and at the same time Thos. Gooding the Executor therein Named appeared & Qualified agreeable to Law. Ordered that Letters Testamentary issue.

Ordered that Isaac Bryan, Whorry Kilpatrick, & Thomas Heath be appointed to Settle the Accts. Of Daniel West & Ferebe Carlton, Adminisx. of Blake Carlton, decd. and report thereon to the next Court. Dr.

Dan'l West has permission to keep Public House of entertainment at his House upon his entering into Bond of £[illegible] with Malachi Russell his Secy.

Ordered that Aaron Arnold, James Gatlen and Charles Williams be appointed to Settle and Divide the Estate of Joseph Willis decd. between the Widow & Children of said decd. and report thereon to the next Court. Issd.

Ordered that William Lawley have Letters of Admn. upon the Estate of Sarah Mitchell decd. Upon his Qualifying and entering into Bond of £20 with Stephen Harris & Charles Williams his Securities. (Bond taken & Letters issd.)

Adjourned 'till 3 oClock this afternoon.

89 — Met pursuant to Adjournment. Present the Worshipful Wm. M. Herritage, John Daly, Hardy Gatlin Esqrs.

Ordered that Benjamin Griffin have the Courses of his Land altered agreeable to his Patent and Petition filed.

Ordered that Eunice Franklin be appointed Guardian of William Conway a Minor upon her entering into Bond in the sum of £500 with Thomas Hyman & James Hyman her Securities.

Ordered that James West aged eleven years be bound to John West Senr. to learn the trade of a Cooper.

Ordered that Levi Dawson, John Biggs, & William Shine be appointed to Audit the Accts. of James Hyman Executor of Michael Hyman decd. with the Estate of said Decd. and report thereon to this Court.

Adjourned 'till tomorrow morng. 10 oClock.

Wednesday 12 Decr. 1792. Met Pursuant to adjournment. Present the Worshipful James Gatlin, Wm. M. Herritage, Francis Lowthorp, Southy Rew, Esqrs. Jno. F. Smith, Jacob Johnston, Spyers Singleton, William Tisdale, Jno. Dawson, Esqrs.

90 — Ordered that Jacob Johnston Senr. have Letters of Administration upon the Estate of John Barry decd. upon his entering into Bond of £20 with John F. Smith & F. Lowthorp his Securities. (Bond taken.)

Whereas William Henry who was appointed Sheriff of Craven County yesterday has failed to appear and Qualify and enter into Bond when called upon required agreeable to Law, the Court proceeded to appoint another Person to Act the Office of Sheriff and Edward Pasteur Esqr. was unanimously elected to the Office of Sheriff upon his Qualifying and entering into Bond agreeable to Law. Whereupon the said Edward Pasteur Qualified and entered into Bond of £5000 with William M. Herritage, Jno. F. Smith, Southy Rew, & Charles James his Securities. (Rescinded.)

Ordered that William Johnston be appointed Guardian of Margeret Rew [Rice?] Orphan of Beverly Rew [Rice?] decd. upon his entering into Bond of £1000 with Edward Pasteur & Wm. M. Herritage Abner Neale his Securities. (Bond taken.) Issd.

Ordered that William Johnston Guardian of Margret Rew [Rice?] sell at Public Vendue for six months Credit the Perishable part of said Orphans Estate.

Ordered that Mary Bohannon have Letters of Administration upon the Estate of William Bohannon Decd. upon her entering into Bond of £200 with Austin Prescott & Daniel West her securities.

91 — Ordered that Elijah Pope aged 15 years be bound to John Hay to learn the Shoemakers Trade. (Inds. made out.)

No. 3. John Den on demise of Joseph Allen vs. Richd. Fen &
Thomas Fish} Eject. The following Jury empanelled & Sworn.
No. 1 William Cox 2. Jas. Gatlin 3. Brittain King 4. Walter
Jones 5. John Phillip 6. William Moore } Jury of Venue   7.
Charles James 8. Joseph Nelson 9. James Nelson 10. Thomas
Webber 11. Jacob L. Benners 12. William Anthony} Original
Panel.
Find the defendt. Guilty and assess 6d Dam. & 6d Costs.
Appeal prayed & allowed the Defendt. upon his filing reasons
and entering into Bond of £250 with John Phillips & William
Moore Securities.

John Sears Esqr. returned a List of Taxable property in Capt.
Thomas Phillips district for the year 1792.

Ordered that Joel King have permission to keep a Public
House of Entertainment at his House in Craven County. Issd.

Adjourned until ½ past 4 oClock in the afternoon. Met
Pursuant to adjournment. Present the Worshipful Levi
Dawson, Isaac Guion, Francis Lowthorp, Henry Tillman, Jno.
Dawson.

Levi Dawson Esqr. returned the list of Taxable property in
Capt. Danl. Wests District for the year 1792.

92 — The jury appointed to lay of a Road from Swifts Creek to William Bryan's Mill upon Mauls run made a return of their proceedings. Which return was objected to by John Bryan. The Court after hearing the arguments offered for and against the Road are of opinion that the Road should be layd out agreeable to the aforesaid Return. John Bryan being dissatisfied with the determination of the Court prayed an Appeal to the next Superior Court which was granted upon his entering into Bond for prosecuting said appeal. (_____ made up.)

Adjourned till tomorrow morning, 10 oClock.

Thursday, Decr. 13, 1792. Met pursuant to adjournment. Present the Worshipful Levi Dawson, Spyers Singleton, Isaac Guion, Frans. Lowthorp, Henry Tillman, John Dawson} Esqrs.

Francis Brown vs. Giles Riggs} Judgment upon appeal a Warrant. Tried before Henry J̶n̶o̶. Tillman, Esqr. and Execution issued for £6.7.0.by Henry Tillman Esqr. which was returned by Clayton Carruthers Constable in these Words. Executed upon One hundred & ten Acres of Land, no personal property to be found — but about £3 worth that have taken by different Execution. Ordered that Vende. Exponas issue directed to the Sheriff to sell the Land agreeable to Law. (_____ with Clayton Carruthers, Cons. & his Res_).

93 — Francis Brown vs. Giles Riggs} Judgment for £6 and Execution issued & Levied the same as before mentioned. Ordered that Vene. Exponas issue agreeable to Law. Debt & Cost settled with Clayton Carruthers Consle. & his Re__.

Joseph Franklin admr. Peter Franklin vs. Giles Riggs} Judgt.
upon a Warrant tried before Joshua Fulsher Esqr & Execution
issd. by Henry Tillman Esqr. for £7.7.0 & 4/ Costs and
returned by Clayton Carruthers Constle. Levied as above.
Ordered that Vene. Exponas isse. to sell the Land agreeable to
Law. Debt & Costs afterward ____ with Clayton Carruthers
Consl. & his Receipt.

Jno. Ince vs. Joseph Crispin} Case. The following Jury
empanelled & Sworn. To wit:
No. 1. Charles James 2. Joseph Nelson 3. James Nelson 4.
James Hyman 5. Edward Tinker 6. Thomas Webber 7.
William Anthony 8. Jacob L. Benners 9. William Hill 10. Jesse
Bryan 11. William Davis 12. Geo. Ellis find the Defendant
did assume and assess £26.1.0 Dam & 6d Costs. Appeal
prayed & allowed.

Ordered that ^Luke Moore daughter of^ Ruth Moore aged
three years be bound to William Dudley. (Indentures
executed.)

Ordered that John Powell be appointed Guardian of Anner
Coleman Orphan of Thos. Coleman decd. upon his entering
into Bond of £200 with Thos. Fisk & William Moore his
Securities. (Bond taken.)

Ordered that Abimeleck Sutton have letters of adminisn. upon
the Estate of Solo. Meddleton upon his Qualifying & entering
into Bond of £100 with William Moore & John Powell ~~Thomas
Fisk~~ his Securities (Bond taken.)

94 — Then was the following Insolvent and absen___ allowed
the Sheriff out of the Taxes for the year 1791. To wit. 23 White
polls, 40 Black do. 7034 ½ Acres of Land & £200 Value Town
Property.

Ordered that William Slade & William Mitchell the Admrs.
Thos. Collier decd. have permission to sell at Public Vendue
two Negroes Viz. Juno & Daniel belonging to the Estate of
said decd. in order to pay the Debts of said Decd.

Adjourned till ½ past 3 oClock. Met Pursuant to Adjournment.
Present the Worshipful Francis Lowthorp, Jno. F. Smith,
Henry Tillman} Esqrs.

John Green survg. Executor David Barron vs. William Davis
Exr. James Davis decd.} Case. The following Jury empanelled
& Sworn. To Wit. No. 1. Charles James
2. James Nelson 3. Edwd. Tinker 4. Thos. Webber 5. James
Hyman 6. Joseph Nelson 7. Willm. Hill   8. Jas. Wharton 9.
Lucas J. Benners 10. Wm. Williams 11. Amos Wade 12. Jno.
Smalwood find the Defendants Testator did assume & assess
£13.4 Dam. & 6d Costs and they further find that ___
Defendants Testator did not assume within t___ ____
Judgment for Defendt.

95 — Jno. Smallwood & William Gibbs are appointed
Inspectors of the Poll of Election to be opend on Friday &
Saturday for a Member for the Town of Newbern to represent
said Town in the General Assembly now setting in the room
of Richard D. Spaight, Esqr.

Then was John C. Bryan Esqr. Sheriff of Craven County for the
~~last~~ present year allowed the sum of Twenty five pounds to be
paid him by the County Treasurer.

Then was Samuel Chapman Clerk of Craven County Court allowed the sum of Twenty pounds for his extra Services the present year. Also the sum of Five pounds for Stationary &c. furnished & Court to be paid him by the County Treasurer.

Then was John McGraw Cryer of this Court allowed him the sum of Twenty five pounds for his Services the present year taking due of the Court House &c to be paid him by the County Treasurer. (Paid.)

Then was Francis Lowthorp, James Ellis and Samuel Chapman appointed Assessors of Town property for the year 1792.

Then was Thomas York, Joshua Carraway, John Carruthers Senr. & Alex. Carruthers are appointed patrollers in Capt. H.G. Tillman's district.

96 — Then were the following Gentlemen appointed to serve as Jurors at the next Superior Court. Vizt. 1. Francis Lowthorp 2. Isaac Guion   3. Jno. F. Smith
4. Wm. M. Herritage 5. William McClure 6. John Sears 7. John Green
8. Levi Dawson 9. Isaac Bryan

Adjourned till tomorrow Morning, 9 oClock.

Friday, Decr. 14, 1792. Met Pursuant to Adjournment.

Present the Worshipful William M. Herritage, Levi Dawson, Isaac Guion, Francis Lowthorp, Henry Tillman} Esqrs.

Martin Stevenson of age to Choose a Guardian appear'd in
Court and made Choice of John Gooding for his Guardian
which was approved of by the Court upon his entering into
Bond of £500 with Wm. M. Herritage & Edwd. Tinker his
Securities. (Dr.)

Then were the following Gentlemen appointed to attend at the
next as Jurors—1. William Lovick   2. Thomas G. Fonvielle 3.
Wm. B. Fonveille 4. Andw. Richardson
5. Ambrose Jones 6. Francs. McIlwean (Issd.)

97—7. John Biggs 8. William Whitty 9. Thomas Nelson
10. John Morris 11. Thomas Harper 12. Chrisr. Wharton 13.
David Wharton 14. John Wheadon 15. Joshua Lewis 16.
Nathanl. Lewis 17. Amos Squires Sen 18. Cason Fulsher 19.
James McCafferty 20. William Shepard 21. Stephen Tinker
22. John Devereux 23. William Mitchell 24. Hardy Heukins
25. John Broughton 26. Oliver Hall 27. Thomas Delamar 28.
Peter Vendrick 29. James Vendrick 30. John Bryan (Ads.
Creek) 31. Joseph Mason 32. John Nelson 33. Joseph Masters
34. Jonathan Frizel 35. Joseph Allen 36. David Lewis

James Brightman has permission to keep a Public House of
Entertainment in Newbern.

Joseph Shute vs. Titus Ogden} Appeal. The following Jury
empanelled & Sworn Vizl.
No. 1. Joseph Nelson 2. James Nelson 3. Edwd. Tinker 4.
Thomas Webber 5. Lucas J. Benners 6. James Hyman 7.
William Williams 8. Isaac Hollis 9. Irvin Sampson (Chs.
Sanders) 10. Daniel Brinson 11. Charles Williams 12. Thos.
Parsons find for the plantiff £12..0..0 & 6d Costs.

The Auditors appointed to Settle the Accounts of William
Slade & William Mitchell Admrs. Thos. Collier decd. made a
return of the Accounts and find a Ballance of £139.13.2 due
from the Estate to the sd. Administrators. Ordered that the
said Accounts be filed.

98 – No. 156. William Henry Atto. Thos. Sugdon vs. Saml.
Pryor} Appeal by Plff.
The same Jury as in the last Cause except Charles Saunder
Junr. In the room of Irvin Sampson empanelled & Sworn find
for the plaff. £2:3:9 & 6d Costs.

No. 157. Wm. Henry Atto Thos. Sugdon vs. Peter Wingate}
Appeal by Plff. The same Jury as in the last Cause empanelled
& Sworn find for the Plff. £3.2.3 & 6d Costs.

No. 160. Thomas ~~Hyman~~ Parsons vs. William Tyre} Appl. By
Plff. The same Jury as in the last Cause except Thomas Hyman
in the room of Thos. Parsons empanelled & Sworn find for the
plantiff £5.6.11 and 6d Costs.

An Inventory of the Estate of Sarah Saunders decd. was
returned by the Administrator (Dr. 4/)

No. 118. William Henry Atto. Thos. Sugden vs. William M.
Herritage} Appeal. The following Jury empanelled & Sworn.
No. 1. Joseph Nelson 2. James Nelson
3. Edwd. Tinker 4. Thos. Webber 5. Lucas J. Benners 6. James
Hyman 7. William Williams 8. Chs. Saunders 9. Danl.
Brinson 10. ~~Jno. Gooding~~ Thomas Hyman 11. Robt. Hetfield
12. William Mitchell find for the Plantiff £14.0.5 and 6d Costs.

99 – Adjourned till 4 oClock this afternoon. Met Pursuant to
Adjournment. Present the Worshipful Levi Dawson, Isaac
Guion, Henry Tillman} Esqrs.

Ordered that the County Treasurer be directed to furnish the County ~~Treasurer~~ Register with a Bound Book for Recording Deeds &c.

No. 187. Admx. Valentine Richardson decd. vs. Frederick Lane & Thomas A. Green} Appeal. The following Jury empanelled & Sworn. Viz. No. 1. Joseph Nelson
2. Jas. Nelson 3. Thos. Webber 4. Lucas J. Benners 5. James Hyman 6. Thomas Hyman 7. William Mitchell 8. William Anthony 9. James Bruce 10. William Paxton 11. John Green 12. Charles Saunders find for the Plantiff £12.0.0 & 6d Costs.

Adjourned till tomorrow Morng. 10 oClock.

Saturday, Decr. 15, 1792. Met Pursuant to adjournment. Present the Worshipful Isaac Guion, Francis Lowthorp, Jno. F. Smith} Esqrs.

100 — John Gooding vs. Nathan Smith} Appeal by Defend. The following Jury empanelled & Sworn. No. 1. Joseph Nelson 2. James Nelson 3. William Anthony
4. Edward Tinker 5. Thomas Webber 6. Lucas J. Benners 7. James Hyman 8. Charles Saunders Jr. 9. David Ambrose 10. James Pearce 11. James Carter 12. Geo. Holston find for the Plantiff £15.2.0 & 6d Costs.

Ordered that David Martin have Administration upon the Estate of Joseph Martin decd. upon his entering into Bond of £200- with George Holton and Joseph Nelson his Securities. Inventory filed & Bond taken.

Henry Tillman Esqr. returned the List of Taxable Property in his District for the year 1792.

John Barrington Constable is allowed £9.12.0 for his attendance upon the Court four Terms. Ordered that the County Treasurer pay the same. (Issd.)

Whereas Martin Stevenson who was bound to John Harvey is desirous to be released from his Indentures and Mr. Harvey being willing to give him up. Ordered that he be bound to John Dewey to learn the Trade of a House Carpenter (aged 15 years) {Inds. made out}

An Account Sales & Invo. of the Estate of William Sho___ decd. and filed.

101 — Ordered that Charles Williams have Letters of Administration upon the Estate of John Burroughs decd. upon his entering into Bond of £200- with Henry Tillman & Francis Lowthorp his Securities.

Jos. Shute vs. T. Ogden} Motion by F. X. Martin for new Trial (On argument no new Trial granted.)

Adjourned till 5 oClock. Met Pursuant to Adjournment. Present the Worshipful John Tillman, John Daly, Levi Dawson, Henry Tillman} Esqrs.

Thomas Crew is appointed Constable to attend next Court.

Isaac Guion vs. Marquis De Britegny} Att. Daniel Carthy, Agent for the Marquis De Britegny appeared in Court in this cause and ~~discharged himself~~ [illegible word stricken] replevied the Goods attached by the Sheriff in his hands and acknowledged himself Special Bail and offered Benja. Williams & Thomas Turner his Securities who acknowledged themselves Liable also to abide by and perform the Judgment of the Court in this cause.

Ordered that John Allen, John Fonvielle & Richard Cogdell be appointed to divide the Estate of Wright Stanly between his Widow & Children agreeable to Law and make return of the proceedings to the next Court.

102 — Where [illegible dark smudges] Sheriff [illegible] resigned his Com[illegible] up to the Court [illegible] William Henry was appointed to the Office of [illegible] and he having failed to Comply with the requi[illegible] of the Law Edward Pasteur was afterwards appointed and it being suggested that the said John C. Bryan could not con[illegible] the Law resign his Commission until the Expiration of his year. Ordered that all proceeding respecting the appointment of Sheriff at this Term be rescinded and the said Jno. C. Bryan be continued in the Office of Sheriff until the expiration of his year and the Court further direct that the Bond entered into by Edward Pasteur Esqr. be cancelled & delivered up to him.
J. Tillman, J.P.
John Daly, J.P.
Is. Guion, J.P.
Levi Dawson, J.P.
H. Tillman, J.P.

103 — At a County Court of Pleas & quarter Sessions begun & held for the County of Craven at the Court house in Newbern on the Second Monday in March being the Eleventh day of the Month 1793 & In the Seventeenth year of American Independence.

Present the Worshipful John Tillman, John Daly, T.A. Green, Joshua Fulcher}Esquires
John Fonvielle, Wm. M. Herritage, Levi Dawson, Jno. Frink Smith, Fras. Lowthorp} Esquires.

The last will of Stephen Wright was proved by the oath of Charles _illiams and the said Charles qualified as Executor thereto __dered to be recorded.

Samuel Hover Senior administrator of the rights & Credits goods and Chattels &c of the Estate of Elizabeth Hollis deceased: returned the Accounts of Sales of said Estate.

Ordered that Frederic Heath have letters of administration on the estate of Agatha White on entering into bond in the sum of £50 with John Dawly, Tho. A. Green securities.

Ordered that he have leave to sell the personal estate of his intestate.

104 — The following Gentlemen were empanelled and Swo__ as Grand Jurors for this Term:
1. John Devereux Foreman 2. William Lovick 3. Thomas G. Fonvielle 4. William B. Fonvielle 5. John ~~Biggs~~ Bryan 6. David Wharton 7. Joshua Lewis 8. Nathanl. Lewis 9. Cason Fulsher 10. James McCafferty 11. William Sheppard   12. Thomas Delamar 13. Peter Vendrick

Ordered that Jonathan Perkins, Charles Williams, and G___ Barrington be appointed to settle the Accounts of Samuel Hover Admr. &c of the Estate of Hezekiah Hollis and that they make return to the ~~next Court~~ This Term. (2/ pd.)

The last Will and Testament of Francis Roundtree was produced in open Court and proved by the oath of Joel Willis and Moses Roundtree qualified as Executor thereto. Ordered to be recorded.

The Worshipful John Brag Esqr. appeared and took his ____

Ordered that Isaac Read be allowed the usual Sum as an Invalid being [illegible] 20.

Ordered that the Executors of Stephen Wallace have leave to sell the perishable part of their Testators Estate. Rule issd. (2/ pd. 2/ pd.)

105 — Then were John and Bazil Foster appointed Administrators &c on the Estate of William Shepard Foster deceased and the said John & Bazil entered into Bond with John Blanks and Carney as Securities in the Sum of Two Thousand pounds.

Then were John and Bazil Foster appointed Guardians to Perrin Foster son of Frederick Foster deceased upon entering into Bond with the same securities as last above mentioned in the sum of Five hundred pounds.

Then were Spiers Singleton, John Blanks and Fredk. Foy appointed to divide the Negroes of William Shepard Foster decd. among the heirs and make return of Such division to the next Term.

Moses Roundtree Executor of the last Will and Testament of Francis Roundtree produced in Court an Inventory of the Estate of the deceased which was duly proved by the oath of the sd. Executor.

Ordered that John Fonvielle, Richd. Nixon & Farnifold Green be appointed to divide the Estate of Mrs. Hannah Reed decd. agreeable to ~~Law~~ her Will.

Ordered that John Fonvielle, Richd. Nixon & Farnifold Green be appointed to divide the Estate of James Emery deceased agreeable to Law.

Joseph Brinson administrator &c of James Horesheens decd. produced in Court an Inventory and acct Sales of the Estate his Intestate which were duly proved by the oath of said Joseph Brinson.

106 – The last Will and Testament of John Philips Decd. was produced in open Court and proved by the oath of Samuel Branton Senr. one of the Subscribing Witnesses thereto – and John and Thomas Philips qualified as Executors thereto – at the same time Thomas Philips returned on oath an Inventory of the said deceased Estate.

Ordered that Letters of Administration on the Estate of Benjamin Balance deceased be granted to Sarah Balance on her entering into Bond in the Sum of Five hundred pounds with John Biggs and Jo__ Dawson Securities.

175. Mary Vance vs. Wilson Exr. of Bingham} Case Default}
The following Jury being empanelled and Sworn viz. 1. Simon Bexley   2. Joseph Carter 3. Jonathan Perkins 4. Richard Johnston 5. James Arnold 6. John Gatlen
7. John West Sen. 8. Wm. Gaskins 9. James Hyman 10. Oliver Hall 11. Wm. Mitchell 12. John Biggs find that the ~~Defendant did assume and assess the~~ Plaintiff has sustained damage to thirty four pounds nine shillings and six pence and six pence Costs.

Nancy Wright widow of Stephen Wright deceased comes into Court and enters her Dissent to the Will of the Said.

Ordered that Charles Williams be appointed Guardian __ Nancy Wright, Orphan of Stephen Wright decd. upon his entering Bond of £1200 with Gardy Gatlin & Levi Dawson Esqrs. his Security (Bond taken.)

107 — Cullen Pollock Guardn. Of George Pollock vs. John Smallwood} Case Default} Same Jury as in the last cause being charged find the Plaintiff hath sustained damage to the sum of one hundred and ninety ~~three~~ six pounds, thirteen shillings and three pence and 6d Costs.

Then was James McCafferty of NewBern Inn Keeper appointed Administrator &c of Michael Venters deceased upon entering into Bond in the sum of One hundred pounds with Simon Bexley and Hardy Hewkins as Security.

On Motion Mary Booth an Orphan Girl bound last March term to William Hawley was by Consent ___aid Hawley and by order of the Court taken from ___ and bound to George Kennedy (Inds. Exd.)

A division of the estate of Edward Rumley was __turned signed by Levi Dawson, Moses Ernell & _harles Williams who were appointed by the __urt for that purpose. Also there report on the _state of Mary Rumley.

Jesse Hofman returned an inventory of the __tate of Frelove Chapman.

Ordered that Thomas Willis, James Gatlen & Joshua __llis be appointed to audit the accounts of Susan__ Miller against the estate of Ephraim Pearce ___ ke return thereof.

__rderd that Abner Neale's Negro man Achilles ____ leave to carry a gun on said Neale's land ___r Newbern said Neale complying with the _____

108 — Ordered that George Lane, William Cox & Daniel West be appointed to audit the accounts of Robert Fosset administrator of Ann Lambert decd.

Ordered that Thomas Oliver have administration on the estate of Mary Granbury decd. the late wife of Edward Ingram entering into bond of five hundred pounds with Joseph Oliver & James Oliver his securities. (B.W. Dr.)

Jonathan Perkins, Charles Williams & Isaac Barrington who were appointed to audit & settle the accounts of Samuel Hoover admr. of Hezikiah Hol__ made return thereof. (for nothing ℘ court.)

Ordered that John S. West have license to keep a public house at the Ferry ten miles from Newbern (paid).

Ordered that Charles Williams be allowed £5..4 for attending the Superior Court as a Constable at Sept. Term 1793 as ℘ his certificate from Silas Cooke Esqr. Clerk of sd. Superior Court.

109 — Court adjourned till tomorrow 9 Oclock.
Court Tuesday, March 12, 1793

Court met according to adjournment.

Present the worshipful John Carney, J.F. Smith, W.M. Herritage, Henry Tillman, Levi Fulshire.

Ordered John Barrington an Orphan boy be bound to Wm. Hawley for the term of Six _ears from the first of May next to learn _he trade of a Taylor.

An exemplified Copy of the last Will and Testament of Thomas Pollock, from the Records of the prerogative Court in the Secretary's Office in Burlington __ the State of New Jersey, under the great Seal __ the said State; was produced in Court, and __dered to be recorded and Letters Testamen_tory to issue accordingly.

Ordered that Edward Wiggins have Letters of Administration on the Estate of Samuel Wiggins decd. upon his entering into bond with [blank] his Securities in the Sum of £200 — who at the same time _eturned an Inventory of said Deceased's Estate.

110 — Read the petition of Joseph Fipps and Ann his wife, Winifed Kemps & Sarah Kemp_ minors, by John Bryan & James Gatlin their Guardians for the appointment of Commissioners to divide the Land of John Kemps decd. Ordered that the prayer of said petition be granted & that Jarvis Fullingham, Jacob Johnson, John S. West, Hardy Gatlin & James Gatlin be appointed Commissioners therefore. Issd.

Ordered that Jessee Bryan be allowed the Sum of £5.4.0 for attending the Superior Court as a Juror, thirteen days, ℘ his Certificate from S. Cook Esqr. Clerk of sd. Court.

Ordered that ~~Humphrey Jones~~ remitted, Philip Turner, (Alexander Duguid remitted,) Delinquent Jurors, be fined Ten Shillings each and George Ellis.

10. Jos. Shute Exr. of Tho. W. Person vs. Titus Ogden, surviving Copartner of Thomas & Titus Ogden} Case. The following Jury impaneled to wit:

1. Oliver Hall 2. William Mitchell 3. John Biggs 4. Amos Squires 5. Thomas Harper } Origl. 6. Wm. Hawley}Tale.   7. Abram Vendrick 8. Thos. Hyman 9. Edward Wigans 10. Stephen West 11. Jonathan Perkins 12. Walter Allen} Tales. Find

111 — Juror withdrawn. No plea having been entd.

_6. Adms. Stephen Hill vs. Saml. Coleman} Attd. Same Jury as in the last Cause except Malacha Russell in the place of Stephen West find that the Defendant did assume & assess the plaintiffs damage at £10.7.0 and Costs.

Ordered that Stephen West, a delinquent Juror, be fined Ten Shillings.

George Emmerson vs. Francis Lowthorp, adm. Jno. Whitehouse} Case. The following Jury impaneled 1. Oliver Hall   2. William Mitchell 3. John Biggs 4. Amos Squires 5. Thomas Harper 6. Wm. Hawley 7. Abram Vendrick 8. Thomas Hyman 9. Edward Wigans 10. Stephen West 11. Hardy Hukins 12. Walter Allen find for the Plaintiff £14.3.4 & Costs.

George Lane, Wm. Cox, and Daniel West, who were appointed to audit & settle the accounts of Robt. Fossett administrator of Ann Lambeth decd. made return thereof.

112 — Sarah Balance returned an Inventory of the Estate of Benjamin Balance decd. ordered that She have leave to sell the perishable part of said Estate & a Negro. Issd.

Ordered that Philip Knowis be cited to settle his accounts as administrator of James Granberry a minor decd & render the same to the next Court (issued)

Adjourned 'till Tomorrow 9 oClock.

Wednesday, March 13, 1793

Met pursuant to adjournment. Present the Worshipful John Dawson, Levi Dawson, F. Lowthorp, Hardy Gatlin, John Allen

Mrs. Mary Heath renewed her Tavern License.

Orderd that Lewis Savins [?] have License to keep a House of Entertainment upon enterg. into bond with James Hyman & Hardy Hukins his Securities.

James Butler on entering into bond with James McMain & F. Lowthorp his securities to have License to keep Tavern. Pd. 10/

113 — Mary Bohannan returned an account Sales of the Estate of Wm. Bohannan.

Mrs. Susanna Stanly is appointed Guardian to her Children, Wright Cogdell Stanly, Lydia Duncan Stanly & John Wright Stanly upon _ntering into bond with her Securities Richard Dobbs Spaight _nd John Daly Esqrs. in the Sum of Ten Thousand Pounds.

__ 12. Lewis Bryan vs. Malacha Russell} Detinue. The following Jury impanneled
1. Thomas Harper. 2. Amos Squires 3. Hardy Hukins 4. Wm. Mitchell 5. Oliver Hall 6. Joseph Nelson 7. John Biggs 8. Walter Allen 9. Alex. Duguid 10. James Arnold 11. John West 12. Wm. Murphy find the Defendant doth not detain &c.

John Carpenter returned an account Sales of the Estate of George Carpenter decd.

John Daw returned an Inventory of the Estate of Hugh Tingle Decd.

114—14. Henry Tillmand vs. Adms. And. Blanchard} Judgt. Vs. Land

Ordered that Mrs. Mary Graham have Letters of Administration on the Estate of Robert Graham decd. on entering into bond of £100 with James McCafferty and Saml. Gooding her Securities.

Order'd that Elizabeth Saunders & Charles Saunders jur have Letters of Administration on the Estate of James Saunders decd on entg. into bond of £500 with Thomas Hyman & Wm. Carter, their Securities. Pd. 16/

17. Hardy Coker vs. Daniel West& Nathn. Wetherington} Case. The same Jury as in the last Cause impanneled & Sworn, find for the Plantif Damage £50.0.0 also the cause of action vs. West.

Ordered that Roderego Latesta have License to keep Public House in the Town of Newbern, upon entering into bond of £[blank] with ~~George~~ James Ellis & John Goulding his Securities.

115—19. Isaac [?] Barrington Indorsee for vs. John Banks }Case. The same Jury as in No. 12 impanneled and Sworn. Find for the Plantiff & assess his Damages at £31..15 & Cost. Appeal prayed & granted. Wm. M. Herritage & Wm. Hoover, Securities.

Elisabeth Saunders & Charles Saunders admrs. of James Saunders decd. returned an Inventory of sd. decd. Estate.

Ordered that the Admins of James Saunders have leave to sell a Negro woman Rose.

The Court adjourned 'till four oClock in the afternoon.

Court met according to adjournment. Present the Worshipful Levi Dawson, John Dawson, Spiers Singleton, Willm. McClure}Esqs. Wm. M. Herritage, Joshua Fulcher, John Allen} Esqs.

20. The Executors of Thomas Delamar vs. Cormack Higgins} Debt. The following Jury being impannelled and Sworn. 1. Thomas Harper 2. Amos Squires 3. Hardy Hukins 4. Wm. Mitchell 5. Oliver Hall 6. Joseph Nelson
7. John Biggs   8. Wm. Murphy 9. Humphry Jones 10. Thos. Curtis 11. Jesse Lester 12. John Thomas find that the Writing

118 — obligatory is the Act and deed of the Defendant [illegible] assess the Plaintiffs damage to £9.9 & 6d Costs.

21. Walter Allen vs. James McCafferty} Case. The same Jury as in the last cause being impannelled find that the defendant doth assume and assess the plantif's Damage at £120.8.0 & Costs with which the Defendant being dissatisfied prayed an appeal.

Ordered that John Bedscott of New Bern have License to keep tavern in the town of New Bern for the space of one year upon entering into bond according to Law in the sum of [blank] with John Latham and Walter Allen Securities. Issd.

Adjourned 'till Tomorrow 9 oClock

Met according to adjournment. Present, The Worshipfull
Levi Dawson,   John Dawson }
Joshua Fulshire, Wm. Henry } Esqrs.
Jacob Johnson,   }

117 — Then were the following Gentlemen appointed to attend
as Jurors at the next Term: 1. James Stewart 2. Richard Hunley
3. George Ellis 4. William Good 5. Enoch Alexander 6. James
Little   7. William Anthony
8. William Hawley 9. Wilson Blount 10. John Kenedy 11.
James McKinlay 12. John Harvey 13. Edward Tinker 14.
James Davis 15. Joseph Clark 16. Wm. Lawrence 17. James
Coor 18. Thomas Cox 19. Joseph Oliver
20. John Moor   21. Jacob Cook 22. Jesse Bryan 23. Stephen
Tinker 24. Rob. Hunt   25. Wm. Paxton 26. Fred. Foy   27.
James Bruce 28. Thomas Hyman 29. Wm. Ross
30. John Green 31. Thomas Oliver 32. John Clark   33. Charles
Saunders Senr. 34. John Knox [?]
35. Aaron Arnuld 36. Francis Fonville

Ordered that Paul Sparrow have Leave to keep a public Ferry
over Adam's Creek from his house to Charles McLins Farm at
the Following Rates: Single Man 1/- , Man & Horse 2/-.

118 — Sarah Kemps, of lawfull age to choose a guardian
appeared in Court and chose James Gatlin Esqr. her Guardian;
who offered John S. West & Hardy Gatlin as securities which
was approved. Ordered that they enter in bond £two
thousand Pounds One thousand Pounds.

Winifred Kemps, of age to choose a Guardian appeared in
Court & chose James Gatlin Esqr. her Guardian, who was
approved of by the Court.

84

On [ink blot] Ordered that John Bryan & James [blot]n, Guardians of Winifred Kemps be discharged of their Guardianship, and that She choose another, Whereupon She cose chose James Gatlin—who offered John Spence West & Hardy Gatlin as Securities, & they were approved of. Ordered that they enter into bond of One Thousand Pounds.

Ord[ered th]at a Citation issue to John Bryan [blot] appear at the next Court; and file an [a]ccount of his Guardianship. (issued)

By Consent of Wm. Mitchell & Isaac Bryan ordered, that said Mitchell be appointed as a Juror to attend the next Superior Court in the Room of said Bryan.

Levi Reel, is appointed Constable in Capt. Arnolds District & gave Levi Dawson & James Reel, his Securities.

119—22. David Witherspoon et Uxor vs. Adms. Justina Nash} Case—Issue. The following Jury impaneled and Sworn: 1. Amos Squires 2. Hardy Hukins 3. Tho. Harper 4. Wm. Mitchell 5. Oliver Hall 6. Joseph Nelson. [First six jurors marked "Orig'l panel"] 7. Wm. Gaskins 8. John West 9. Nathaniel Streets 10. Isaac Kemp 11. Thomas Philips [Jurors 7-11 marked "Talesmen"] 12. John Biggs—origl. Find the Defendant's Intestate did assume & assess the plantiff's Damage at £121.18.11 & 6d Cost, & they further say that she did assume within Three years.

Jacob Johnson, administrator of the Estate of John Barrie decd. returned an Inventory of said Estate—and an acct. Sales of same.

Ordered that Moses Arnul, Charles [blot]ams, and Joseph
Willis, be appointed to audit & Settle the accounts of William
Seales — Administrator of John Griffin decd.

24. Tho. Haslen vs. David Wetherspoon} Case. The Same Jury
as in the last Cause except Wm. Hawley & Joseph Loftin in the
room of John West & Nath. Streets — find for the plantiff &
assess the Damages at £173.12.0 & 6d Cost. With Which the
Defd. Being dissatisfied prayed an appeal & offered Levi
Dawson & Wm. Henry Securities — granted.

120 — 25. John Lines vs. Wm. Davis} Covenant. The same Jury
as in the last cause impaneled and Sworn, find that the
defendant hath broken his covenant & assess the plaintiffs
damage to £70 & 6 costs.

Adjourned till half after 3 oClock.
Met according to adjournment. Present, The Worshipfull
John Dawson, Jacob Johnson, Levi Dawson, Wm. M.
Herritage, Joshua Fulshire.

Elisabeth Vail returned an Inventory of the Estate of Sarah
Vail, decd.

James Hyman, Joshua Fulshire, Francis Delemar, and John
Biggs, returned a settlement of the Accounts of Joseph
Franklin Admr. of Peter Franklin with the Estate of said
Intestate.

Also the Division of the Negroes of the said Intestate between
the Heirs — Also a Settlement of the Accounts of the Estate of
Jos. Franklin with the heirs of James Conway.

121 – 27. Elisabeth Haslen vs. Wilson Blount} Case. The following Jury impaneled & Sworn: 1. Hardy Hukins 2. William Mitchel 3. Oliver Hall
4. Joseph Biggs 5. William Davis 6. Joseph Nelson 7. Robert Hunt 8. Stephen Dun 9. ~~Humphry Jones~~ Tho. Harper, Origl. 10. Will. Williams 11. James Nelson 12. Jesse Bryan find the defendt. guilty & assess Plff. Damgs. 30 pds. 6 costs & Court

Ajournd till 9 oClock tomorrow morning.
Met according to adjournment. Present the Worshipfull Levi Dawson, John Dawson, Joshua Fulshire, F. Lowthorp, Wm. M. Herritage, Wm. McClure} Esqrs.

James McMains is appointed Constable in the Town of Newbern upon entering into bond with John Goulding & James McCafferty his Securities.

37. Ann Webber vs. John Norris} Case. The following Jury impaneled & Sworn.
1. Hardy Hukins 2. Will. Mitchell 3. Oliver Hall   4. John Whitehead 5. Jacob Cooke 6. Joseph Masters 7. James McCafferty 8. Levi Fulshire 9. James Nelson 10. Chr. Sanders 11. Nathan Smith 12. John Cox Find the plantiff has sutain'd Damage £20.13.7 & Costs.

122 – State vs. Penelope Tear} Ind. Assault. The Same Jury as in the last Cause impaneled & Sworn find the Defendant Guilty – upon which the Court fined her Six pence.

State vs. Rhody Sawyer} Ind. Assault. The Same Jury as in the last Cause, impaneled & Sworn find the Defendant Guilty upon which ordered that She be fined one penny.

J.C. Bryan Esqr. Sheriff, surrendered the Body of Cormick Higgins who for want of further Security was ordered to Jail.

John Frink Smith Esqr. is allowed the Sum of £5.4.0 for attending as a Juror at the last Surperior Court, per the Clerks Certificate.

State vs. John Williams} petit Larceny. The following Jury impaneled & Sworn.
1. John Biggs   2. Joseph Nelson 3. Enoch Alexander 4. Philip Knowis 5. Tho. Hyman 6. John Clark   7. Thomas Harper 8. Will. Lawley 9. Will. Adams 10. Joshua Balance 11. Thomas Webber 12. James Hyman
find the Defendant Guilty, upon which Ordered that he John Williams, receive thirty-nine Stripes upon his bare back, between the hours of one & three this Eveng. & be committed until his fees are pd.

123 — State vs. John Nagall} Ind. Assault. The same Jury as in No. 37 impannel'd find the Defendant Guilty upon which the Court proceeded to ~~pass~~ Fine the Defendant Six Pence.

On Motion Francis Lowthorp and William Tisdale are appointed to divide, between Ephemia Tinker (formerly Snead) and Leah Snead, a lot of half Acre of Land in [illegible] town of New Bern No. 292 which said Lot was purchased by sd. Euphemia & Leah by Deed bearing date January 31st. 1772 & Registered in Book H No. 2, page 241 of this Office (issued).

On Motion Ordered that Farnifold Green Senr., John Fonville and Richard Nixon be appointed to Divide the Estate of Silas S. Stevenson decd. among the Children agreeable to Law and return the Proceedings to next Court.

State vs. Wm. McKerral} Idt. Assl. John Goulding Prosr.
The same Jury as in No. 37 Impaneled and Sworn find the Defendant Guilty.

On motion of Benjamin Wood, & affidavit of Philip Knowis Ordered that ~~John S.~~ A writ brought by Justices Warrant by John Bedscot against Philip Knowis and tried before John Tillman Esquire be brought up before this Court on appeal.

124 — Ordered that James Murchie have ~~Leave~~ License to keep public house in the Town of Newbern, & he gave as Securities David Terry and Fred. Clements.

Adjourned till ½ past 4 oClock.
Met pursuant to Adjournment. Present Levi Dawson, John Dawson, J.F. Smith, Francis Lowthorp, Joshua Fulshire} Esqrs.

Ordered that the Executor have leave to sell the perishable part of the estate of Stephen Wright decd.

State vs. McKerral} The Defendant having been found Guilty, the Court proceeded to Fine him Ten Shillings.

Ordered that John Gooding be added to the Commissioners to divide the Estate of S.S. Stevenson between the Heirs & that either three of them be a majority for that purpose.

125 — State vs. Jeremiah Parsons} The following Jury impaneled and Sworn.
1. Hardy Hukins 2. Wm. Mitchell 3. Oliver Hall 4. John Whitehead 5. Jacob Cooke 6. Joseph Masters 7. Levi Fulshire 8. James Nelson 9. Charles Saunders 10. James McCafferty 11. Thomas Weber 12. James McKinlay
find the defendant Not Guilty.

State vs. Wm. McKerral} Same Jury as in the last Cause except Wm. Anthony instead of James McKinlay. Jury called one failing to answer — Mistryal.

State vs. Francis Gardner} The following Jury, impaneled & sworn. 1. Wm. Hawley 2. John Banks 3. John Biggs 4. John Gooding 5. Wm. Ross 6. Tho. Harper 7. Joshua Balance 8. John Shuffield 9. James Carney 10. Ed. Pasteur 11. Wm. Tignor 12. Wm. Shepard find the Defendant Not Guilty.

126 – State vs. James Cleary} Same Jury as in the last Cause except Tho. Hyman, James McMains & David Brothers in the place of James Carny, Ed. Pasteur, & Wm. Shepard, nol. Pros.

Adjourned till Tomorrow 9 oClock.
Met pursuant to adjournment. Present J.F. Smith, Wm. McClure, Levi Dawson, Francis Lowthorp, John Dawson, Isaac Guion} Esqrs.

Ordered that Isaac Lewis, a free molatto boy, aged seventeen years, the 25th Octr. Last, be bound apprentice to Capt. Isaac Mackee. (Indrs. Executed)

Ordered that Philip Knowis be appointed Constable in Capt. Daniel West District (in the room of John Latham) upon entering into bond with Levi Dawson & Charles Williams his Securities.

Richard Hunley, John Smith, and James Moor, or any two of them, are appointed to audit the accounts of Wm. McClure Executor of Elisabeth Egleston Decd. & make return to next Court.

Ordered that David Spelman, a free black boy aged nineteen years next July be bound to George Emmerson to learn the Carpenters Trade.

127—Ordered that Alexander Duguid and Thomas Turner have Letters [blot] of Administration on the Estate of Monsr. Volpellier, decd. upon entering into bond of £2000 with William Mitchell and ~~William Shepard~~ Edward Pasteur their Securities, upon which A. Duguid qualified as Adm. Tho. Turner also Qualified.

Eliza Haslen vs. Wilson Blount} Motion for newTrial made by Defendant. Court being divided the motion fell to the Ground. Appeal prayed ~~& Granted~~ by Defendant & Granted upon entering into bond with William Slade and John S. West.

Walter Allen vs. James McCafferty} Appeal prayed by Defendant who gave for Securities John Allen Esqr and John Dawson Esqr. (Bond taken)

Wm. Henry, Atty for Thomas Sugden vs. John Darby} Appeal by Plantff. The following Jury impaneled and Sworne viz. 1. Hardy Hukins 2. William Mitchel
3. Oliver Hall   4. John Banks   5. William Lawly 6. John Gatlin 7. Thomas Webber 8. Joseph Masters 9. Robert Hunt 10. Alexander Duguid 11. Joshua Balance 12. David Brothers find for the Plantiff Two pounds & Cost.

128—William Henry atto. to Sugden vs. Daniel West} Appl by Defd. The following Jury [blot]nelled & Sworn viz. 1. John Biggs   2. Joseph Nelson 3. Thos. Hyman 4. Edward Tinker 5. Jas. McCafferty 6. Charles Binders
7. Jeremiah Parsons 8. James Hollis 9. John Kenedy 10. James Nelson 11. John Clark   12. William Tigner find for Plaintiff and Assess Seventeen Shillings Damages & 6d Costs.

172. François X. Martin vs. William Ross & Levi Dawson} Appl. By Pltff. Same Jury as in the last Suit duly Impanelled. Jury called one failing to answer. Mistrial.

The nuncupative Will & Testament of William Gatlin decd. reduced to writing by William Tisdale, was produced in Court, and proved in proper form by the oaths of James Hollis and Nancy Arthur. Ordered that Letters of Administration with the will annexed issue to Amy Gatlin his widow.

129 – An Inventory & Acct. Sales of the Estate of Peter Reel decd. was returned by the Admx.

The Court adjourned till 4 oClock in the Evening. Court met according to adjournment. Present The Worshipful Francis Lowthorp, Levi Dawson, Joshua Fulcher, John Dawson, Isaac Guion} Esquires.

Wm. Lawley, Administrator to the Estate of Sarah Mitchell decd. returned an Inventory and Account States of said Estate.

P. Thomequez vs. Charles Saunders} Appeal. The following Jury impaneled and Sworn.
1. Joseph Nelson 2. John Biggs 3. Ed. Tinker 4. James McCafferty 5. Nathan Smith 6. Thomas Webber 7. Wm. Lawley 8. John Kenedy 9. Tho. Hyman 10. John Clark 11. John Gatlin 12. Robert Hunt Find for the plantiff £19.19 Nine pounds 19/11 & Costs.

130 – Ordered that Isaac Guion, Francis [illegible] and J.F. Smith Esqrs. or any two of them ~~Audit~~ be appointed Auditors to settle the Accounts of Jno. Devereaux Admr. of the Estate of Patric Cleary decd. and make return thereof to ~~next~~ Court.

Ordered that George Worsley, an orphan boy be bound apprentice to James Brightman to learn the Trade of a Blacksmith.

Age to be ascertained when Indentures taken.

Ordered that the administrators have leave to sell the perishable part of the Estate of Monsr. Volpellier decd.

Emmerson vs. Adms. Whitehead} The Defendant being dissatisfied with the verdict, prayed an Appeal; upon entering into bond with Levi Dawson & John Banks — Granted.

Ordered that Thomas Crew be allowed Two Pounds eight Shillings for attending the Court & Grand Jury this Term.

131 — Joshua Fulsher, Levi Dawson, F. Lowthorp, J.P.

[June 1793]
132 — At a County Court of Pleas & Quarter Sessions begun and held for the County of Craven at the Court House in Newbern on the second Monday in June being the 10th day of the Month in the Seventeenth year of American Independence A.D. 1793.

Present the Worshipful Joseph Leech, John Tillman, Wm. M. Herritage, Spyers Singleton, John Bragg, John F. Smith, Jacob Johnston, Francis Lowthorp} Esqrs.

The Sheriff of Craven County (To wit) John C. Bryan Esqr. returned the Venire for Jurors duly summoned to attend this Court in these Words "Executed."

Ordered that Nancy Lewes have Letters of Administration upon the Estate of her Deceased Husband Jesse Lewis upon her entering into Bond of £1000- with David Lewis and Jacob Cooke her securities.

Ordered that a fine of £5.0.0 adjudged against Nathan Tisdale at the last Court for his non attendance as a Juryman be remitted upon his paying fees.

Ordered that Christopher Norwood, an orphan Boy aged 13 years and six months be bound to Benja. Foscue to learn the Trade of a Shoemaker. Issd.

Ordered that Jacob Johnston Esqr. William Phipps and Joseph Palmer be appointed to Divide the Estate of Samuel Wiggins decd. between the Widow & Heirs of said Deceased.

133 — Then was the following Gentlemen Sworn as Grand Jurors. To wit. 1. James McKinley, Foreman   2. Edward Tinker 3. Frederick Foy 4. William Ross 5. Enoch Alexander 6. John Kennedy 7. Geo. Ellis 8. Jesse Bryan   9. William Good 10. John Clark   11. Jacob Cooke 12. John Moore 13. William Paxton Thos. Crew, Constable.

The last Will & Testament of Neale Watson decd. was Proved in Open Court by the Oath of John Carmack a subscribing Witness thereto, and at the same time Joseph Watson one of the Executors therein named appeared in Court and Qualified agreeable to Law, ordered that Letters Testamentary issue thereon accordingly.

An Inventory of the Estate of Richard Carlton decd. was returned by the Executor & filed.

An Inventory of the Estate of Jesse Lewis was returned by the Admx. & filed.

An Inventory and Account Sales of the Estate of William Sheppard Foster was returned & filed.

A Division of Negroes belonging to the Estate of Wm. Sheppard Foster decd. was returned by the persons appointed at last Term to divide the same, and ordered to be Recorded.

A Division of Negroes between William McClure & James R. Emery of the Estate of Thomas James Emery decd. was returned by ~~the~~ John Fonveille & Richard Nixon two of the Referees appointed at last Term for that purpose.

134 – A Division of Negroes of the Esate of Ha____ _____ was returned by John Fonveille & Richard Nixon two of the Referees appointed at last Term for that purpose.

Ordered that Richard Daugherty have Letters of Administration upon the Estate of Nehemiah Randall decd. the W[idow?] of said Decd. having resigned her right of Admn. To him upon his entering into Bond of £50 with John Cox & John Carmack his securities. (Letters iss.)

Ordered that John S. West have Letters of Admin. upon the Estate of Benjamin Burton decd. upon his entering into Bond of £100- with John Tillman & Jacob Johnston Esqrs his securities.

Ordered that John Daly, Isaac Bryan, John Holloway, John Fonvielle, John Cox, & Wm. M. Herritage or any five of them be appointed to Divide the Estate of John Green decd. both Real & Personal, between the Widow & Child of said decd. and make return of the Proceedings to the next County Court. Issd. Dr.

Adjourned till 3 oClock this afternoon. Met Pursuant to adjournment.

Present the Worshipfull Joseph Leech, John Tillman, John Bragg, Francis Lowthorp} Esqrs.

A Division of the Cattle of Stephen Wallace decd. was returned & ordered to be filed.

George Lane to have Tavern License upon entering into Bond of £100- with Isaac Bryan & John Cox securities. Dr.

An Account Sales of the Estate of Stephen Wallace Decd. was returned by the Sheriff & filed.

135 – Mary[?] Wrenford vs. Heirs of Jno. Green Jr. decd.} Sci. Fa. Judgment final against the Lands agreeable to the Judgment given by the Justice upon the Warrant.

George Barrow vs. Exr. Benoni Barnard} Cos. Default. The following Jury impaneled 1. James Coor   2. James Stewart 3. James Bruce 4. James Little 5. John Harvey 6. Thomas Cox 7. John Green   8. Thomas Oliver 9. John Knox   10. Thomas Hyman 11. William Anthony 12. William Hawley Find the Plantiff hath sustained damage to amount £12.9.9- and they assess 6d Costs.

Mary Nelson vs. Josias Jones and Thomas Sparrow} Debt. The same Jury as in the last Cause. Find the writing obligatory to be the act and Deed of the Defendants, and assess £8.11.8 damage & 6d Costs, and they further find that the sum of £5 has been paid.

Elizabeth Peters vs. Thomas Phillips} Motion for Rule to shew cause why an Execution issued against the Defendant should not be set aside.

An Account Sales of the Estate of Agness White was returned by the Sheriff & ordered to be filed.

Read the Petition of John Bryan praying leave to Build a Toll Bridge over Swifts Creek upon the Main Road Leading from West's Ferry to Washington, where he had a Bridge. Ordered that the prayer

136 — of said Petition be granted. The said John Bryan Building a good and Sufficient Bridge over the said Creek and Keeping the same in good repair during the time the same shall be vested in him. Provided the Bridge is Built & Compleated within three months from this term. Which Bridge when Built shall be vested in the said John Bryan his Heirs and assigns for and during the Term of thirty years from the 10th day of September next he entering into Bond of Five hundred Pounds with James McCafferty & Joel King his Securities for the faithful Building said Bridge and keeping the same in repair during the Term of Term aforesaid, --and the said John Bryan his Heirs Executors Administrators & Assigns are hereby empowered to ask Demand & receive the following Toll. Vizt. (fees paid)

The above order Rescinded.

Mr. Bryan to continue to keep the Ferry untill a Bridge is Built by Jacob Johnston Esqr. & William Bryan who have engaged to Build the Bridge at their own Expense at the same place where the former Bridge stood.

Adjourned till 8 oClock in the Morng.

Tuesday, June 11, 1793. Met Pursuant to Adjournment. Present the Worshipfull John Tillman, John Allen, Henry Tillman, Wm. McClure} Esqrs.

137 – [Ord]ered that William Hawley a defaulting Juror be fined [tw]enty Shillings (remitted).

[Tho]mas Turner, Executor Jno. W. Stanley decd. vs. [J]no Green Admr. of [J]ames Green junr. decd.} Case. The following Jury empanelled Vizt.
1. James Coor   2. James Stewart 3. James Little   4. James Bruce 5. Thomas Cox 6. Thomas Oliver 7. John Knox   8. Thomas Hyman 9. Wilson Blount 10. John Harvey 11. William Hawley 12. William Anthony Plantiff called & non prossd.

An account sales of the Perishable part of the Estate of Margaret Rew ~~decd. was no~~ Orphan of Beverly Rew decd. was returned & filed.

A Settlement & Division of the Estate of Beverly Rew decd. was returned and ordered to be filed.

Present the Worshipfull Joseph Leech, Jno. Tillman, Jno Fonvielle, John Daly, Jacob Johnston, Richd. Nixon, Jno. Allen, Jno. Carney, Adam Tooley, Isaac Bryan, Wm. M. Herritage, Levi Dawson, Southy Rew, John Bragg, James Gatlin, Spyers Singleton, Isaac Guion, Thos. A. Green, Jno. F. Smith, William M.Clure, Henry Tillman, John Dawson, Francis Lowthorp.

The Court proceeded to appoint a Sheriff for Craven County when on casting up the Votes it appeared that

138 – William Henry Esqr. had thirteen Votes for Sheriff including his own Vote and Edward Pasteur thirteen Votes including the Vote of Abner Neale, Esqr.

An Inventory of the Estate of James Pearce decd. was returned by the Executors of said Decd.

No. 14 Joseph Shute Exr. of Thos. W. Pearson vs. Titus Ogden Survg. CoPartner of Thos. & Titus Ogden} Case. The same Jury as in the last cause Except Jno. Green in the room of Wm. Anthony find the Defendants did assume, and assess the plantiffs Damages at £443.15.6 & 6d Costs, and they further find that the Defends. Did assume within three years and that there is no Sett off.

Ordered that Moses Ernull, Charles Williams & Joseph Willis be appointed to Settle and Divide the Estate of Jno. Griffin decd. amongst the Heirs of said Decd. with William Surles Admr. of said Estate also to Divide the Estate of said Decd. amongst the Heirs of said Decd. (issd. 3/ pd. Dr.)

Ordered that William Adams have permission to keep Tavern at his House in Craven County upon his entering into Bond of £100 with Levi Dawson Secy. (pd.)

Ordered that John B. Herritage be fined twenty Shillings for his Contempt of this Court in tearing a Paper said to be a Petition which was in the Custody of the Court. (pd.)

Ordered that Elizabeth Green Ex~ of John Green decd. have permission to sell the perishable part of the Estate of said Deceased agreeable to Law. (issd.)

139 — [No.] 18 Stephen Brooks vs. Winston Caswell} Case. The following Jury empanell'd. James Coor, James Stewart, James Little, James Bruce, Thomas Cox, Thomas Oliver, Jno. Knox, Thomas Hyman, John Green, John Harvey, William Hawley, William Anthony find the Defendant did assume & assess the Plantiffs Damages to £75.18.13 & 6d Costs, and they further find the Defends. Did assume within 3 years.

No. 19. Administratrix of Jno. Allmand decd. vs. Bridget Conner} Detinue. The same Jury as in the last Cause empanelled find the Defendant did not detain the Negroe in Question. Appeal prayed & allowed. Wm. Good & Sarah Burney Securities.

State at the Instance of Colo. Dawson vs. John Latham} Peace Warrant. The defendant appeared and entered into Recognizance in the sum of £300, with John West and Edward Perkins his Securities each in the sum of £150 to be Levied upon the Goods & Chattels Lands and Tenements for the use of the State, to be Void nevertheless if the said John Latham shall well & truly keep the peace towards all the Good Citizens of this State & more particularly towards Levi Dawson Esqr. for the term of twelve months from this date.

140 — Adjourned till tomorrow Morng. 8 oClock.

June 12, 1793. Met pursuant to adjournment. Present the Worshipfull
John Tillman, John Carney, Adam Tooley, Wm. M. Herritage, John Bragg} Esqrs.

Ordered that David Underhill aged 14 years be bound to Thomas Oliver to learn the Trade of a House Carpenter. (Inds. made out)

Ordered that Jarvis Burton [Buxton] Esqr. Coroner of Craven County be allowed the sum of £3.18.0 for taking an Inquisition upon the Body of Wm. Hartley who was Drowned. (issued)

Robert Donnell vs. Stephen Stevenson} The following Jury empanelled, To Wit. 1. James Coor   2. William Hawley 3. James Stewart 4. Frederick Lane 5. James Bruce 6. Thomas Hyman 7. John Green   8. Thomas Oliver 9. Jno. Knox   10. Wm. Anthony 11. John Harvey 12. Frans. Fomvielle Find the Defends. did assume & assess the Plffs. Damages at £63.5.0 & 6d Costs.

Ordered that Adam Tooley Esqr. and Levi Fulsher be appointed to Audit the Accounts of Peter Physioc Executor of Joseph Brittain decd. and make a return to the next Court. Issd.

Ordered that Adam Tooley Esqr. & Levi Fulsher be appointed to Audit the Accounts of Joseph Brittain decd. who was Guardian of the Orphans of Thos. Roe and make a return to the next Court. Issd.

141 — Ordered that James Little & Thomas Cox defaulting Jurors be fined twenty shillings each. (fine cancelld.)

No. 22 James Saunders vs. Jacob Mills alias Jarrell} [illegible] Assault & Battery. The same Jury as in the last Cause except Thomas Cox in the room of Frederick Lane empanelled find the Defendant Guilty and assess the Plantiffs Damages £5.0.0 & 6d Costs.

Henry Livingston & William Gibbs renewed their Tavern License.

No. 23 Henrion & Constantin vs. Thomas Haslen} Case. The
same Jury as in the last Cause empanelled find the Defendant
did assume and assess the Plantiffs Damages at £173.12 & 6d
Costs. Appeal prayed & allowed giving Elizabeth Haslen &
Danl. Carthy Securities.

Ordered that Francis Lowthorp, James Ellis & Samuel
Chapman assessors of Town property for the year 1792 be
allowed forty shillings each.

A Division of the Estate of Wright Stanly decd. was returned
by the Referees appointed for that purpose and ordered to be
filed.

A Division of the Estate of Silas S. Stevenson decd. was
returned by the persons appointed for that purpose & filed.
[writing in the margin illegible]

142 – No. 24. Jno. Smallwood assignee &c. vs. Thomas Haslen}
Case. The following Jury empanelled & Sworn.   1. William
Hawley 2. James Stewart 3. Thomas Cox 4. James Bruce 5.
Thomas Hyman 6. John Green 7. Thomas Oliver 8. Jno. Knox
9. William Anthony 10. John Harvey 11. Frans. Fonvielle 12.
James Little find the Defendant did assume and assess the
Plantiffs Damages at £133.6.6 Damages & 6d Costs.

No. 209 Henrion & Constantin vs. Thomas Turner Admr.
Wright Stanly decd.} Case. The same Jury as in the last Cause
empanelled find the Defendants Intestate did assume & assess
the Plantiffs Damages at £132.15.8 & 6d Costs.

Fairwell Coit vs. William Henry} Case. The same Jury as in the
last Cause except Frederick Lane in the room of Thomas Cox
empanelled, find that the Defendant did not assume.

Then were the Grand Jury discharged. Adjourned till 3 oClock.

143 — Met Pursuant to Adjournment. Present the Worshipfull John Tillman, Levi Dawson, Francis Lowthorp} Esqrs.

An Account Sales of the Estate of James Saunders decd. was returned by the Sheriff.

No. 26 Richard Fen on demise William Slade vs. John Den, and Nathan Smith, Tenant} Eject. The same Jury as in No. 24. empanelled find the Defendant Guilty and assess 6d Damage & 6d Costs. Appeal prayed by the Defendants Attorney which is granted upon his filing reasons and entering into Bond of £100 with John Green & James Little his securities.

No. 29. Titus Ogden Survg. Copartner &c. vs. William M. Herritage} Covt. The same Jury as in the last Cause empanelled. Plantiff called Non suit.

No. 30. Bibby Bush vs. Francis Lowthorp} Case. The same Jury as in the last Cause empanelled find the Defendant did assume & assess the Plantiffs Damages at £20 & 6d Costs.

144 — No. 31. James McKinlay vs. Edmund Perkins} Case. The same Jury as in the last Cause empanelled find the Defendant did assume & assess the Plantiffs Damages to £56.1.11 and 6d Costs.

No. 32. Thomas Turner vs. Edmund Perkins} Debt. The same Jury as in the last Cause empanelled find the Writing Obligatory is the Act & Deed of the Defendant and assess the Plantiffs Damage to £13.12 & they further find that no payments have been made. Appeal Judgement accordingly Sci. Fa.

No. 33, Thomas Turner vs. Edmund Perkins & ~~Leah Coll~~
William Slade & William Mitchell Admrs. ~~of Th~~ De Bonis non
of Thomas Collier decd.} Debt. The same Jury as in the last
Cause empanelled find the Writing Obligatory in the Act and
Deed of Edmund Perkins and Thomas Collier and further find
that no payments have been made and that William Slade &
William Mitchell have fully administered upon all the
property of the said Thomas Collier decd. which have come to
their Hands &c and assess the Plantiffs Damages at £6.18.6 ½
& 6d Costs. Judgement accordingly and Sci. Fa. to issue to the
Heirs of Collier to shew Cause why the Lands should not be
sold &c.

Ordered that Thomas Webber, William McClure & Francis
Lowthorp be appointed to Audit the Accounts of Francis X.
Martin Executor of the last Will & Testament of Duryvault D
St Leger decd. & make return to the next Court.

145 – [No.] 35 [?]. Joseph Leech vs. John Williams} The same
Jury as in the last Cause empanelled find the Defendant did
assume and assess the Plantiffs Damages at £40.19.0 & 6d
Costs.

No. 35. Thomas Turner vs. Geo. Duffy and James Ellis} Debt.
The same Jury as in the last Cause empanelled find the
Writing Obligatory is the Act and Deed of the Defendants and
that no payments hath been made and assess the plantiffs
Damages at 6d & 6d costs. Judgment accordingly. Appeal
prayed & allowed the Defendants.

No. 36. William Hannis vs. Nathaniel Willis} Case. The same
Jury as in the last Cause empanelled find the Defendant did
assume and assess the Plantiffs Damages at £39.17.9 & 6d
Costs.

No. 37. Thomas Cox vs. Joshua Knight} The same Jury as in the last Cause empanelled. Plantiff called Non pros.

No. 40. James McKinlay vs. Geo. Duffy} Case. The same Jury as in the last Cause empanelled find the Defendant did assume & assess the Plantiffs Damages at £33.3.1 and 6d Costs.

146 — Bazell Smith Esqr. appeared in Court and took his Seat upon the Bench and Voted for William Henry Esqr. as Sheriff for Craven County which vote was objected to by Doct. Pasteur. Mr. Henry also Objected to the Vote of Abner Neale Esqr.

Doctor Pasteur at the same time Objected to Mr. Henrys Voting for himself.

Adjourned till tomorrow Morng. 8 oClock.

Thursday, 13th Jun 1793. Met Pursuant to Adjournment. Present the Worshipfull John Tillman, William McClure, John Carney, John Sears}

No. 44 Jeptha Utley vs. Gabriel Kingsbury Exr. &c of John Kingsbury decd.} Sci. Fa. To revive Judgt. The following Jury empanelled To wit. 1. James Stewart 2. James Little 3. William Hawley 4. John Harvey 5. James Coor 6. Thomas Cox 7. James Bruce 8. Thomas Hyman 9. John Green 10. Thomas Oliver 11. John Knox 12. Francis Fonvielle Find the Record of Judgment and that no Payments have been made & assess £14.16.8 Damage & 6d Costs.

147 — Then was Joshua Fulsher & Thomas York appointed Inspectors of the Poll of Election at Smith Creek in August next and Samuel Chapman & John Fonveille inspectors of the Poll of Election at Newbern in August next.

Ordered that Edward Fields an Orphan Lad aged nine years the 2d March last be bound to James Meeks to learn the Taylors Trade (indentures made out). Issd.

The Admrs. Peter Franklin vs. Joseph West & Jno. West} The same Jury as in the last Cause except William Anthony in the room of Thomas Hyman empanelled find the Defendants did assume and assess £33.16.4 Damage & 6d Costs.

No. 192. Benja. Williams vs. James Wallace & Danl. Burdoc} Default & Enqy. The same Jury as in No. 44 except William Anthony in the room of Thomas Cox empanelled assess the Plantiffs Damages to £47.10 and 6d Costs.

No. 50 John Coart vs. George Lovick} The same Jury as in No. 44 except William Anthony in the room of Thomas Hyman empanelled find the Writing Obligatory is the

148 — Act and Deed of the Defendants and that no payments have been made and they assess the Plantiffs Damages to £6.10.1 & 6d Costs.

No. 49. Thomas Turner Survg. Partner &c. vs. David Witherspoon} Case. The same Jury as in the last Cause empanelled find the Defendant did assume, and that he did assume within three years, and they assess the Plantiff Damages to £24.15.0 & 6d Cost and they further find that there is no Setts off.

Motion for Arrest of Judgment — overruled & Judgment on Motion.

No. 56. Ann Webber vs. Francis X. Martin, Exr. De S Ledger decd.} Case. The same Jury as in No. 44 except Wm. Anthony in the room of James Little empanelled find the Defendants Testator did assume and assess £59.17.0 Damages & 6d Costs and that there are no assetts in the hands of the Executor.

No. 59. Wm. Dove assignee Thomas Cox ~~Assignee Wm. Dove~~ vs. John West of Moseley's Creek} Case. The same Jury as in No. 44 except Wm. Anthony in the room of Thos. Cox empanelled find the Defendant did assume and assess the Plantiff's Damages to £45.18.0 & 6d Costs appeal prayed and allowed giving Danl. West & Wm. M. Herritage securities.

149 — No. 74. John Simpson vs. John Smallwood} Case. The same Jury as in No. 44 except William Anthony ~~against~~ in the room William Hawley. Plantiff called. Non. Pros.

Motion for Rule to shew Cause the Judgment of Non Pros should not be set aside — on argument dismissed.

An Inventory of the Estate of Samuel Smyth decd. was returned by the Administrators.

No. 84. Levin Clark vs. Anthony Inloe} Case. The same Jury as in the last except Edmond Perkins in the room of Thomas Cox find the ~~Defendants Intestate did assume~~ Plantiff hath sustained £63.1.4 Damages and assess ~~the Plantiffs Damages to £63.1.4~~ and 6d Costs.

Adjourned till Three oClock this afternoon.

Met Pursuant to Adjournment. Presnet the Worshipfull John Tillman, Wm. M. Herritage, Francis Lowthorp, Wm. McClure} Esqrs.

Ordered that Nancy Smith have Letters of Administration upon the Estate of her decd. Husband Jesse Smith upon her Qualifying and entering into Bond of £50 with Thomas P. Ives & John Williams her Securities. Whereupon the said Nancy Qualified & entered into Bond accordingly and rendered an Inventory of said Estate.

Ordered that Nancy Smith have permission to sell the perishable part of said Estate.

150 — Ordered that Mathew Burnis have Letters of Administration upon the Estate of Michael Flood Decd. upon his entering into Bond of £300 with Southy Rew Esqr and William Johnston his Secrys., and Qualifying agreeable to Law. Letters issd.

Ordered that the said Mathew Byrnes have Permission to sell the perishable part of the said Michael Flood's Estate, agreeable to Law. Issd.

Four Accounts of Sales of the Estate of Charles McLin decd. was returned by the Admr. signed by the Sheriff and ordered to be filed. (Chargd.)

No. 64. James Ellis suvivg. Partner of Richard & James Ellis vs. David Witherspoon Admr. Debonis non of Abner Nash who was Bail for John Howell.} The following Jury empanelled to Wit. 1. James Stewart   2. James Little   3. William Hawley 4. James Coor   5. Thomas Cox 6. James Bruce 7. Thomas Hyman 8. John Green   9. Thomas Oliver 10. John Knox   11. Francis Fonvielle 12. William Anthony   P. Harvey T. Webber
find there is such an Record as set forth in the Scire Facias and that a Writ of Capias ad Sates faciendum was issued previous to the issuing Scire Facias.

Ordered that John Sears Esqr. have Letters of Administran. upon the Estate of his Father James Sears decd. upon his Qualifying and entering into Bond of £500 with Francis Lowthorp & William Sears his Securities.

151 – No. 65. David Witherspoon Adminr. De Bonis non of Abner Nash decd. vs. James Ellis} Sci. Facias to reverc [?] Judgment. The same Jury as in the last Cause except John Harvey in the room of Thos. Oliver empanelled find that there is such an Record as set forth in the Sci Facias and that £65.16.6 hath been paid, and that there remains due to the Plantiffs the sum of £231.13.5 ¼ and they assess 6d Damage and 6d Costs.

No. 80. Richard D. Spaight Esqr. vs. Francis X. Martin} Case. The same Jury as in No. 64 except John Harvey in the room of Thomas Oliver, and Thomas Webber in the room of John Knox empanelled & Sworn. Nonsuit.

Adjourned till tomorrow morning 9 oClock
Friday 14 June 1793. Met Pursuant to adjournment. Present the Worshipfull John Tillman, John Carney, Wm. M. Herritage, John Bragg} Esqrs.

Ordered that Joshua Fulsher, Francis Delamar & John Biggs be appointed to Audit the Accounts of Thomas Hyman Administrator of Joseph Franklin decd. and make return to the next Court.

152 – No. 164. John Mansfield vs. David Murdock} Appeal. The following Jury empanelled &c. To wit. 1. James Stewart 2. James Little   3. William Anthony 4. John Harvey 5. Thomas Cox 6. James Bruce 7. Thomas Hyman 8. Thomas Oliver 9. William Hawley 10. Francis Fonvielle 11. John Green 12. James Coor Juror withdrawn & contd. by Consent.

Executors of Hezekiah McCotter decd. vs. James Clark} Appl by Defendt. The same Jury as in No. 64 empanelled find the Defendant did assume & that he assumed within here years and Assess the Plffs. Damages to £3.12.0 & 6d Costs and that no payments or sett offs have been made.

Gilbert Gray vs. Isaac Guion} appeal by Plantiff. The same Jury as in the last Cause empanelled find the Defendant did assume and assess the Plantiffs Damages to £12.0.0 and 6d Costs.

The Nuncupative Will & Testatment of John Smith decd. reduced to Writing by Richard Nixon Esqr. and Sworn to by Benajah Bogey was produced in Court and Ordered to be Recorded and at the same time Pearcy Smith Widow of the

153 – [dec]d. appeared in Court and prayed for Letters of Administration with the Copy of the Will Annexd. Which was granted upon her Qualifying and entering into Bond of £200 with Simon Bexley & Benajah Bogey her Securities. Whereupon the said Pearcy Smith Qualified & entered into Bond and also rendered an Inventory of the said Decds. Estate.

[No.] 206 – John Conner vs. Frans. X. Martin Exr. Duryl. D.S.Leger decd.} Appl. By Plantiff. The same Jury as in the last Cause empanelled find the Defendants Testator did assume and that he assumed within three years and that he hath assetts have come to the Executors Hands to the amount of twenty pounds and they assess £4.7.6 Dama. & 6d Costs.

Read the Petition of Nathan Smith praying leave to Build a Public Water Grist Mill upon Otter Creek where he owns Land upon Westernmost Side of said Creek and Christopher Merchant owns the Lands upon the Opposite side of said Creek. Ordered that Geo. Lovick, [blank] Bailey & [blank] Fooks be appointed to Lay off and Value two Acres of Land upon the said stream, belonging to the said Smith & Merchant and make a return of their proceedings to the next Court and that Sci. Facias issue to the said Chrisr. Merchant to appear at the next Court and shew Cause if any &c &c, [illegible] issd.

James McCafferty Admr. D. Herron decd. vs. Abner Nash decd.} Appeal by Defendt. The same as in the last Cause empanelled & Sworn. Plantiff called Non Pros.

154 – Then was the following Gentlemen appointed Jurors for the next Term viz.
1. Richard Hunley 2. Joseph Oliver 3. Wilson Blount

4. William Dudley ____ ~~Turner~~ [Illegible, stricken] 5. Robert
Hunt 6. James McCafferty (Newbern) 7. William Smyth (S.
Creek) 8. Benjamin Brinson 9. David Lewis 10. George
Lovick 11. James Davis 12. John Morris 13. John Whiding 14.
Andrew Richardson 15. Michael Willis

16. William Winn 17. Francis Carraway 18. Enoch Masters
19. Thomas York 20. Mathew Neal 21. John S. Nelson 22.
Amos Squires 23. James Whitfield
24. Willis McCoy 25. Thomas G. Fonville 26. Joseph Clark
27. William Cox 28. Jonathan Wadsworth 29. John Gooding
30. Southey Jorden Rew 31. Edw. Pritchet 32. Jno. Jones
(Clubfords Creek) 33. Jno. Cummings 34. Evan Jones 35.
Frederic Turner 36. Benja Mason
37. Aaron Ernull 38. ~~Joseph~~ William Clark (Issd.)
And the following to attend the Superior Court for Newbern
District, Sept. Term 1793.
1. John Carney 2. Southey Rew 3. Jno. F. Smith 4. Jno. C.
Bryan 5. Francis Lowthorp 6. Thomas A. Green 7. Hardy
Gatlin 8. John Green 9. Thomas Oliver

Saml. Gooding vs. Abm. Comron} appeal by Pltff. The same
Jury as in last Cause find the Defendant did assume & that he
did assume within three years, & assess the Pltffs Damage to
£4.5 & Costs.

155 — Read the Petition of John Bryan praying leave to Build a
public water Grist Mill upon Poplar Branch on both sides of
Swifts Creek where he owns Land & Praying that Citation
may issue against John West who Claims Land adjoining
thereto returnable to the next Court &c.

_o. 1. John Saul vs. Charles Saunders Junr.} Appeal by Defend. The same Jury as in the last Cause empanelled find the Defendant did assume & that he was not an Infant at the time of assuming and assess the Plantiff's Dama. To £12.10.0 & 6d Costs.

Thomas Turner vs. Edmund Perkins} The defendant prayed an appeal in this Cause to the Superior Court and offered for Security Andrew Richardson & James McCafferty his Securities. Granted.

Adjourned untill 3 oClock. Met Pursuant to Adjournment. Present the Worshipfull John Tillman, Southy Rew, Wm. McClure} Esqrs.

Charles Crawford & Wife vs. William M. Herritage} Appeal by Defendt. The following Jury empanelled. To Wit.

156 – 1. James Stewart 2. James Little 3. William Anthony 4. Jno. Harvey 5. Thos. Cox 6. James Bruce 7. Thomas Hyman 8. Thomas Oliver 9. Wm. Hawley 10. Francis Fonvielle 11. John Green 12. William Mitchell
Juror Withdrawn & Cause Contd.

No. 3 appeals} George Duffy vs. William Henry} Appeal by Defendt. The same Jury as in the last Cause except James Coor in the room of Wm. Mitchell empanelled find the Defendt. did assume & that he assumed within three years and they assess the Plantiffs Damages to £6.13. ~~Dam~~ and 6d Costs.

Ordered that Daniel a Negroe Slave belonging to Wm. Slade Esqr. have permission to carry a Gun upon his entering into Bond of £100 with Samuel Chapman & James McMains his Securities.

Adjourned till tomorrow Morng. 8 oClock.

Saturday June 15th 1793. Met Pursuant to adjournment.
Present the Worshipfull John Tillman, Levi Dawson, Wm. M.
Herritage, John Bragg, Wm. McClure} Esquires.

Ordered that John Knox and Francis Fonvielle defaulting
Jurors be fined. Jno. Knox forty shillings & Francis Fonvielle
twenty shillings nisi. (issd.)

157 — Ordered that John Fonvielle, John Daly & Francis
Lowthorp be appointed to Audit the Accounts of Silas S.
Stevenson decd. as Guardian of the Orphans of John
Stevenson decd. and report thereon to the next Court.

Whereas Letters of Administration was granted at the last
Term of this Court to Alexander Duguid and Thomas Turner
upon the Estate of Monsr. Laurence Volspelier decd. which
appears to have been Illegally done, the said Decd. being a
Citizen of the French Nation. Therefore Ordered that the said
Letters of Administration be Revoked and Annulled and that
the Bond given by the said Duguid & Turner be given up and
Cancelled and the aforesaid Letters of Administration
returned to the Clerks Office.

__ 23. State vs. Monsr. Chaponell} Indictt. Petit Larceny,
Misdemeanor &c.
The following Jury empanelled & Sworn. To wit.
1. James Stewart 2. James Little 3. Wm. Anthony 4. John
Harvey 5. Thomas Cox 6. James Bruce 7. Thomas Hyman 8.
Thomas Oliver 9. William Hawley 10. John Green 11. David
West 12. Danl. Carthy. find the Defendant not Guilty.

The last Will & Testament of Jeremiah King decd. was proved by the Oath of Jeremiah James one of the Subscribing Witnesses thereto and ordered to be Recorded and at the same time William Phipps one of the Executors therein Named appeared in Court and Qualified as Such. Order'd that Letters Testamentary issue thereon accordingly.

158 – An Inventory of the Estate of Jeremiah King decd. was returned & filed.

No. 9. State vs. Wm. M. Herritage} Indt. Assault & Batty. The same Jury as in the last Cause except William Gaskins in the room of David West and Francis McIlwean in the room of Danl. Carthy find the Defendt. Guilty. fined forty shillings & Costs.

Mathew Gooding vs. James Carney, Admr. &c Charles McLin decd.} Refered. Referees returned an Award in this Cause and do find a Balance due from the said McLin's Estate to the said Mathew Gooding £161.9.10 to be discharged agreeable to return if the Referees. Judgment Pursuant to the award. (filed).

No. 10. State vs. William Henry} The same Jury as in the Cause No. 9 empanelled & Sworn find the Defendant is not Guilty. Ordered that Wm. M. Herritage the Prosecutor pay the Cost of this Suit.

Ordered that John Fonvielle, John Daly & Francis Lowthorp Esqrs. be appointed to Audit the Accounts of John Gooding and Mary White Admrs. of Saml. White decd. and report thereon to the next Court. (issd. Charged.)

159 – State vs. Benjamin Gilstrap} Indt. Assault.
The same Jury as in No. 9. empanelled & Sworn. find the Defendant Guilty. fined six pence.

State vs. John West} Indt. Petit Larceny.
The same Jury as in No. 23. except James Coor in the room of David West and Francis McIlwean in the room of Danl. Carthy—empanelled & sworn—find the Defendant not Guilty.

Ezekiel de la Statius renewed his Tavern License.

Dr. Mons. Fab__ & __e_h Oliver renewed their Tavern License. William Geb_ _lso renewed his Tavern License. John McGraw also to have License. Saml. Chapman Security w/- John Knowles. De.

The Referees appointed to Audit the Accounts of William McClure Executor of Elizabeth Eggleston decd. returned the said accounts which were approved of by the Court & ordered to be filed.

State vs. Wm. M. Herritage} Indt. For Assault & Batty. upon Geo. Lane.
The same Jury as in the last Cause empanelled & Sworn find the Defendant Guilt. fined forth shillings.

State vs. Wm. M. Herritage} Indt. For Rescue. The same Jury as in the last Cause empanelled & Sworn. Juror withdrawn & Cause Continued.

160—State vs. Wm. McKerald} Indt. Assault etc.
The same Jury as in the last Cause empanelled find the Defendant Guilty. fined six pence.

Ordered that Richard Hunley, William Johnston & James Carney be appointed to Audit the Accounts of William Slade & William Mitchell Guardians of the orphans of Yelverton Probate decd. and make return of their proceedings to the next Court. (Issd. Chgd. 2/-. Wm. Slade)

Ordered that John Daves[,] James Carney & James Daves be appointed to Audit the Accounts of David Witherspoon Admin~ De bonis non of the Goods & Chattels &c of Abner Nash decd. and report thereon to the next Court. Dr.

It being suggested to this Court that the South west Bridge adjoining this County[,] Lenoir County & Jones County is out of Repair. Ordered that Isaac Bryan Esqr. be appointed to meet Col. Robert White and the Commissioner to be appointed for Jones County and consult and agree as they may think proper respecting the rebuilding or repairing the said Bridge.

State vs. John Hobday} Indictment Assault & Battery. The same Jury as in the last Cause empanelled & Sworn find the Defendant Guilty fined £20.

161 — Ordered that Joseph Clark & Aaron Ernull be fined five pounds for Nisi for non attendance at this Court as Jurors agreeable to Summons.

Ordered that Joseph Allen, William Sears & Ambrose Jones are appointed Patrollers in Captain Phillips District and that John West, David West, Phillip Knowes & James Daw are appointed Patrollers in Capt. Daniel Wests District.

No. 9. Thos. Turner Exr. Jno. W. Stanly Decd. vs. John Green Adm~ of James Green Jr. Decd.} Non Pros. Motion by Mr. Woods for Rule __ _hew Cause why the suit should not be reinstated — on argument — Rule discharged. — Appeal prayed & allowed on entering into Bond with William Shepard & Danl. Carthy Suys.

On the Execution issued at December Term the Clerks Office against Andrew Grear directed to the Sheriff of Edgcomb County. Ordered that the Sheriff aforesaid be fined twenty Pounds Nisi for Neglecting to make return of the said Executor agreeable to the tenor thereof.

The Court Proceeded to appoint Processioners agreeable to the last Act of Assembly and Divided the County into Districts as follows.
No. 1. on the North side of Neuse River Beginning at Adams Ferry Leading with the main Road
162 — to the Flatt Swamp Containing all the Lands Binding on the Lines of Beaufort & Pitt Countys and upon Neuse River to the upper part of the County. Stephen Harris Processioner.

District No. 2} All the Lands on the North side of the Neuse River below the first District. Henry Tillman Esqr. Processioner.

District No. 3. From Trent River including all the Lands upon the South side of Neuse River from the Fork of said Rivers to the upper part of the County Lines. Geo. Lane Prosr. (issd)

District No. 4. Upon the South side of Trent River & Neuse River down to the Mouth including all the Lands within the County upon the Southernmost side of said Rivers. Southy Rew Esqr. Processioner. (issd.)

Ordered that the Justices who received the lists of Taxables for the year 1792 receive the lists in their ~~different~~ Several Districts for the present year except William Tisdale Esqr in the room of Wm. McClure Esqr. and that Notice issue accordingly. (issued)

James McKinlay vs. Geo. Duffy} Motion in Arrest of Judgment by Wm. Duffy Atto. for Defendant on Argument. Motion overruled. Appeal prayed & allowed the Defendt. on filing Reasons and entering into Bond ~~with~~ of £[blank].

163 — Present the Worshipfull Joseph Leech[,] John Bragg[,], John Tillman[,] Jno. F. Smith[,] Levi Dawson[,] Henry Tillman[,] Isaac Guion[,] Francis Lowthorp[,] Jno. Allen[,] Jno. Daly[,] John Carney[,] Wm. McClure[,] Southey Rew[,] William Henry[,] Abner Neale[,] Wm. M. Heritage.

The Court proceeded to appoint two Coroners in addition to Jarvis Buxten who was heretofore appointed when on Casting up the Votes it appeared that William Dudley & William Moore were appointed. Whereupon the said William ~~Duffy~~ Moore appeared in Court & Qualified by taking the Oaths prescribed agreeable to Law and ~~entering into Bond of~~ Offered James Coor & William Mitchell his Securities. William Dudley also Qualified and offered Isaac Bryan & Jno. C. Bryan Esqrs. his Securities. The said William Dudley & Wm. Moore also took the Oath of Allegiance to this State & also the Oath of Allegiance to the United States.

~~William Green vs. Furnifold Green Jr.}~~

Sam. Chapman vs. Wm. Lovick} Debt. Defendant called and failing to Appear Judgment fined according to Specialty filed.

164 — James Davis vs. Daniel Salt} Atto. ~~Debt~~. Case. The Defendant being Solemnly called and failing to appear and Answer Judgement ~~fined~~ by Default & Enquiry.

Henrion & Constantin vs. Thomas Turner Admr. Wright Stanly} Appeal prayed by Defendt. Granted on filing reasons and entering in__ Bond with Wm. Shepard & Danl. Carthy Securities.

Mr. M Mains Allowed as Constable forty Eight Shillings (issued)

J. Tillman, J.P.
John Carney
John Bragg
W. McClure

165 — [Blank]

[September 1793]
166 — At a County Court of Pleas & Quarter Sessions be__ and held for the County of Craven at the Court Hou__ in Newbern on the second Monday in September __ being the 9th day of the Month A.D. 1793.

Present the Worshipfull Levi Dawson[,] Francis Lowthorp[,] John Sears} Esqrs.

Wm. Dudley Esqrs. one of the Coroners for Craven County returned the Writ of Venue for Jurors summoned to attend this Court at this Term "Executed."

An Inventory of the Estate of Neal Watson Senr. was returned by the Executor.

Ordered that William Johnston & James Carney be appointed to Audit the Accounts of William Good Exr. of William Wood Decd. and report thereon to this Term.

Ordered that Josiah Huckins aged 13 years the 4th January next be bound to Daniel Bradley to learn the Trade of a Brick layer.

John Fonvielle Esqr. Returned the lists of Taxable property in Capt. Lewis District for 1793.

Acct Sales of the Estate of James Ives decd. was returned by the Coroner Wm. Dudley.

167 — The last Will and Testament of John Muse was produced in Court and Proved by the Oath of Caleb Muse one of the Subscribing Witnesses thereto and at the same time Sarah Muse the Executrix therein named Qualified as such agreeable to Law, Ordered that Letters Testamentary issue accordingly.

Ordered that Jane Buxton & William Ross have Administration upon the Estate of William J. Buxton decd. upon their Qualifying and entering into Bond of £800 — with Isaac Guion & Humphrey Jones Secuy.

The last Will & Testament of Joseph Tingle decd. was proved by the Oath of Joseph Burney one of the Subscribing Witnesses thereto and at the same time David Tingle and Shadrach Tingle the Executors therein named appeared in Court and Qualified as such agreeable to Law. Ordered that Letters Testamentary issue at the same time the Exrs. returned an Inventory of sd. Estate.

Ordered that Elijah Copes aged 10 years be Bound to John Godett to learn the Trade of a Cooper. (Inds. Exd.)

Ordered that Anna Daw have administration upon the Estate of John Daw decd. upon her Qualifying & entering into Bond of £300 with Joseph Brinson & Thomas Speight her securities.

Ordered that William Surles be appointed Guardian of Mary & Ephraim Pearce Orphans of Ephraim Pearce decd. (Susanna Miller late Susanna Pearce having resigned the Guardianship of said Orphans.) upon his entering into Bond £500 with Jas. Gatlin & Levi Dawson securities.

168 — Ordered that Aaron Ernull & Moses Ernull & Ephraim Willis be appointed to Audit the Accounts of Susanna Miller, late Susanna Pearce — Guardian to the Orphans of Ephraim Pearce decd. — and Divide the said Decd. Estate between the Widow & Children of said Decd. Issd.

Ordered that the Widow of John Mason decd. be cited to appear this afternoon to shew Cause if any why administration should not be granted to Robert Hatfield.

Ordered that John Carpenter be appointed Guardian to William Carpenter (a Minor) upon his entering into Bond of £100 with Levi Dawson & James Hyman his Securities.

Present: Joseph Leech, John Fonvielle, John Tillman, Richard Nixon, Jacob Johnston, John Sears, Wm. M. Herritage, Jno. F. Smith, Hardy Gallen [Gatlin?], Levi Dawson, Isaac Guion, James Gatlin, Spyers Singleton, Francis Lowthorp, Isaac Bryan, Wm. Henry} Esqrs.

Mr. Enoch Alexander applied to this Court to be appointed Inspector in the Town of Newbern — the Court are of Opinion that there is no Occasion of appointing another inspector.

Ordered that the Court Proceed upon the appointment of a Sheriff for Craven County tomorrow at 12 oClock.

Ordered that Mrs. Daw Admx. John Daw decd. have permission to sell the Perishable part of said Decd. Estate.

169 — Adjourned until 4 oClock this Afternoon.

Met Pursuant to Adjournment. Present the Worshipful Levi Dawson, James Gatlin, Hardy Gatlin}

Ordered that James Jewks an orphan Lad aged 12 years in April last be bound to John Ferguson to learn the Trade of a Shoe maker. (Inds. Exd.)

Then was Evan Jones reappointed Inspector of Produce at Slocumbs Creek upon his entering into Bond of £500 with Geo. Lovick & John Jones his Securities.

Ordered that Robert Hatfield have Administration upon the Estate of John Mason decd. (the Widow of said Decd. being summoned to appear & shew cause &c and having failed to appear) upon his entering into Bond of £100 with Francis Lowthorp & Henry Purss his Securities.

Adjourned till tomorrow morng. 9 oClock.
Met Pursuant to Adjournment.
Present the Worshipful Levi Dawson, Wm. M. Herritage, James Gatlin} Esqrs.

Then was the Grand Jury empanelled & Sworn. To Wit.
No. 1 James David (foreman)   2. Jas. McCafferty 3. Geo. Lovick 4. John Wheeding 5. William Winn
6. Amos Squires 7. Mathew Neale 8. Jas. Whitfield 9. Willis McCoy 10. William Cox 11. John Jones

12. Evan Jones 13. Aaron Ernull

170 — Ordered that Robert Hatfield Admr. of John Mason
decd. have permission to sell the perishable part of said Decd.
Estate.

The Referees appointed at this Term to audit the Accounts of
Wm. Good Executor of William Wood decd. made a return of
the Accounts of said Executor settled by them which was
approved of by the Court and ordered to be filed.

Then was John Vendrick appointed Guardian of Sarah
Carpenter Orphan of Geo. Carpenter decd. upon his entering
into Bond of £100- with Levi Dawson & Joseph West his
Securities.

Ordered that Jonathan Perkins, Joseph West & John Biggs be
appointed to Settle and Divide the Estate of George Carpenter
decd. between the Widow & Heirs of said Decd.

Ordered that Roderigo Le Taste have Letters of
Administration upon the Estate of James McDaniel Decd.
upon his entering into Bond of £80 with Nathan Smith &
Joseph Crispin his Securities.

An Inventory of the Estate of Stockwell Bright decd. was
returned.

Ordered that Ephraim Green aged 12 years lad may be bound
to David Bryan to learn the Trade of a Shoemaker. Dr. 8/)

On Motion of James Carney, Administrator of Charles McLin decd. praying that the Bond given by him for the Administration wherein John C. Bryan & Richard D. Spaight were his Securities may be cancelled and a new Bond given for the administration by the said James Carney with the aforesaid Richard D. Spaight and Joseph Leech Esqr. his Securities. Changd. Dr. 8/

171 – No. 9. Amos Wade & Wife vs. John Carney Exr. of John Bryan decd.} Debt. The following Jury empanelled & Sworn. Viz. No. 1. Thomas Hyman 2. Robert Hunt
3. John Morris 4. William Smith 5. Joseph West 6. Joseph King 7. James Potter 8. Obadiah Allway 9. John Allway 10. Wm. Good 11. John West 12. Alexr. Carruthers. Find the Writing Obligatory is the Act & Deed of the Defendts. Testator and they further find all the several issues in favour of the Plantiffs and assess 6d Dam. & 6d Costs.

Present the Worshipful
Joseph Leech, Issac Guion, Francis Lowthorp, Levi Dawson, John Tillman, John Allen, James Gatlen, John F. Smith, Wm. McClure, Hardy Gatlen, Wm. Henry, Richd. Nixon, Wm. M. Herritage, John Sears, John Dawson, John Fonvielle, Isaac Bryan, John Daly, Henry Tillman, Jacob Johnston, Thomas A. Green, Adam Tooley, Spyers Singleton.

The Court proceeded to appoint a Sheriff for Craven County when on casting up the Votes they appeared as follows.
For William Henry   for Edward Pasteur
Isaac Guion   1   Joseph Leech   1
Levi Dawson   2   Francis Lowthorp 2
John Tillman   3   Jno. F. Smith   3
John Allen   4   John Sears   4
James Gatlen   5   William M. Herritage 5
Wm. McClure   6   John Dawson   6

Hardy Gatlen   7   Jacob Johnston 7
William Henry 8   Adam Tooley   8
John Fonvielle 9   Spyers Singleton 9
Isaac Bryan   10
John Daly   11
Henry Tillman   12
Thos. A. Green 13
Richard Nixon   14
172 — The Court are of Opinion that William Henry Esquire is
duly Elected to the Office of Sheriff for Craven County and
Order that the Clerk make out a Certificate of his appointment
in order that he may Obtain a Commission from his
Excellency the Governor.

Adam Tooley Esqr. returned the List of Taxables in Capt.
Dunn's District for the year 1793.

Motion by Joseph Leech Esqr. to enter a Protest upon the
Minutes against the Appointment of William Henry Esqr. to
the Office of Sheriff he being and suggesting that he was not a
freeholder, which motion was overruled by the a majority of
the Court.

The Court Present the Worshipfull
Jno. Tillman, Henry Tillman, Isaac Guion, John Allen, John
Daly, Richd. Nixon, Hardy Gatlen, Jas. Gatlen, Levi Dawson,
Isaac Bryan, Thos. A. Green, Wm. M. Herritage, Adam Tooley,
Jno. Dawson, Jno. F. Smith} Esqrs.

The Court having reconsidered of the Necessity of appointing another Inspector of Produce for the Town of Newbern are of Opinion that another should be appointed. Whereupon William Hannis was appointed to that Office upon his Qualify___ and entering into Bond with Richard Nixon, John Daly & John Allen his Securities. Whereupon the said William Hannis Qualified and entered into Bond with Security as aforesd.

173 – Adjourned untill 4 oClock this Afternoon.
Met Pursuant to adjournment. Present the Worshipfull
Levi Dawson, James Gatlen, Wm. M. Herritage} Esqrs.

An Acct. Sales of the Estate of Jeremiah King decd. was returned by Wm. Moore Coroner & filed.

James McKinlay vs. Malcolm Gillies} Case. The following Jury empanelled & Sworn.
Viz. 1. Edward Pritchard 2. Thos. Hyman 3. Robert Hunt   4. Wm. Smith 5. Joseph West 6. Joel King 7. James Potter 8. Ignatius Wadsworth 9. Obadiah Allways 10. John Allways 11. Alexander Carruthers 12. Wm. Good
find the Defendant did assume & that he assumed within three years & assess the Plantiffs Damages to £194..19..1 and 6d Costs.

Present the Worshipfull John Allen, Wm. M. Herritage, Hardy Gatlen, Henry Tillman, Levi Dawson.

William Henry Esqr. produced a Commission from His Excellency the Governor appointing him Sheriff for the County of Craven Whereupon the said William Henry Qualified by taking the Oath of Allegiance to this State and also to the United States and the Oath of Office and entered into Bond in the sum of Five thousand Pounds with John Tillman, John Daly, John Fonvielle, Levi Dawson,

174 — Henry Tillman, John Allen, Frederick Lane, Richard Nixon, Thomas A. Green, James Whitfield, John Blanks, & Isaac Guion his Securities.

Adjourned till tomorrow Morning 9 oClock.

Wednesday Septemr. 11th, 1793.
Met Pursuant to adjournment. Present the Worshipful
Levi Dawson, James Gatlen, Hardy Gatlen} Esqrs.

An Inventory and Account Sales of the Estate of John Green decd. was returned & filed. (Dr. J.B.H. 3/)

A Settlement of the Accounts of Joseph Brittain decd. Guardian to the Orphans of Thomas Roe decd. was returned by the Referees appointed at the last Term and Ordered to be filed.

A Settlement of the Accounts of Peter Physioc Executor of Joseph Brittain decd. was returned by the Referees appointed at the last Term & ordered to be filed.

No. 2. Francis Lowthorp vs. Nathan Smith} Case. The following Jury empanelled & Sworn. To wit No. 1. Thos. Hyman 2. Robert Hunt 3. Wm. Smyth 4. Edward Pritchard 5. Benja. Mason 6. James McCafferty 7. Jno. C. Bryan 8. John Devereux 9. Francis McIlwean 10. John Smallwood 11. John Gatlen 12. Thomas Speight find the Defendant did assume & Assess the Plantiffs Damages to £414..18..6 & 6d Costs.

175 — Ordered that Conelius Lovitt be exempt from Mustering and Working upon the Roads on Account of his Infirmities.

Peter Gero__ renewed his Tavern License.

Motion by Francis X. Martin Esqr. that Administration granted to Robert Hatfield on the Estate of John Mason decd. be revoked and that the Widow of said Decd. have Administration upon sd. Estate on Argment Overuled — Appeal prayed & allowed upon entering into Bond of £100 with F.X. Martin Security.

Read the Petition of Joshua Balance son of Benja. Ballance decd. praying hat Commissioners may be appointed to Divide the Real Estate of the said Benja. Ballance between the Heirs of said Decd. Whereupon Ordered that Joshua Fulsher, Francis Delamar, John Biggs, Thomas Sparrow & Jesse Lester be appointed to Divide the Real Estate of the said Benja. Ballance decd. between the Heirs and make a return of their proceedings to the next County Court. Issd.

Ordered that Zadock Rumley who was bound to John Khun to learn the Trade of a Shoemaker and by consent of Parties the Indentures cancelled — he bound again to Luther Hyde to learn the Trade of a Blacksmith.

Ordered that Francis Lowthorp, John F. Smith and William Johnston be appointed to Audit the Accounts of Benja. Grenade Administrator of the Estate of Arthur Smith, decd.

Adjourned untill 4 oClock.
Met Pursuant to Adjournment.

176—Present the Worshipful.
Isaac Guion, Levi Dawson, Jas. Gatlen, Hardy Gatlen} Esqrs.

Ordered that Samuel Copper aged sixteen years the 9th October last be bound to Robt. Williams to learn the Trade of a Painter. (Inds. made out & signed.) Issd.

Ordered that John Riggs aged about sixteen years be bound to Thomas Steel to learn the Trade of a Hatter. Issd.

On Motion by Francis X. Martin Esqr. Ordered that Administration granted to Robert Hatfield at this Term upon the Estate of John Mason decd. be revoked and that the Bond given by Mr. Hatfield cancelled and made Void and that Ann Mason Widow of the said Deceased have Administration upon the said Estate upon her Qualifying & entering into Bond of £100 with James McCafferty and William Henry her Securities.

Present the Worshipfull Levi Dawson, John Allen, John Tillman, Hardy Gatlen, James Gatlen, John F. Smith, Wm. M. Herritage, John Sears} Esqrs.

On motion, Ordered that Administration be granted to Isaac Guion upon the Estate of the Marquis De Bretigny, he being the greatest Creditor.

Thomas Turner E. who also applied for the said Adminstration being dissatisfied with the Decree of the Court prayed for an Appeal to the Superior Court of Law to be held for the district of Newbern.

177 — Adjourned till tomorrow Morning 9 oClock.

Thursday Septmr. 12th 1793. Met Pursuant to Adjournment.
Present the Worshipful
Levi Dawson, James Gatlen, Hardy Gatlin} Esqrs.

3. Nathan Smith vs. Francis Lowthorp} Case. The following Jury empanelled & Sworn. To wit. 1. Thomas Hyman 2. Robert Hunt 3. William Smyth 4. Edwd. Pritchard 5. Benja. Mason 6. Daniel West 7. Thomas Webber 8. Jesse Bryan 9. John Carruthers 10. William Lovick 11. Thos. Parsons 12. Jeremiah Reddings find the Defendant did assume & assess the Plantiffs Damages to £33.11.0 and 6d Costs.

Then was the Grand Jury discharged.

No. 4. Nathan Smith vs. Francis Lowthorp & John Benners} Case. The same Jury as in the last cause empanelled &c. To wit find the Defendants did assume and assess the Damages of the Plantiff to £752.5.0 & 6d Costs.

No. 5. Nathan Smith Francis Lowthorp vs. Nathan Smith} Origl. Atta. The same Jury as in the last Cause empanelled find the Defendant did assume & that he assumed within three years and assess the Plantiffs Damages to £217.14.7 & 6d Costs.

178 — Southy Rew Esqr. returned the list of Taxable property for the year 1793 in Capt. Masters District.

No. 17. William Thompson vs. John Physioc & Charles Jones junr.} Case. The same Jury as in the last Cause empanelled find the Defendants Guilty and assess the Plantiffs Damages to £3.0.0 & 6d Costs.

Adjourned till 4 oClock.
Met Pursuant to Adjournment. Present the Worshipful Levi Dawson, Isaac Guion, Francis Lowthorp}

~~The Fo~~
No. 13. James Herriott vs. Mary Vance} Replevin. The following Jury empanelled & Sworn. To Wit. No. 1. Thomas Hyman 2. Robert Hunt   3. Lewis Bryan
4. Edwd. Pritchard 5. Benja. Mason 6. Jesse Bryan   7. John Carruthers 8. Thomas Parsons (W. Smith   9. Jeremiah Redding 10. William Lovick 11. John Gooding 12. John B. Herritage find for the Avowant £15.13.3 Damages & 6d.

Then was the Sheriff of Craven County allowed the following Insolvents for the year 1792. (To Wit)
3327 Acres of Land
108 Polls.

179 — No. 18. Willoughby Knowes vs. Philip Knowes} Case. The same Jury as in the last Cause empanelled. Juror withdrawn & cause continued.

No. 19. Josiah Parsons by his Father & Next Friend vs. Herman Harris} Tus.. A.B.Y.
The same Jury as in the last Cause except Wm. Smyth in the room of Thos. Parsons empanelled, find the Defendant Guilty and assess 6d Damage & 6d Costs.

Adjourned till tomorrow Morng. 9 oClock. Met Pursuant to Adjournment. Present the Worshipful Levi Dawson, Francis Lowthorp, Hardy Gatlin} Esqrs.

A Settlement of the Accounts of William Slade & William Mitchell ~~Administration of~~ Guardians of the Orphans of Yelverton Probart decd. was returned by the Referees appointed for that purpose and Orderd to be filed.

State vs. John Physioc} Indictment. The following Jury empanelled & Sworn. To Wit.
No. 1. Thomas Hyman 2. Robert Hunt 3. Edwd. Pritchard 4. Wm. Smyth 5. Benja. Mason 6. John B. Herritage 7. Edwd. Tinker, Jno Biggs 8. Humphry Jones, Wm. Lovitt 9. Ambrose Jones 10. James Roe
11. Sampson Morris 12. James Nelson find the Defendant is not Guilty.

180 — Wm. Slade Esqr. Attorney for Leven Clark paid into the Court £8.15.0 being as he suggested the Amount of a Judgment & Costs obtained upon a Warrant before Francis Lowthorp Esqr. from which Judgment the plantiff To wit. Moses Griffin appealed to Court.

Orderd that John Fonvielle, John Daly, Francis Lowthorp, & John Sears Esqrs. be appointed to Audit the Accots. of Silas S. Stevenson decd. as Guardian of the Orphans of John Stevenson decd. and report thereon to this Court (or any three of them). Issd.

Ordered that Jno. Fonvielle, John Daly, Francis Lowthorp & John Sears Esqrs. be appointed to Audit the Accounts of William M. Heritage Guardian of the Orphans of John Stevenson decd. and report thereon to this Court. — or any three of them. Dr. (Jno. Gooding) (Iss. Changd).

Ordered that Jno. Fonvielle, John Daly, Francis Lowthorp & John Sears Esqrs. be appointed to Audit the Accots. of John Gooding & Mary White Admrs. of Samuel White decd. and that any three of them make a Return of their Proceedings to this ~~next~~ Court. (Jno. Gooding) Dr. Chagd. Issd.

State vs. Edwd. Tinker} Indt. A.B. The same Jury as in the last Cause except John Biggs & William Lovick in the room of Edwd. Tinker and Humphry Jones empanelled & Sworn find the Defendant Guilty of an Assault in manner & form &c as charged in the Bill of Indictment. Judgment of the Court that Tinker be fined £3.0.0 & Costs.

Ordered that Isaac Guion, George Ellis and Samuel Chapman be appointed Assessors of Town Property for the year 1793.

181 — State vs. William Low} Indt. Petit Larceney. The same Jury as in the last Cause empanelled and Sworn find the Defendant Guilty in manner & form as Charged in the Bill of Indictment, new Trial Granted.

State vs. Wm. Jones} Indt. Assault. The defendant submits and fined three pounds & Costs.

John Gooding is appointed a Juror in the room of William Henry Esqr. to the next Superior Court.

Joshua Fulsher Esqr. returned the list of Taxable property in Joseph West & Francis Delamar's Districts.

Adjourned till 4 oClock.
Met Pursuant to adjournment. Present the Worshipful Levi Dawson, Isaac Guion, Francis Lowthorp} Esqrs.

Ordered that Mary Noland aged 10 years be bound to Mary Low to learn to be a Spinster.

Ordered that Roderigo Le Taste have permission to sell the perishable part of the Estate of James McDaniel decd.

Ordered that Anna Mason have permission to sell the perishable property of the Estate of her decd. Husband Jno. Mason.

182 — Francois X. Martin vs. Levi Dawson & William Ross}
Appeal. The same Jury as in the last Cause empanelled & Sworn. Asses the Plantiffs Damages to £20.0.0 & 6d.

Stephen Brooks vs. William M. Herritage} Appeal. The following Jury empanelled & Sworn. Viz. No. 1. Thos. Hyman 2. Robt. Hunt 3. Edwd. Pritchard 4. Wm. Smyth 5. Benja. Mason 6. John Biggs 7. James Roe 8. James Nelson 9. Richd. Barrington 10. John Blank 11. Thos. Webber 12. Francis Delamar find the Defendant did assume & assess £8.10.7 Damages & 6d Costs.

Ordered that Celia King be allowed by James McCafferty nine pounds for maintaining said a Bastard Child for nine months which Child was sworn to the said James McCafferty. (Fi.Fa. issd. March Term 1794)

John Mansfield vs. David Murdock} Appeal. The following Jury empanelled, to Wit.
1. Tho. Hyman 2. Robt. Hunt [?] 3. Edwd. Pritchard 4. Wm. Smyth 5. Benja. Mason 6. John Biggs 7. James Nelson 8. Jesse Bryan 9. Thos. Webber 10. Francis Delamar 11. Wm. Lovick 12. Sampson Morris
find the Defendt. did assume & assess the Plantiffs Damages to £3.19.4 & 6d Costs.

183 – Adjourned till tomorrow Morning 9 oClock.
___day. Met Pursuant to adjournment. Present the
Worshipfull Levi Dawson, Francis Lowthorp, Jas. Gatlin}
Esqrs.

John Allen Esqr. returned the list of Taxable property in Capt.
Jones District for the year 1793.

Ordered that John Charles have Adminisn. upon the Estate of
William West upon his Qualifying and entering into Bond of
£200 with Levin Dickerson & Charles Saunders jr. his
securities. Wereupon the said Jno. Charles Qualified, entered
into Bond & returned an Inventory of said Decd. Estate.

Ordered that Daniel Bryan have administration upon the
Estate of Mary Ann Brown decd. upon his entering into Bond
of £100 with Levi Dawson & James Gatlin his securities.

Thomas Turner who prayed an appeal for the adminisn. of the
Estate of the Marquis De Britigeny offered Nathan Smith &
Francis Hawks for his securities. Ordered that they enter into
Bond of £100 for prosecuting said appeal.

Levi Hill vs. Francis Hill} Judgt. & Execution upon two
Warrants for £20 each upon which Jas. McMain retured [blot]
no Goods & Chattels to be found. Levied upon 300 acres of
Land lying upon Goose Creek.

Ordered that Vende. Expenas issue agreeable to Law. Vende.
Expenas not issued by the Plantiffs directions and Cost posed
by him in Office. Constable 16/
Clerk 4/   pd. J. McMains Constable £1.0.0

184 — Levi Dawson Esqr. returned a List of Taxable property in Capt. Danl. Wests District for 1793.

No. 2. Francis Lowthorp vs. Nathan Smith} Appeal prayed by the Defendt. which was granted upon his entering into Bond with John C. Bryan & Jas. McCafferty his Securities & filing reasons &c.

No. 3. Nathan Smith vs. Francis Lowthorp} Appeal prayed by the plantiff which was granted upon his entering into Bond with John C. Bryan & Jas. McCafferty his Securities and filing reasons &c.

No. 5. Francis Lowthorp vs. Nathan Smith} Appeal prayed by the Defendt. which was granted upon his entering into Bond with Jno. C. Bryan & Jas. McCafferty his Securities and filing reasons &c.

James Gatlin Esqr. returned a list of Taxable property in Capt. Ernull's District for the year 1793.

Hardy Gatlin Esqr. returned a list of Taxable property in Capt. Jno. Bryans District for the year 1793.

A Division of the Lands of John Kemp decd. was returned by the Commissioners appointed for that purpose which was ordered to be filed.

Thomas Speight to have Tavern License upon entering into Bond with Wm. Speight his security.

Isaac Bryan Esqr. returned the list of Taxable property in Capt. Cox's District for the year 1793.

185 – Then were the following Jurors appointed to attend the next Term. Viz.
1. Richard Hunley 2. Wilson Blount 3. Joseph Carter 4. Benj. Brinson 5. Francis Carraway 6. Thomas York 7. Jno. S. Nelson 8. Southy Jordan Rue 9. Wm. Clark 10. Levi Hill 11. William Gaskins 12. John Arthur 13. Thomas Smyth 14. Joseph Gaskins 15. John Ernull 16. William Dixon 17. Saml. Sparrow 18. Joseph Brinson 19. Cason Brinson 20. John Fell 21. Thomas Hall 22. Samuel Willis 23. Caleb Willis 24. Joseph Willis 25. Jarvis Fillingham 26. Jacob Johnston Jun. 27. Joseph Phills 28. Michael Mitchell 29. Jeremiah James 30. Lewis Jones 31. John Potter 32. Mathew Stevens 33. Lucas J. Benners 34. William Lovick 35. Moses Lambert 36. Joseph Loftin 37. Sampson Morris 38. Jonathan Perkins

Ordered that Isaac Guion Esqr. have Letters of Administration Pendente Lite upon the Estate of the Marquis De Britigny decd. upon his Qualifying and entering into Bond in the sum of £200 with Jno. C. Bryan & Levi Dawson Esqrs. his securities.

An Inventory and Account Sales of the Estate of Benjamin Burton decd. was returned & filed.

Nathan Smith vs. Francis Lowthorp & John Benners} Appeal prayed by the Defendant upon which was granted upon their entering into Bond with Wm. M. Herritage & Levi Dawson Esqr. Securities & filing Reasons &c.

186 – Ordered that Isaac Barrington be allowed the sum of two pounds six shillings and six pence for the Prison fees and Costs of a process instituted by the State against a Negro named Ben who was discharged and acquitted by the Court held for his Trial and that the County Treasurer pay the same. (issd.)

On Motion of Benja. Woods Esqr. on behalf of Robt. Hunt in a suit brought by said Hunt agains [blank] Norman by Original Attachment that a Vende. Exponas issue directed to Jno. C. Bryan Esqr. late Sheriff of Craven County Commanding him to sell the property which appears in his Returns of said Attachment to be in his hands ~~and~~ to satisfy the Judgment obtained in sd. suit.

Elizabeth Potter vs. Heirs Edwd. Potter decd.} Petn. for Dower. Ordered that a Writ of Venire issue directed to the Sheriff of Craven County Commanding him to summon 12 freeholders to meet upon the premises and lay off the Dower of the Petitioner in the Lands & Tenements of Edwd. Potter junr. decd. agreeable to Law. (Venire issd.)

John Porter has permission to keep a public House of Entertainment in Craven County for one year upon his entering into Bond with Francis Lowthorp his Secy.

James McMains Constable is allowed £2.8.0 for his attendance at this Term. Ordered that the County Treasurer pay the same.

Thomas Hyman Admr. Peter Franklin decd. produced his Accots. and vouchers against said Decd. Estate which was examined by the Court and Ordered to eb filed.

187 — Whereas in the suit instituted by the Executor of Thomas Delamar against Carmick Higgins & the Admr. of Peter Franklin which was not brought forward by mistake. Ordered that the said Cause be reinstated in it proper place at the next Term.

Adjourned till 4 oClock.

Met Pursuant to adjournment. Present the Worshipful Levi Dawson, Isaac Guion, Francis Lowthorp} Esqrs.

John Latham appeared in Court and took the Oath of Deputy Sheriff also the Oath of Allegiance to this State and the United States.

Joseph West et Uxr. Vs. Admr. & Guardn. of the Heirs of Jas. [?] Perkins, decd.} Petition for Dower. On Hearing the Petition Recd. Ordered that a Write of Venire issue directed to the Sheriff of Craven County to lay off Dower agreeable to the Petition and Act of Assembly.

Philip Knowis appeared in Court and took the Oath of Deputy Sheriff also the Oath of Allegiance to this State & the United State.

Levi Dawson, J.P.
Is. Guion, J.P.
Jas. Gatlin, J.P.
F. Lowthorp, J.P.

188 – [page blank]

December 1793 Term
189 – At a County Court of Pleas & Quarter Sessions begun and held for the County of Craven in the State of No. Carolina __ the Court House in Newbern on the second Monday in December in the eighteenth year of our Independence A.D. 1793 being the 9th day of the month. Present the Worshipful John Fonvielle, Henry Tillman, John Sears} Esqrs.

Wm. Henry Esqr. Sheriff of Craven County returned the Writ of Venire Facias for Jurors to this Court in these Words "Executed in full."

The last Will & Testament of Thomas Morriss decd. was produced in Court and proved by the Oath of Francis Fonvielle one of the Subscribing Witnesses thereto and at the same time Mary Morris the Executrix therein named appeared in Court & Qualified agreeable to Law. Ordered that Letters Testamentary issue — at the same time the Executrix rendered an Inventory of said Estate.

An Inventory of the Estate of Hugh Tingle decd. was returned & filed.

The last Will & Testament of Daniel Yates decd. was proved by the Oath of James Witherington one of the Subscribing Witnesses thereto and at the same time David Yates one of the Executors therein named appeared in Court and Qualified agreeable to Law and rendered an Inventory of said Estate.

190 — Ordered that Mrs. Jennett Adams have Adminn. upon the Estate of Charles Adams decd. upon her Qualifying and entering into Bond in the sum of £3000 with James Davis & William Bartl__ her Securities.

Ordered that John Clark have administration upon the Estate of John Clark Senr. upon his Qualifying and entering into Bond of £300 with Henry Tollman & Wm. Harford his Securities.

Then was the following Grand Jury empanelled, To wit. 1. Lewis Jones Foreman 2. Joseph Loften 3. William Lovick 4. John Fell 5. Jacob Johnston jun. 6. William Gaskins 7. Sampson Morriss 8. Joseph Willis 9. Joseph Carter 10. John Arthur 11. Jarvis Fillingham 12. Benja. Brinson 13. Michl. Mitchell

Ordered that Joseph Peddy aged nine years be bound to Thomas Cox to learn the Trade of a House Carpenter. (Inds. made out). Dr.

Ordered that Jesse Horshends aged fifteen years be bound to Philip Knowes to learn the Trade of a Cart Wheelwright. (Dr.)

Ordered that Martin Black aged 13 years & Sharper Black aged 11 years be bound to William Carter to learn the Turners Trade. (Inds. made out.) Dr. 16/

Ordered that Jack Charles aged 14 years be bound to Abner Nash to learn tobe a Barber. Dr.

191 — Ordered that Thomas Webber have administration upon the Estate of Ann Webber decd. upon his Qualifying and entering into Bond of £3000 with Joseph Leech & Charles William his Securities.

Ordered that Leah Saunders & Malachi Russell have Administration upon the Estate of John Saunders decd. upon their Qualifying and entering into Bond of £[blank] with John West & Moses Lambert their Securities — whereupon they entered into Bond Qualified and returned an Inventory of said Decd. Estate — letters issd.

Ordered that William Dudley & William Moore Coroners of Craven County be allowed three pounds two shillings & six pence each for their extra services for three months past. (issd. for Moore) & Dudley.

Adjourned till tomorrow Morning 9 oClock.

Tuesday Decr. 10th 1793
Met Pursuant to adjournment. Present the Worshipful Levi Dawson, Spyers Singleton, Henry Tillman, Isaac Bryan, Jno. F. Smith, Jno. Daly} Esqrs.

Read the Petition of John Foster for Division of the Real Estate of Wm. Shepard Foster decd. amongst the Heirs. Ordered that Prayer of said Petition be Granted and that John Blanks, John Porter, Richard Hickman, Benja. Tolson & Robert Johnston be appointed commissioners to lay off & ~~Divide~~ Appropriate the said Estate agreeable to Law.

192 — An Inventory of the Estate of James Sears decd. was returned by John Sears Esqr. Administrator & filed. Dr. 2/

Exrs. Of Evan Swan decd. vs. Heirs of Evan Swann decd.}
Contested Will, by Lewis Tyre, Thos. Wise, Thomas Clements & John West. The following Jury empanelled viz.
1. William Clark 2. Joseph Brinson 3. Cason Brinson 4. Saml. Willis 5. Caleb Willis 6. Moses Lambert 7. Jonathan Perkins 8. Jeremiah James 9. Alexr. Carruthers 10. Danl. West 11. William Hollis 12. John Green. find the Writing produced to be the last Will & Testament of Evan Swann decd.

The last Will & Testament of Evan Swann decd. was proved by the Oath of Nathaniel Street and Thomas A. Green, the subscribing Witnesses thereto and at the same time Shadrach Swann the Executor therein named appeared in Court and Qualified agreeable to Law. Ordered that Letters Testamentary issue.

The last Will & Testament of Thomas Forgason decd. was proved in Open Court by the Oath of William Wetherington one of the Subscribing Witnesses thereto and at the same time Hannah Forgason & Robert Wetherington the Executrix & Executor therein named appeared in Court & Qualified agreeable to Law. Ordered that Letters Testamentary issue.

Daniel West renewed his Tavern License for one year.

193 – The last Will & Testament of Thomas Gatlin decd. was produced in Court and Signed but no Subscribing Witnesses being thereto the Hand Writing of the said
Thomas Gatlin decd was proved by the Oath of Hardy Gatlin, Daniel West & Joseph Loften agreeable to Law. James Gatlin & John Gatlin two of the Executors therein Named appeared in Court and Qualified as such accordingly. Ordered that Letters Testamentary issue.

Ordered that Nathan Bunn have Administration upon the Estate of Daniel Bradley Decd. upon his Qualifying and entering into Bond in the sum of £400 with William Johnston, Wm. Mitchell Securities.

William Vendrick who also applied for Letters of Administration upon the said Decd. Estate being dissatisfied with the Judgment of the Court prayed an Appeal to the Superior Court of Law to be held for the District of Newbern in March next which is Granted upon his entering into Bond in the sum of £100 with Levi Dawson & Jos. West his Securities for Prosecution &c. (Bond taken.) (Records sent up.)

Ordered that Nathan Bunn have Letters of Administration Pendenti Lite upon the Estate of Daniel Bradley decd. upon his Qualifying and entering into Bond of £400 with Wm. Johnston & Wm. Mitchell his Securities.

Ordered that Joshua Fulsher, John Dawson & Jno. Biggs be appointed to Settle with the Guardians of the Orphans of James Perkins decd. and allot and lay off to Alexander Carruthers and Peggy his Wife (formerly Peggy Perkins) her proportion of part of said Decd. Estate agreeable to Law and make a Return of their proceedings to the next Court.

194 — Ordered that Francis Lowthorp, George Lane & Danl. Lane be appointed to Settle the Accounts of William Bryan Executor to the Estate of Hardy Bryan decd. and make return of their proceedings. (issd.)

An Account of Sales of the Estate of Alexr. McAuslan decd. was returned and filed.

Ordered that James Coor, William Shepard & Saml. Chapman be appointed to Settle the Accounts of John Green Exr. of James Green Senr. decd. and report thereon to this Court.

Adjourned till Tomorrow Morning 9 oClock.
Wednesday Decr. 11 1793.

Met Pursuant to adjournment. Present the Worshipful Levi
Dawson, Henry Tillman, Frans. Lowthorp} Esqrs.

No. 7. James McKinlay vs. Malcolm Gillies} Case. The
following Jury empanelled & Sworn vizt. 1. Southy Jordan
Rew   2. William Clark 3. Thos. Smyth
4. Joseph Brinson 5. Cason Brinson 6. Caleb Willis 7. Moses
Lambert   8. Jonathan Perkins 9. Joseph West (S. Willis) 10.
William Whitford 11. William Tyre 12. Wm. Vendrick find
the Defendant did assume and that he assumed within three
years and assess the Plantiffs Damages to £192.3.6 & 6d Costs
and that no payment or sett off hath been made. Motion in
Arrest of Judgment reasons filed.

195 — The last Will & Testament of Michael Hyman decd. was
proved by the Oath of Philip Turner one of the Subscribing
Witnesses thereto agreeable to Law and at the same time
James Hyman the Executor therein named appeared in Court
and Qualfied. Ordered that Letters Testamentary issue.

Ordered that James Hyman Executor of Michl. Hyman decd.
sell the perishable part of said Estate agreeable to Law.

An Account of Sales of the Estate of Patrick Cleary decd. was
returned & filed.

Ordered that Bazell Bratcher be bound to William put under
the care & Guardianship of William Holland upon sd.
Holland entering into Bond of £200 with Mathew Stevens &
Philemon Holland his Securities.

Ordered that Thomas B. Adam Tooley Levi Fulsher and
George Lovick be appointed to settle the Accounts of Thos. [?
Blotted] Bratcher, Executor of Roger Bratcher decd. and make
a Return to the next Court.

Then was the Grand Jury discharged.

An Account of Sales of the Estate of Charles Edwards decd. was returned by the Sheriff.

The Nuncupative Will of Jeremiah Wood decd. was produced in Court and proved by the Oath of William M. Herritage and Ordered to be Recorded. Ordered that Jesse Gardner Sen. have Administration with the said Will annexed upon his entering into Bond in

196 – in the sum of Two hundred pounds with William M. Herritage & William Mourning his securities – at same time he returned an Inventory of said Decd. Estate.

Ordered that William Honey Esqr. have Adminn. upon the Estate of Thomas Duncan decd. upon his entering into Bond of £100 with Levi Dawson & Thomas Lowthorp his Securities.

John Kennedy vs. William Bowen} Case. The same Jury as in the last Cause except Samuel Willis in the room of Joseph West empanelled &c. Juror withdrawn by Consent and Cause continued.

The last Will & Testament of William Trewhitt decd. was proved by the Oath of Jeremiah Masten one of the Subscribing Witnesses thereto and at the same time Levi Trewhitt the Executor therein named appeared & Qualified as such – ordered that Letters issue.

No. 21. John Whitehurst vs. Elijah Vail} Covt. The same Jury as in No. 7 except Samuel Willis in the room of Joseph West empanelled find the Convenant is Broken and assess the Plantiffs Damage to £2.10.0 & 6d Costs — On argument judgment arrested — appeal prayed & allowed — appeal withdrawn and Writ of Error granted.

197 — The Referees appointed to settle the Accounts of Susannah Miller late Guardian of the orphans of Ephraim Pearce decd. and also to Divide the Estate of said Decd. made a report of their proceedings which was ordered to be filed.

Adjourned to the Palace 'til 9 oClock tomorrow.

Thursday Dec. 12, 1793. Met pursuant to adjournment. Present the Worshipful John Daly, Levi Dawson, Henry Tillman} Esqrs.

An Account of Sales of the Estate of Nehemiah Randal decd. was returned by the Coroner, and filed.

No. 22 James Carney Atto. John Jones Assignee &c vs. George Lovick} Debt. The following Jury empanelled viz. 1. Southy J. Rew 2. William Clark 3. Thos. Smyth 4. Joseph Brinson 5. Cason Brinson 6. Saml. Willis
7. Caleb Willis 8. Moses Lambert 9. Jona. Perkins 10. Thos. Webber 11. Wm. Tyre   12. Amos Squires (T. Oliver) find the Writing Obilgatory is the Act & Deed of the Defendant and assess £11.17.4 Damages & 6d Costs and they further find the Statute Limitations does not Bar & that no payment hath been made — Appl. prayed & allowed Jno. C. Bryan & Wm. Moore Securities.

An Inventory & Account Sales of the Estate of William Buxton decd. was returned & filed.

Ordered that Thomas York, Joseph Good & Henry Tillman be appointed to Settle the Accounts of John Thomas Guardian to the Orphans of Thomas Delamar decd. and make a return to the next Court.

An Inventory of the Estate of John Daw decd. & also an Account of Sales was returned & filed.

198 — No. 23. James Carny Atto. for John Jones Assgne &c. vs. George Lovick} Debt. The same Jury as in the last Cause empanelled find the Writing obligatory is the Act & Deed of the Defendant and assess £14.__.__ Damages & 6d Costs and they further find that the Statu__ of Limitations does not bar. & that no payments have been made — Appl. prayed by Defent. & allowed Jno. C. Bryan & William Moore Securities.

No. 29 John Cuyler vs. John Sheffield} Case. The same Jury as in the last Cause empanelled find the Defendant and assume and assess £26.14.7 ¾ Dam & 6d Costs — and they further find that no payment hath been made & that he assumed within three years.

Read the Petition of William McClure Setting forth that he is owner of Lands upon both sides of Brices Creek and Praying leave to Build a Public Water Grist Mill upon said Streatm. Ordered that the Prayer of said Petition be Granted. 10/ Dr. Chayd.

An Inventory & Account of Sales of the Estate of Mary Ann Brown decd. was returned & filed.

No. 28. Henry Livingston vs. John Archer} ABy. The same Jury as in the last Cause empanelled & Sworn — find the Defend. not Guilty.

199 — No. 30. James W. Stanly vs. Amos Squires} 2 C F. The same Jury as in the last Cause except Thomas Oliver in the room of Amos Squires — Plantiff called Nonsuit. Appeal prayed.

No. 31. Levi Dawson vs. John Latham} Covt. The following Jury empanelled vzt.
1. Southy J. Rue 2. William Clark 3. Thomas Smith 4. Cason Brinson 5. Samuel Willis 6. Caleb Willis 7. Moses Lambert 8. William Tyre 9. Amos Squires 10. Thomas Hyman 11. Thomas Oliver 12. James Hyman
find the Defendt. has not broke his Covenant.

Ordered that Clara Brown a free Negro Girl be bound to Mathias Rose to learn to be a Spinster aged eight years (Inds. End)

Henry Tillman Esqr. returned his list of Taxable proper[ty] in Capt. [blank] District for 1793.

Adjourned till tomorrow Morning 9 oClock.

200 — Friday Dec. 13, 1793
Met Pursuant to Adjournment.
Present the Worshipful John Daly, Wm. M. Herritage, Henry Tillman} Esqrs.

State vs. David Brothers, Overseer of the Roads} Indt. The following Jury empanelled & Sworn to wit: 1. Southy Jordan Rew 2. Wm. Clark 3. Thos. Smyth
4. Joseph Brinson 5. Cason Brinson 6. Saml. Willis 7. Caleb Willis 8. Moses Lambert 9. Jona. Perkins 10. Sampson Morris 11. William King 12. Levin Dickenson find the Defendt. not Guilty.

No. 119. William Keeler vs. John Neggle} Appeal by Defendt. The same Jury as in the last Cause empanelled find for the Plantiff & assess £4.15 Damages & 6d Costs.

No. 120. Thomas Hyman Admr. Peter Franklin vs. John Banks} Appeal by Defendt. The same Jury as in the last Cause empanelled find for the Plantiff & assess £8.12 Dams. & 6d Costs.

201 — Ordered that John Read alias John Hurley aged nine years last September be bound to Nymphus Price to learn the Art of a Mariner.

No. 133. William Lawrence [?] vs. James McCafferty} Appeal by Defend. The same Jury as in the last Cause empanelled find no Cause of Action.

Ordered that William Davis have permission to keep a Ferry from Green Spring to Newbern and that he take the following Rates. Viz. for Man & Horse 4/
for a Single passenger 2/ for every Carriage Wheel 2/

upon his entering into Bond with Nathan Smith & William McClure his Securities.

Ordered that the said William Davis have permission to keep a Public House of Entertainment at said Place for one year from the date hereof upon his entering into Bond with Wm. McClure Security agreeable to Law.

Ordered that Levi Fulsher have Letters of Administration upon the Estate of Joseph Holland decd. upon his Qualifying and entering into Bond in the sum of £200 with Henry Tillman & Francis Delamar his Securities — the said Levi Fulsher Qualifd. & entered into Bond &c. & also filed an Inventory of said Decd. Estate.

Ordered that Edmund Bryan aged 18 years the 9th July last be bound to Archibald McCalap to learn the Taylors Trade.

202 — Ordered that James Ruff aged Eighteen years be bound to Capt. William Bartlett to learn the Art of a Mariner (inds. End.)

No. 150. Moses Griffin vs. Levin Clark} Appl. by Plff. The same Jury as in the last Cause except James Roe in the room of Levin Dickinson empanelled find for the Plantiff £8.4 Dams. and 6d Costs.

Ordered that Ezekiel Johnston aged eleven years on the 25th Inst. be bound to Edmund Perkins to learn the Trade of a Shoemaker. Dr.

Ordered that Levin Dickenson pay unto Bathsheba Calaham Ten Pounds per year for the maintainance of an Illegitimate Child of which he is the reputed Father. Dr.

Moses Griffin vs. Levin Clark} On motion of Mr. Graham The Court Ruled that monies should not be recd. but upon payment of Cost up to the time of the Motion of the Defendants Attorney to pay the Money into Court.

Then were the following Gentlemen appointed to attend as Jurors at the next Superior Court, Vizt. 1. Levi Dawson 2. Francis Lowthorp 3. Joseph West

4. Charles Williams 5. James Gatlin 6. Hardy Gatlin 7. Isaac
Bryan
8. Southy Rue   9. Charles James [issd.]

203 — Then were the following Jurors appointed to attend at
the next County Court vzt. 1. Wilson Blount 2. William Good
3. William Shepard
4. Charles Roach 5. William Dickson 6. Daniel Lane   7.
Frederick Lane
8. William Surles 9. James ~~Hollis~~ Vendrick 10. Stephen W.
Dunn
11. Thomas Tyre 12. Lucas J. Benners 13. John S. Nelson 14.
Levi Hill
15. John Ernull 16. John Moore 17. David Lewis 18. Enoch
Masters
19. William Bryan S. Creek 20. John Bryan Ads. Creek 21.
Thomas Masters
22. Abraham Vendrick 23. Daniel Brinson 24. Jesse Holton
25. James Brinson junr. 26. Thomas Holton 27. Thomas
Sparrow
28. William Carraway   29. Francis Delamar 30. Demson
Delamar
31. Thomas Pittman   32. Zacker Dubberly 33. Andw.
Richardson
34. Moses Ernull 35. Aaron Ernull 36. William Carter

Adjourned till tomorrow Morning 9 oClock.
Saturday Decr. 14, 1793 Met Pursuant to adjournment.
Present the Worshipful Levi Dawson, Wm. M. Herritage,
Henry Tillman} Esqrs.

Two Inventory's and Accounts of Sales of the Estate of
Stephen Wright decd. was returned & filed.

Inventory and Account of Sales of the Estate of Michael Flood decd. was returned.

Ordered that Edward Harris Esqr be appointed Guardian to Francis Batchellor an Oprhan of Edwd. Batchellor decd (she having appeared in Court & made choice of him) upon his Entering into Bond of £4000 with William McClure & Francis Lowthorp his Securities.

204 – [No.] 152. William Carraway vs. William Davis} appeal by plantiff. The following Jury empaneled 1. Southy Jourden Rue 2. Thomas Smith 3. Joseph Brinson 4. Cason Brinson 5. Saml. Willis 6. Caleb Willis
7. Moses Lambert 8. Jonathan Perkins 9. Joseph West 10. William Tyre 11. John Moore 12. James Nelson find that £10.12.6 of the Note has been paid and that the balance of £19.17.6 remains unpaid & assess 6d damages and 6d Costs.

153. James Roe vs. Wm. King} appeal by Defendt. The same Jury as in the last cause assess the Plantiffs Damages to £4.5 & 6d Costs.

Ordered that Bridget Biggs have Administration upon the Estate of James Biggs decd upon her Qualifying and entering into Bond of £500 with John Biggs & Francis Delamar her Securities Whereupon she Qualified, entered into Bond & returned an Inentory of said Decd. Estate.

Read the Petition of Esther Johnston praying that persons be appointed to Divide the Estate of ~~John~~ Charles Johnston decd. Whereupon Ordered that John Knox, John Blank & Spyers Singleton be apponted to Divide said Estate agreeable to the last Will & Testament of the Deceasd. Dr.

205 — Read the Petition of Charles B. Stevenson praying that Commissioners may be appointed to lay off and Divide the Real Estate of [stricken smudge] his Deceasd Father Silas S. Stevenson agreeable to the Act of Assembly in such Case made & provided. Whereupon Ordered that John Fonvielle, Richard Nixon, John Gooding, Farnifold Green and Stephen Harris be appointed Commissioners to lay of said Decd. Estate and that they make a return of their proceedings to the next Court.

A Division of the Real Estate of Benjamin Balance decd was returned by the Commissioners appointed at the last Term and ordered to be filed.

Ordered that William Sawyer aged 19 years in March next who was bound to Sylvester Pendleton and given up by him be bound to William Bartlett to leart the Art of a Mariner (inds. Exd.)

Thomas Cox has permission to Keep a Tavern in Newbern for one year upon entering into Bond with Francis Lowthorp his Security.

Charles Williams appeared in Court and resigned his Guardianship of Nancy Hill Wright. Whereupon she appeared in Court and made Choice of Isaac Barrington for her Guardian, which was approved of by the Court upon his entering into Bond in the sum of £1000 with Charles Williams and Levi Dawson his Securities.

Ordered that Levi Dawson, Francis Lowthorp & Henry Tillman be appointed to Audit the Accounts of Charles Williams Guardian of Nancy Hill Wright a Minor and make a return of their proceedings to the next Court, or any two of them.

206 – Isaac Barrington vs. Peter F. Palaton} Appeal by Defend.
The following Jury empanelled Vzt. No. 1. John Thomas 2.
John Biggs 3. Thomas Webber
4. John Green 5. Charles Williams 6. James Hyman 7.
Edmund Perkins 8. David Lewis 9. Jonathan Perkins 10.
Joseph West 11. Jeremiah Parsons
12. Simon Bexley [verdict not recorded]

No. 80. Thomas Hyman vs. Jas. Brinson, Exr. Peter Hyman
decd.} Petition.

Thos. Turner vs. Heirs & Devisees of Thos. Collier decd.} Sci.
Fa. to shew Cause &c. Why the Real Estate should not
be sold to pay the plantiff; according to Former Judgment –
Judgment aga___ the Real Estate accordingly – no Execution
to issue but on Motion to the Court.

Henry Purss resigned his appointment of Keeping the
Standard Weights &c of Craven County. Whereupon James
McMains was appointed to take Charge of the same & Execute
the office agreeable to Law & said James McMains Qualified,
and entered into Bond with Sam Chapman & Francis
Lowthrop Securities. Dr.

207 – On Motion of William Slade Esqr. Guardian to the
Robert Collier Probart Devisee of Thomas Collier decd. setting
forth that Judgment hath been obtained against the Lands and
Tenements as Devised to the said __ Robert by the said
Thomas Collier decd. praying an Order of Sale, Pursuant to
Act of Assembly in such Case made & provided. Ordered that
the said Guardian proceed to sell the Lands at Public Vendue
for six months Credit Pursuant to the said Act.

Whereas at the last Court, Isaac Guion Esqr. was appointed Administrator upon the Estate of the Marquis De Bretigny — from Which Appointment Thomas Turner Appealed to the Superior Court — Which Appeal is withdrawn by Consent.

Ordered that the said Thomas Turner have joint administration upon the Estate of the said Marquis De Britigny with the said Isaac Guion — upon his entering into Bond with Security and Qualifying agreeable to Law Whereupon the said Thomas Turner Qualified and entered into Bond of Five hundred Pounds with Francois X. Martin & William Henry Securities.

Ordered that John C. Bryan Esqr. former Sheriff of Craven County be allowed twelve pounds ten for his Extra Services for six months. __sd.

Ordered that John Latham Constable be allowed £3.12.0 for his attendance at September & this Term. __sd.

208 — Ordered that John McGraw Cryer of this Court be allowed the sum of Twenty five pounds for his services taking Care of the Court House &c. (issued)

Ordered that Samuel Chapman Clerk of this Court be allowed the sum of Twenty Pounds for his Extra Services the present year. issd.

Ordered that Samuel Chapman be allowed five pounds for Stationary &c furnished the Court the present year. issd.

William ~~& James~~ Probart of Age to Choose a Guardian appeared in Court and made Choice of William Hawley for his Guardian which was approved of by the Court upon his entering into Bond of £400 with Wm. Henry & William Slade his Securities. Dr.

James Probart of Age to Choose a Guardian appeared in Court and made Choice of Wm. Slade Esqr. for his Guardian which was approved by the Court upon his entering into Bond of £400 with William Henry & Wm. Hawly his Securities. (Changd.)

On Motion of William Slade Esqr. in behalf of Benjamin Brinson & others for a Rule to ~~shew~~ be served on Daniel West, Guardian to the Orphans of Cason Brinson decd. to appear at the next (issd.)

209 – Court and shew Cause &c Why the Guardianship should not be taken from him &c.

Ordered that James McMains be allowed for his attendance as Constable at this Term £2.8.0.

Ordered that Thomas Crew be allowed for his attendance at June & September Court as Constable the sum of four pounds sixteen shillings.

Ordered that the Sheriff Summon Edmund Perkins and Isaac Barrington Constables to attend at the next Term.

On Motion of Wm. Slade for a Rule to be served on ~~Joseph~~ William Carter to shew Cause why Martin Black & Sharpen Black who was ordered to be bound to him should not be liberated from his Service &c.

The Referees appointed to Settle the Accounts of John Devereux Administrator of Patrick Cleary decd. return the Accounts as Settled by them which was approved of by the Court & Ordered to be Recorded.

John Daly, J.P.
H. Tillman, J.P.
F. Lowthorp, J.P.

210 – [Page blank]

[March 1794]
211 – At a County Court of Pleas & Quarter Sessions begun and held for the County of Craven at the Court House in Newbern on the second Monday __ March being the 10th day of the Month A.D. _794.

Present the Worshipfull John Fonvielle, John Carney, Jno. F. Smith} Esqrs.

Ordered that James Carney have Letters of Adminisn. upon the Estate of Isaac Blanchard decd. upon his Qualifying and entering into Bond in the sum of £100 with John Carney & Wm. Shepard his Securities.

The Last Will & Testament of James Brightman decd. was proved by the Oath of Massey Pyner a subscribing Witness thereto, and at the same time Sally Bridghtm__ the Executrix therein named appeared in Court and Qualified agreeable to Law. Ordered that Letters Testay. _ssue.

Ordered that Jacob Carter a free Negro Boy aged Ten years ro thereabouts be bound to William Jone_ to Learn to be a Cooper (Inds. Exd.)

Ordered that Joseph Carter a free Negro Boy aged five years or thereabouts be bound to John Jones to learn to be a Cooper (Inds. Exd.)

212—Ordered that John Forguson be appointed Guardian to Adam Forguson (Minor) upon his entering Bond __ the sum of £300 with Jno. Carney & John Bryan Secuys.

Read the Petition of John Harris setting forth th__ he is proprietor of Lands on Both sides of Kitts Bridge Branch and prayed leave to Build a public Water Grist Mill upon said Stream ordered that the prayer of the Petitioner be Granted.

Then was the following Grand Jurors appointed & Sworn vizt. 1. William Good, Foreman 2. Wilson Blunt 3. Wiliam Shepard 4. Wm. Dixon 5. Jno. S. Nelson 6. John Arnold 7. Jno. Moore 8. David Lewis 9. Jno. Bryan 10. Abraham Vendrick 11. James Brinson junr. 12. Thomas Holton 13. Wm. Carraway

The Referees appointed to settle the Accounts of John Griffin's Estate with Wm. Surles Admr. made a Return of their proceedings which were Ordered __ be filed. Pd. 5/

McGrath & Wife vs. Ross & Clark} Appeal by Plff. Ordered that the Execution issd. for Costs be sett aside & that the Cause be reinstated on the Docket upo_ the Plantiffs entering into Security for Prosecutio_ &c—Whereupon Francis Lowthorp offered himself a Security agreeable to Law.

213—Ordered that John Cox, Jesse Skean & Stephen Gulen be _ppointed to Audit the Accts of Rd. Doherty Adminr. __ Nehemiah Randall decd.

Ordered that the Administrators of Silas S. Stevenson decd. produce there Accounts Properly stated on Friday next in Order for a Settlement. On Motion further time allowed until next Court.

The last Will & Testament of Jacob Rathburn Decd. was proved in Open Court by the Oath of Elizabeth Emmerson a subscribing Witness thereto and at the same time Nancy Rathburn the Exx. therein appeared in Court and Qualified agreeable to Law. Ordered that letters issue.

The last Will & Testament of Levi Hill decd. was proved in Open Court by the Oath of Charles Williams one of the Subscribing Witnesses thereto and at the same time Simon Rouse & Richard Hill the Executors therein named appeared in Court and Qualified agreeable to Law. Ordered that Letters issue.

Admrs. Sam. Smyth vs. Levi Dawson} Caveat. Ordered that the Execution issd. against the Defendant in the Cuase for Costs be set aside — being issued illegally — no judgment being entered in said Cause.

Nancy Stevenson of age to choose a Guardian appeared in Court and made Choice of John S. West, which choice was approved by the Court upon his entering into Bond in the sum of £1000 with Jacob Johnston & Hardy Gatlin Securities.

214 — March 1794
Ordered that Jonathan Baily have Letters of Admin upon the Estate of John J. Baily decd. upon his Ent__ into Bond in the sum of £100 with John Ives & John Taylor his securities. Letters issd.

Ordered that Enoch Alexander have Letters of Admin. upon the Estate of William Howard decd. upon his Qualif___ & entering into Bond in the sum of £100 — with John Bedscott jr. & John Taylor his Securities. 2/

Ordered that Isaac Reed who was wounded at the Battle of Alamance be allowed the Sum of Twenty Pounds to be paid him out of the County Tax. Issd.

Ordered that David Yeats Exr. of Danl. Yates decd. have leave to sell the personal Bequeathed to Esther Yates Decd. by her Husband the aforesaid Dl. Yates.

Present the Worshipful Richd. Nixon, Jno. Carney, Hardy Gatlin, John F. Smith, Wm. Tisdale} Esqrs.

Ordered that Nancy James have Administration upon the Estate of Jeremiah James decd. upon her entering into Bond of £100 with Joseph James & Fran. D. James Sec__

Ordered that Joseph Heartly aged fourteen years be bound to Lawrence Blakey to learn to be a Cooper. Dr.

Ann Butler to have Tavern License F. Lowthorp & Jas. McMains Secy.

215 — March 1794

The Nuncupative Will of Mary Heath decd. was produced in Open Court, reduced to Writing and Sworn to by Robert Fossett and Hannah Phillips. Evidence thereto — & ordered to be Recorded — at the same time Ordered that Robert Fossett have Letters of Administration with a Copy of the said Nuncupative Will annexed upon his Qualy. & entering into Bond in the sum of £250 with John Gooding & Richard Johnston his Securities.

Ordered that Jonathan Fellows have permission to keep a public House upon his entering into Bond with Thomas Hyman his Security.

Ordered that James Powell aged nine years the _2d Inst. Be bound to Jno. Hayes to learn to be a Shoemaker. Inds. Exd.

The last Will & Testament of William Murphy decd. was proved in Open Court by the Oath of Isaac Guion Esqrs. one of the Subscribing Witnesses thereto agreeable to Law and at the same time Stephen Harris Jacob Johnston jr & William S. Murphy the Executors therein Named appeared & Qualifyed Agreeable to Law & rendered an Inventory of said Estate. Ordered that Letters issue &c.

Ordered that John Taylor have Adminisn. upon the Est. Rebecca Taylor his Sister upon his Qualy. & entering into Bond in the sum of Fifty Pounds with John Ives & Jno. Williams his Securities.

216 — March 1794

Ordered that William Trippe have Letters of Admn. upon the Estate of Jesse Bryan decd. upon his Qualifyg. and entering into Bond in the sum of £3000 with John Carney & James Carney his Securities.

Ordered that John Taylor Admr. Rebecca Taylor d__ have leave to sell the perishable part of said De__ Estate agreeable to Law.

Ordered that William Hill aged 12 years be bound to Thomas Parsons to learn the Trade of a Blacksmith. Dr.

Adjourned till tomorrow Morng. 9 oClock.
Tuesday, March 11th 1794. Met Pursuant to Adjournment. Present the Worshipful Jacob Johnston, John F. Smith, John Dawson} Esqrs.

Ordered that Lucretia Allen aged 13 years be bound to Sarah Gooding to learn to be a Spinster. Dr.

On the Petition of John Ferguson for the Division of the Lands of Adam Ferguson decd. between the petition__ and his Brother Adam Ferguson. Ordered that the following Commissioners be appointed to lay off & Divide the said Lands & make return to the next Court Vzl. Jno. Carney, Southy Rew, Joseph Masters, Benj. Mas___ & Wallace Stiron.

Ordered the above Persons be likewise appointed to Divide the personal Estate of the sd. Adam Ferguson decd. amongst the Children of said Heirs & make return to the next Court.

217 — March 1794

Miss Clarissa Carney Bryan of age to choose a Guardian appeared in Court and made choice of William Trippe which was approved of by the Court upon sd. Trippe's entering into Bond in the sum of £1000 with John Dawson & William Henry Esqrs. his Securities.

Ordered that Charles Roach, Enoch Masters, Thomas Masters, Jesse Holton, Demson Delamar, Thomas Pittman ~~Zacker Dubberly~~ Moses Ernul & Aaron Ernul Defaulting Jurors to this Term be fined agreeable to Act of Assembly & that Sci. Fa. issue.

Ordered that Francis Lowthorp, Jno. F. Smith, James Coor, Wm. Johnston & James Carney be appointed to Divide the Personal Estate of Jesse Bryan Decd. between the Heirs of said Decd.

Ordered that John Biggs, Jno. Dawson & Thomas York be appointed to Divide the Negroes belonging to the Estate of Thomas Delamar decd. between the Heirs & Representatives of said Decd. & make return to the next Court.

Ordered that John Purify aged fifteen years be bound to John Bedscot jr. to learn to be a Shoemaker. (Inds. made out)

Ordered that Edward Purify aged Eleven years or thereabouts be bound to Frederick Clements to learn to be a Shoemaker.

On the Petition of James Gatlin & Jno. Gatlin Exr. of Thos. Gatlin Decd. praying leave to sell a Negro Boy named Limbo who was bequeathed to Mitchell Gatlin, who Died before the Testator — Ordered that the prayed of said Petitioners be granted and that said Negro be sold at ~~Nine~~ Six Months Credit.

218 – March 1794

Charles Crawford & Wife vs. William Henry & Wife} Peto. For Dower.

The following Jury. – withdrawn.

No. 3 Den, on Demise of Geo. Thomas Pollock vs. Rd. Fen & Nathl. Streets} Eject.

The following Jury empanelled vizl. No. 1. Danl. Lane 2. Stephen W. Dunn 3. Lucas J. Benners 4. Frans. Delamar 5. James Hollis 6. Fredk. Metts 7. William Tyre 8. Hardy Bush 9. Jno. Ives 10. Evan Thomas 11. Thos. Wayne 12. James Nelson find for the Defendant not Guilty.

Appeal prayed by the Plantiff and allowed upon Entering into Bond in the sum of £100 Jno. Devereux & Thos. P. Monk Secys.

The last Will & Testament of Isaac Bryan Esqrs. Decd. was proved in Open Court by the Oaths of Wm. Bryan & Charles Saunders two of the Subscribing Witnesses thereto and Ordered to be Recorded and at the same time Lewis Bryan & William Cox two of the Executors therein Named appeared in Court & Qualified agreeable to Law Ordered th__ Letters issued.

An Inventory and Account Sales of the Estate of Thomas Gatlin Decd. was returned by the Executors & filed.

An Inventory of the Estate of Thomas Gatlin decd. was returned & filed.

The last Will & Testament of Albert Berry Decd. was Produced & proved by the Oath of J. Brown a subscribing Witness thereto and at the same time Jarvis Burton the one of the Exrs. therein named appeared in Court & Qualified as such agreeablt to Law. Ordered that Letters issue. Dr.

219 — March 1794
Ordered that James Coor, George Ellis & William Shepard be appointed to Audit the Accounts of the Administrators of Alexander McAuslan Decd. and make a return as soon possible.

Ajourned till 9 oClock.
Wednesday, March 12, 1794
Met pursuant to adjournment. Present the Worshipful Richd. Nixon, Jno. F. Smith, Jno. Dawson} Esqrs.

Ordered that John Harris, Jarvis Fillingham & David Pearce be appointed to Audit the Accts of John Bryan Guardian of the Orphans of James Kemp decd. & make return of their proceedings to the next Court.

Whereas Jno. Bryan [stricken illegible words] entered into Bond for the maintainance of two Children that was sworn upon him by Sarah Mitchell — who is since Dead — and the Children being produced in Court it appears that they are Mulattoes. Ordered that the said Bond be Cancelled & said Bryan discharged from the further maintenance of said Children.

Ordered that Lucas J. Benners a defaulting Juror be fined ten shillings. Remitted.

Ordered that Levi Dawson, John Biggs, & Wm. Shine be appointed Settle and the Accounts of James Hyman Exr. of Michael Hyman decd. and also Divide the undevised part of said Decd. Estate between the Heirs & make a return to the next Court.

Mrs. Heath renewed her Tavern License. Issd.

220 – No. 1. Francis Stringer vs. Gordon & Kean} Ansl. Atta. [?]. The following Jury empanelled & Sworn Viz. No. 1 Daniel Lane 2. Stephen W. Dun 3. Francis Delamar 4. Lucas J. Benners 5. Hardy Hawkins 6. Hardy Bush 7. William Gaskins 8. James Potter 9. James Roe 10. John Smallwood 11. Ignatius Wadsworth 12. Robert Hunt find for the Planiff and Assess £871.0.0 and 6d Costs Release as to Rd. Jones the Garnishee.

An account Sales of the Estate of Thomas Forguson Decd. was returned & filed.

An Account Sales of Negroes of the Estate of Andw. Ball decd. was returned & filed.

A Division of the Real Estate of Silas S. Stevenson Decd. was returned by the Commissioners appointed to Divide the same and ordered to be filed. Dr. 16/ Charged.

Daniel Lane, Joseph Loftin & Reuben Heath are appointed Patrollers in Capt. Wm. Cox's Distrit from half Moon to Mosely's Creek. Issd.

An Account Sales of the Estate of Peter Franklin Decd. was returned & filed.

John Sears Esqr. returned the list of Taxables in Capt. T. Phillips District for the year 1793.

Ordered that Thomas A. Green Esqr. be appointed to take the list of Taxables in Capt. Tho: A. Green's District for the year 1793. Mr. Henry being appointed to take the said list and was afterwards appointed Sheriff. Issd.

Ordered that Levi Fulsher, John Porter & Wm. Ives be appd. to Audit the Accounts of Jno. P. Ives Guardian of Sarah Ives & make return to the next Court.

221 — Ordered that John Dawson, John Biggs, & James Hyman audit the the Accounts of Hardy Hawkins Admr. of Hannah Hawkins decd. and also to Divide the Estate of the sd. deceased between the Heirs of said Decd.

Jno. Smallwood a defaulting Juror fin'd 10/. Remitted.

Jas. McCafferty vs. Jeremiah Redding} the same jury as in the last cause one failing to answer. Mistrial.

No. 16. John Kennedy vs. William Bowen} Case. The same Jury as in the last Cause except Jno. Knox in the room of Jno. Smallwood empanelled — find the Defendant did assume & assess £21.13.4 Dam. & 6d Costs. Appeal prayed by Plantiff & granted on filing Reasons & entering into Bond with James Carney & Francis Lowthorp Securities.

An Account of Sales of the Estate of Joseph Holland decd. was returned & filed.

A Division of the Estate of Saml. Wiggins Decd. was returned by the Persons appointed at Steptember Term last to Divide the same & ordered to be filed.

Adjourned till 3oClock.
Met Pursuant to Adjournment. Present the Worshipfull Richard Nixon, Jno. F. Smith, Francis Lowthorp, Jacob Johnston, Wm. M. Herritage} Esqrs.

Whereas in the suit William M. Herritage against George Lovick & Thomas Lovick — Richard Fenner was subpoenaed on behalf of the Plantiff & summons being returned Executed & the sd. Fenner having failed to appear. Ordered that he be fined Ni Si agreeable to Act of Assembly & that Sci. Fa issue to shew Cause &c.

222 — The last Will & Testament of Titus Ogden decd. was proved in open Court by the oath of Wilson Blount one of the Subscribing Witnesses thereto agreeable to Law and at the same time Jno. G. Blount one of the Executors therein named appeared in Court & Qualified agreeable to Law. Ordered that Letters issue.

Ordered that James Roe be find ten shillings fine for delinquency as a Juror. Ca Sa issd.}

No. 22. Isaac Guion vs. William Ryan} Case. The following Jury empanelled & Sworn vzl. No. 1 Danl. Lane   2. Stephen W. Dun 3. Francis Delamar
4. Lucas J. Benners 5. Hardy Huckins 6. Hardy Bush   7. William Gaskins
8. James Potter 9. Danl Cathy   A. McCalop 10. Ignatius Wadsworth
11. Robert Hunt 12. Thomas Dunn find the Defendant did assume & the Plantiffs Damages to £33.0.8 & 6d Costs.

Ordered that William King pay unto Avey Roe Forty shillings for the Maintenance of a Bastard Child son [?] (of which he is the Reputed Father) for two months.

No. 27. Joseph Shute Exr. &c vs. Thomas Parsons} The same Jury as in the last Cause empanelled find the Defend. did Assume & assess £53.7.9 Dam. & 6d Costs. Plantiff remits £4.16

Jno. Dubberly renewed his Tavern License. pd. 10/

223 — No. 28. Jno. Devereux vs. Admr. Silas S. Stevenson}
Case. The following Jury empanelled & Sworn. No. 1. Danl.
Lane 2. Stephen Dun 3. Frans. Delamar 4. Lucas J. Benners 5.
Hardy Hawkins 6. Hardy Bush 7. Wm. Gaskins 8. James
Potter 9. Archd. McCalop 10. Ignatius Wadsworth 11. Thos.
Dun   12. Jno. Smallwood find the Defendants intestate did
assume & that he assumed within three years & they assess
the Plantiffs Dams. to £72.4.7 ½ & 6d Costs.

No. 29. James Lockwood vs. Edward Tinker} Case. The same
Jury as in the last Cause empanelled find the Defendant did
Assume & Assess £120.10.8 & 6d Costs.

No. 30. Joshua Potts for Boretz & Co. vs. Frederick Ward}
Case. The same Jury as in the last Cause empanelled find the
Deft. did assume & assess the Plantiffs Damages to £41.17.5 &
6d Costs appeal prayed by the Defent. & granted. Jno. F.
Smith & Wm. Davis Security.

Adjourned till tomorrow Morng. 9 oClock
Thursday, March 13th 1794.
Met Pursuant to Adjournment. Present the Worshipful
Jacob Johnston, John F. Smith, John Dawson} Esqrs.

224 — Ordered that William Trippe be appointed Guardian to
Elizabeth, Carney & Jesse Bryan Orphans of Jesse Bryan Decd.
upon his entering into Bond in £1000 each with John ~~Bry~~
Dawson & William Henry Securities. Dr. 24/ Chagd)

No. 26. William Borden Senr. vs. John Green Exr. of Richard
Cogdell decd.} Case. The following Jury empanelled & Sworn
vizl.

1. Danl. Lane   2. Stephen W. Dun 3. Frans. Delamar 4. Lucas
J. Benners F. Foy 5. Thomas Webber 6. Hardy Bush   7. John
Fell 8. Benja. Brinson 9. William Ross (J. McCafferty) 10.
Edward Bowen 11. John Blanks
12. John Smallwood find the Defendant did assume & assess
£23.8.1 Dams. & 6d Costs.

No 28 34. James McKinlay vs. John Freebody} Case. The same
Jury as in the last Cause did find the Defendant did assume &
assess £20.16 Dams. & 6d Costs.

Ordered that Sarah Brightman have leave to keep Tavern in
Newbern for one year. Joseph Clark & J. McMains Security.

John Daves vs. James Postlewaite} Case. The following same
Jury empanelled as in the last Cause find the Defendant
Guilty and assess the Plantiffs Damages to £50 & 6d Costs.

225 – An Account of Sales of the Estate of James Sears decd.
was returned & filed.

Jno. Sears Admr. of James Sears decd returned his Acct
against the Estate of said Decd. which was examined by the
Court & allowed.

Joseph Oliver renewed his Tavern License.

Moses Lambert, Thomas Clements, & John Gooding Junr. are
appointed Patrollers in Capt. Greens District.

Wm. Bryan, William Smyth & Enoch Harris Frederick
Johnston are appointed Patrollers in Capt. Jno. Bryan's
District.

No. 40. Willis McCoy vs. Thos. A. Green} Case. The same Jury as in No. 26 except Fredk. Foy & James McCafferty in the room of Thos. Webber & Wm. Ross — empanelled & Sworn find the Defendant did assume & assess the Damages of the Plantiff to £25.19.2 & 6d Costs. Appeal prayed and allowed William Henry & Wm. M. Herritage Securities.

No. 41. Piere Thamegeux vs. James Hyman} Case. The same Jury as in the last Cause empanelled [nothing further]

Ordered that Stephen Taylor aged sixteen years the 26th October next & Abraham Taylor aged thirteen years the 5th Novr. next be bound to Edward Bowen to learn the Trade of a ~~Milling~~ Cart Wheelrights Trade. (Rescinded at June Term 1794)

226 — Ordered that a Free Negro Negro Boy named Sam [illegible] aged thirteen years be bound to Edward Bowen to learn the Trade of a Cartwheelright. (Inds. Exd). 4/ due.

Adjourned till 4oClock.
Met Pursuant to Adjournment. Present the Worshipful Jacob Johnston, Jno. F. Smith, John Dawson}

Then were following Gentlemen appointed to attend at the next Court as Jurors Vzl.
1. George Lane 2. John Clark 3. Charles Saunders 4. John Smallwood 5. William Mitchell 6. Enoch Alexander 7. Danl. Carthy 8. John Devereux 9. John Bryan 10. James Davis 11. Thomas Oliver 12. Joseph Oliver
13. William Smith 14. Thomas Speight 15. Thos. Webber 16. James McCafferty 17. John Blanks 18. Thomas Sparrow Jr. 19. William Anthony 20. John Gooding Wm. McCoy 21. Cason Amory 22. John Gooding Jos. Clark

23. Frederick Foy 24. Francis Hawks 25. James Hollis 26. Frederick Lane 27. Danl. West   28. Moses Ernul 29. Aaron Ernul 30. Andw. Richardson 31. Thomas Cox 32. Francis McIlwean 33. Thos. G. Fonvielle   34. John Kennedy 35. Amos Cutrel. Issd.

Ordered that James McCafferty & Edward Bowen defaulting Jurors be fined ten shillings each & that Execution issue for the same. (Ca sa. Issd. agt. Bowen)

A post Inventory of the Estate of Joseph Holland Decd. was returned by Levi Fulsher & filed.

227 — Admr. Alexr. McAuslan vs. Jesse Barnard & William Speight} Case. The following Jury empanelled viz: 1. Danl. Lane   2. Stephen W. Dun 3. Frans. Delamar 4. Lucas J. Benners 5. Frederick Foy 6. Hardy Bush
7. John Fell 8. Benj. Brinson 9. Hardy Hewkins I.G. 10. Thomas Oliver 11. John Blanks 12. John Smallwood find the Defendant did assume & assess £23.19.2 Dams. & 6d — appeal prayed by Defendt. Levi Dawson & Thos. Speight Security.

Ordered that Hardy Hewkins a defaulting Juror be find ten shillings final & that Execution issue.

No. 44. Administrators of Alexr. McAuslan decd. vs. William Davis} Case. The same Jury as in the last Cause except Jno. Gooding in the room of Hardy Hewkins empanelled find the Defendant did assume & assess £65.3.10 ½ Dams. & 6d Costs and they also find that he assumed within three years.

No. 88. Mathew Neale & Eunice his Wife vs. Jno Carney Exr. of John Bryan decd.} Case. The same Jury as in the last Cause empanelled find for the Plantiff and assess £85.14.2 Dams. & 6d Costs.

228—No. 47. Farnifold Green Jr. Asignee Wm. Clure vs. Wm. McClure Admr. Edwd. Potter jr. Decd.} Case. The same Jury as in the last Cause empanelled find the Defendants Intestate did assume & assess £107.4.0 Dams. & 6d Costs they further find that the Defendant has fully Administered except as to £17.4.6 which they find to be assets in his Hands. Judgement for £17.4.6 and Sci. Fa to issue against the Heirs viz James Potter, George Potter & Joseph Potter as to the Residue to shew Cause &c why the Lands should not be sold agreeable to Law. (Sci. Fa issd.)

No. 49. Isaac Read Asignee &c. vs. Levi Dawson} Case. The following Jury empanelled vzl. No. 1. Daniel Lane 2. Stephen W. Dun 3. Francis Delamar 4. Lucas J. Benners 5. Robert Hunt   6. Hardy Bush   7. John Fell
8. Benja. Brinson 9. Jno. Gooding 10. Thomas Oliver 11. Jno. Blanks 12. Jno. Smallwood find the Defendant did not assume—Appeal prayed & allowed the Plantiffs entering into Bond in the sum of £500 with Wm. Slade & John Fell his Securities, reason filed.

No. 51. Sharpe Blount vs. Abner Nash} Case. The same Jury as in the last Cause empanelled find the Defendant Assumed and that he assumed withing 3 years. [illegible blotted words] and assess £29.13.9 Dam & 6d Costs.

Adjourned till tomorrow Morning, 9 oClock.

229--___day, March 14, 1794, Met Pursuant to adjournment. Present the Worshipful John Allen, Jacob Johnston, John Dawson} Esqrs.

Ordered that John Allen Esqr. be appointed Guardian to Susanna Bryan upon his entering into Bond in the Sum of £1000 — with John Daly & John Tillman Esqrs. his Securities.

__ John Fell vs. Thomas Spikes alias Speight} Case sur words. The following Jury empanelled & Sworn to Wit: 1. Daniel Lane 2. Stephen W. Dun 3. Francis Delamar 4. Lucas J. Benners 5. Thomas Webber 6. Joseph West 7. Ambrose Jones 8. John Gill 9. Charles Saunders jr. 10. William Anthony 11. Solomon Caton 12. John Gooding find the Defendant Guilty & assess forty shillings Damage & 6d Costs.

William Sears is appointed Inspector of Merchantable Commodities at the Warehouse Landing upon Little Contentnea. Francis Lowthorp & Jno. Sears Securities. Dr. Sears being absent ordered that John Sears Esqr. Qualify him out of Court.

Francis Brown to have Tavern License. Jno. Fellows & Jno. F. Smith Securities.

Ordered that James Coor, John Fonvielle & Saml. Chapman be appointed to Audit the Accounts of William Slade & Richard Nixon Administrators of Silas S. Stevenson decd. and report thereon to the next Court.

230 — State vs. Negro Peter belonging to Alexr. Stewart} Felony. The following Jury Impanelled & Sworn, Viz. No. 1. Stephen W. Dun 2. Francis Delamar 3. Thomas Webber 4. Ambrose Jones 5. John Gooding 6. William Gaskins 7. Fisher Gaskins 8. Sampson Morris 9. Francis McIlwean 10. William Smyth 11. John Kennedy 12. Robert Hung find the Prisoner at the Bar, Negro Peter, is not Guilty.

Ordered that Joseph Frelick have permission to keep a Public House of entertainment in Newbern upon his entering into Bond with Jno. C. Osborn & Sam. Chapman his y.

An Account of Sales of the Estate of Daniel Bradley Decd. was returned & filed. D. 2/

State vs. Negro Peter & Bill} Alexander Stewart appeared in Court & entered into Recognizance in the sum of £50_ to be Levied on his Several Goods & Chattels, Lands & Tenements for the use of the State to be Void never theless upon his producing his Negro Peter before a Special Court to be held for the Trial of Negro Will the property of Danl. Carthy who stands Charged with Felony.

Adjourned till 9 oClock tomorrow.
Saturday, March 15, 1794.
Met Pursuant to Adjournment. Present the Worshipful, Levi Dawson, Wm. M. Herritage, Jno. F. Smith, John Dawson} Esqrs.

231 – A Settlement of the Accounts of Charles Williams Guardn of Nancy H. Wright was returned by the Referees appointed to Settle the Same & ordered to be Recorded.

James McKinlay vs. Malcolm Gillies} Case. On argument in Arrest of Judgment. Ordered that the Judgment be arrested. Appeal prayed upon the Plantiff entering into Bond in the sum of £100. John Daves & Geo. Ellis Securities. Reasons filed.

Ordered that John Sears Esqr. be appointed Inspector of Merchantable Commodities at the Warehouse Landing on Little Contentnea upon his Qualifying and entering into Bond in the Sum of £500 with Jno. F. Smith & Francis Lowthorp Securities.

Ordered that Francis Lowthorp, Jno. F. Smith & James Carney be appointed to Audit the Accounts of Charles ~~Sanderson~~ Williams Executor of Stephen Wright Decd. and make return to the next Court.

A Settlement of the Estate of the Orphans of Thomas Delamar Decd. with John Thomas Guardian was returned by the Referees appointed for that Purpose & filed.

232 — State vs. Thomas Roe} Petit Larceny. The following Jury impanelled & Sworn viz. No. 1. Danl. Lane   2. Stephen W. Dun 3. Francis Delamar
4. Lucas J. Benners 5. Joseph West 6. Charles W. Masters 7. Jno. Devereux 8. Solomon Caton 9. William Caton 10. Jno. Lovick 11. Sampson Morris 12. John Blanks find the Defendant Guilty. Judgment that he receive twenty four Lashes upon his bare Back & that the Sheriff put the same in Execution immediately & pay costs.

Ordered that James Carney be appointed Guardian to William Dawson Bryan minor upon his entering into Bond of £1000 with John Daves & William Dudley his Securities. Dr. (Charged)

John Gooding Jr. Sampson Morriss & Thomas Wise are appointed Patrollers in Capt. T.A. Greens District from Core Creek to Stoney Branch. Issd.

James Whitfield, Thomas Clements & William M. Herritage are appd. Patrollers from Core Creek to the Half Moon Branch. Issd.

Read the petition of John Gooding setting forth that a Patent Granted to him by his Excellency Richard D. Spaight Esqr. for 500 Acres bearing date 1 Jan 179_ has one Course left out, Viz: North eighty two poles, the Plat of the said Patent being right. Ordered that an Order issue directed to the Secretary of State directing him to insert the said Course No 12 ____ in the Patent so as to make it Conformable to the Plat.

233 — Ordered that Nehemiah Haddy [?] aged 18 [?] years be bound to John Digner to learn the Trade of a [illegible] (made out)

Ordered that William Tignor be appointed Guardian to Sarah Tignor (Minor) upon his entering into Bond in the sum of £1000 with Wm. Johnson & William Mitchell his Securities.

Ordered that Edmund Per___ [illegible] be appointed to attend at the next Term as Constable.

State vs. William Thomas} Ordered that the Defendant pay unto Polly Hurley £6.17.0 for the maintainance of a Bastard Child sworn by her against him.

State vs. William Arthur} Petit Larceny. The Defendant appeared in Court & entered into Recognizance in the sum of One hundred Pounds & John Arthur and Arthur Ipock entered into Recognizance in the Sum of Fifty Pounds each to be Levied on their Several Goods & Chattels Lands & Tenements to the use of the State to be Void nevertheless if the said William Arthur shall make his Personal Appearacen at the next Court to be held for the County of Craven in June next then & there to abide the Order & Decree of said Court.

Ordered that Francis Lowthorp, Edmund Perkins & Thomas Webber be appointed to Audit the Accounts of John Bedscot, jr. & Jno Bedscot Senr. Guardians to the Orphans of David Purify decd. & make return to the next Court.

234 – Wm. M. Herritage, J.P.
John Dawson, J.P.
F. Lowthorp, J.P.

///

[June 1794]
235 – At a County Court of Pleas & Quarter Sessions begun and held for the County of Craven at the Court House in Newbern on the second Monday in June being the 9th day of the month in the 18th year of our Independence A.D. 1794. Present the Worshipful John Tillman, Jacob Johnston, John Fonvielle, John Carney, Joshua Fulshire, Francis Lowthorp, Wm. M. Herritage, Wm. Tisdale} Esqrs.

The Sheriff of Craven County returned the Writ of Venire facias for Jurors to this Term "Executed."

An Inventory of the Estate of Isaac Blanchard Decd. was returned & filed.

Then was the Grand Jury empanelled Viz.
1. Jno. C. Bryan, Foreman 2. Francis Hawks 3. James Hollis 4. John Devereux 5. James Davis 6. George Lane 7. William Anthony 8. Thomas Speight 9. William Smyth 10. Moses Ernull 11. Joseph Clark 12. Joseph Oliver 13. Enoch Alexander

An Account Sales & Inventory of the Estate of James Brightman decd. was returned & filed.

An Inventroy of the Estate of Jacob Rathburn decd. was returned and filed.

236 — An Account Sales of the Estate of Hester Yeats Widow decd. was returned & filed.

Ordered that Sarah Oliver have Letters of Adminn. upon the Estate of Samuel Oliver decd. upon her Qualifying and entering into Bond in the sum of £300 with John Carney & Joseph Masters, Securities — Bond taken & Inventory returned.

Ordered that Jane Pittman have administration upon the Estate of Obedience Pittman decd. upon her Qualifying and entering into Bond in the sum of £300 with John Carney & Joseph Masters Securities — Bond taken & Inventory retd.

Ordered that Jane Pittman be appointed Guardian to John & Betsy Pittman Orphans of Obedience Pittman decd. upon her entering into Bond of £20_ with John Carney & Joseph Masters Securities.

Whereas Stephen and Abraham Taylor were Ordered to be Bound to Edward Bowen at last Term and the Indentures being not Executed & on Cause shewn. Ordered that the former Order be Rescinded and made Void. Issd.

Ordered that Mrs. Jane Pittman have permission to sell the Perishable Estate of Obedience Pittman decd.

237 — The last Will and Testament of Daniel Daugherty Decd. was proved by the Oath of John West one of the Subscribing Witnesses thereto agreeable to Law and at the same time James Arnold one of the Executors therein named appeared in Court and Qualified as such. Ordered that Letters Testamentary issue.

Ordered that John West, Joseph Palmer & William Bryan be appointed to Audit the Accounts of William Phipps Executor of the Estate of Charles Marshall Decd. and make return to the next Court.

Ordered that Peter Smith be appointed Guardian to Sarah Smith upon his entering into Bond in the sum of £200 with John Taylor & _____ ___sley his securities.

An Inventory of the Estate of Levi Hill decd. was returned & filed.

Ordered that John Cummings have administration upon the Estate of James Cummings decd. upon his entering into Bond in the sum of £200 — with John Carney & Joseph Masters Security's — Bond taken & Inventory filed.

Ordered that John Blanks, Levi Fulsher & Evan Jones be appointed to Settle the Accounts of John Taylor & Benja. Toleson Executors of the Estate of Absalom Taylor decd. and make return to the next Court.

William Gibbs renewed his Tavern License.

238 — The Referees appointed to Audit the Accounts of James Gatlin & John Bryan Guardians of the Orphans of James Kemp Decd. made a return of the Accounts &c which was ordered to be filed.

James Carney renewed his Inspection Bonds and offered John Carney & Joseph Masters his Securities. Dr.

William Johnston renewed his Insection Bond & offered John Carney & Joseph Masters his Securities. Dr.

Ordered that George Sparrow be appointed Guardian to Henry Sparrow upon his entering into Bond in the sum of £150 with John Carney & Jos. Masters Securities.

It being Represented to the Court that William Nelson an Aged Infirm man is incapable of Transacting Business for himself being also Blind. Ordered that Jacob Johnston Esqr. be appointed his Guardian upon his entering into Bond of £200 — with Edward Nelson & Charles Roach his Securities.

Jacob Johnston Esqr. renewed his Inspection Bond & offered Charles Roach & Edward Nelson his securities.

Adjourned till 4 oClock

Met Pursuant to Adjournment. Present the Worshipful John Tillman, Wm. M. Herritage, Joshua Fulsher, Henry Tilman.

239 — A Division of the Real Estate of William S. Foster decd. was returned by three of the Commissioners appointed to Divide the same and ordered to be Rescinded.

An Account of Sales and Inventory of the Estate of William Murphy decd. was returned & filed.

An Inventory of the Estate of Jno. Igs. Bailey Decd. was returned & filed.

Ordered the Defaulting Jurors which were fined at the Special Court held for this County in May last be ~~remitted~~ released from the payment of said fines — also the Jurors that were fined Ni Si at the last Court.

Ordered the fine adjudged against James McCaffert at the last Term for his Default as a Talesman be Remitted.

John Bryan vs. Jno. S. West} Peto. for a Mill. Ordered that Jarvis Fillingham, Joel King, Thomas Green & John Hill be appointed to lay off and Value one Acre of Land upon both sides of the Stream and report thereon to the Next Court. Issd.

Ordered that the County Treasurer be directed & empowered to purchase two Books for the County Register.

James Bryan renewed his Registers Bond, James Carney & Wm. Johnston his Securities.

Ordered that William Johnston, James Carney & Edwd. Pasteur settle the Accts. of Francis Gardner Admr. Esau Tingle decd. and report thereon to this Court.

240 — Adjourned till 9 oClock.
Tuesday, June 10, 1794. Met Pursuant to Adjournment.
Present the Worshipful
John Tillman, William M. Herritage, Isaac Guion, Henry Tillman

Ordered that James McCafferty pay unto Celia King Six pounds for the maintenance of a Bastard Child sworn to hom for twelve months.

Ordered that John Marchment aged fifteen years be bound to Jesse Lester to be a Blacksmith.

An Account Sales of the Estate of James Biggs was returned & filed.

Charles Crawford & Wife vs. William Henry & Wife} Pett. The following Jury empanelled Viz. No. 1 John Clark 2. Charles Saunders 3. William Mitchell 4. Thomas Webber 5. Thomas Oliver 6. Wm. McCoy 7. Cason Amory 8. Aaron Ernull 9. James McCafferty 10. Andrew Richardson 11. Wm. Spencer Murphy 12. James Reel find no Cause of Action.

A Division of the Real Estate of Adam Ferguson De__ was returned & filed.

241 — William Hannis renewed his Inspection Bond. Richd. Nixon & John Allen Security.

William Davis, Joseph ODowde, Shadrack Collins & William Whaley are appointed Patrollers in Captain Parsons District.

Present the Worshipful John Tillman, Levi Dawson, John Allen, Wm. McClure, Levi Dawson [sic], Henry Tillman, James Gatlen, Joshua Fulsher, Francis Lowthorp, John Sears, John Daly, Thos. A. Green, Hardy Gatlin, John Fonvielle.

The Court Proceeded to appoint a Sheriff when William Henry Esqr. was unanimously Elected. Ordered that a Certificate issue that he may obtain a Comission from his Excellency the Governor agreeable to Law.

Ordered that Joshua Fulsher, Francis Delamar & John Dawson be appointed to settle the Account of Bridget Biggs Admx. James Biggs Decd. and also to Divide the Estate of said Deceased between the Widow & Heirs of said Decd.

Ordered that Isaac Kemp have administration upon the Estate of Hannah Gaskins Decd upon his entering into Bond in the sum of £400 with Herman Gaskins & John Arthur his Securities.

Ordered that Aaron Ernull, Moses Ernull, & James Gatlin Esqr. be appointed to Divide the Estate of Hannah Gaskins decd. between the Heirs and make a return to the next Court.

242 – Samuel Chapman Clerk of Craven County Court ____ his Bond agreeable to a late Act of Assembly and offered Isaac Guion & John Allen Esqr for his Securities – which were approved of by the Court and Bond Executed Accordingly – and De__[??] Jno Esqr presiding Chairman.

Adjourned till 4 oClock.
Met Pursuant to adjournment.
Present the Worshipfull John Tillman, Wm. M. Herritage, Joshua Fulsher} Esqrs.

A Settlement of Accounts between the Guardian of Peggy Perkins, Orphan of James Perkins decd. was returned by the Referees appointed for that purpose and Ordered to be Recorded.

John Digsin [??] has permission to Keep Tavern in Newbern Charles Saunders Security.

An Inventory and Account Sales of the Estate of Isaac Bryan Decd. was returned & filed.

Agreeable to Act of Assembly the Justices of this Court Classed themselves as follows.
1st Class — Joseph Leech, Jno. Dawson, Jacob Johnston, Jno. F. Smith, Joshua Fulsher, Richard Nixon, Adam Tooley.
2nd Class. Jno. Tillman, Wm. McClure, Jno. Carney, Wm. Tisdale, Wm. M. Herritage, John Bragg
3rd Class. Jno. Fonvielle, John Sears, James Gatlin, Francis Lowthorp, Levi Dawson, Hardy Gatlin, Isaac Guion
4th Class. John Dawley, Southy Rew, John Allen, Henry Tillman, Spyers Singleton, Thomas A. Green.

243 — Wm. H. Conner, Joseph Clark, & Benajah Bogey is appd. Patrollers in Capt. David Lewis Company.

No. 13. Robert Hunt & Wife vs. David Witherspoon adm. To Abner Nash} Case. The following Jury empanelled. Viz. No. 1. John Clark 2. Thos. G. Fonvielle 3. William Mitchell 4. Thomas Webber 5. Thomas Oliver 6. William McCoy 7. Cason Amery 8. Aaron Ernull 9. James McCafferty 10. Andw. Richardson   11. James Reel
12. William Shepard mil no Ca the Defendt. Testator did not assume. Appeal prayed by Plff.

On Motion of William Slade Esqr. on behalf of James Taylor. Ordered that a Subpoena issue against Mathew Stevens of Craven County Commanding him to appear before the next Court and produce the Will of William Howard Decd. &c.

Adjourned till 9 oClock.
Wednesday, June 11th 1794.
Met Pursuant to Adjournment.
Present the Worshipfull John Tillman, John Fonvielle, Henry Tillman}

A settlement of the Accounts of Silas S. Stevenson Decd. Guardian to the Orphans of John Stevenson decd. was returned by the Referees appointed for that purpose & ordered to be Recorded.

A Settlement of the Accounts of the Admrs. of Saml. White Decd. was returned by the Referees appointed for the purpose & Ordered to be Recorded.

244 – A Settlement of the Accounts of Francis Gardner Admr Esau Tingle Decd. was returned by the Referees appoin___ for that purpose.

Ordered that John Holder aged 14 years be bound to Thomas Cox to learn to be a House Carpenter.

No. 22. Piere Thomageux [??] vs. James Hyman} Case. The following Jury empanelled Viz. No. 1. John Clark 2. Charles Saunders 3. William Mitchell 4. Thomas Oliver 5. Thomas Webber 6. William McCoy 7. Cason Amery 8. Aaron Ernull 9. Andw. Richardson 10. Thomas G. Fonvielle 11. John Kennedy 12. John Good   find the Defendant did assume, and that he assumed within 3 years and assess £65.7.0 Damages & 6d Cos__ Appeal prayed & allowed the Defendt. Thomas Hyman & Philip Knowis Security.

The Referees appointed to Settle the Accounts of Richard Daugherty Admr. Nehemiah Randal Decd made a Return of the proceedings which were approved of by the Court and Ordered to be Recorded.

No. 31. William Gaston by his Guardian vs. Nathan Smith} Tres. Q.C.F.
The following Jury empanelled & sworn. Viz.

No. 1 Spyers Singleton 2. James Davis 3. William Johnston 4. William Mitchell 5. John Devereux 6. Thomas Smith 7. Thomas Dunn 8. Stephen W. Dunn 9. William Davis 10. Thomas Hickman 11. Thomas Oliver
12. John Clark   find the Defendant Guilty and assess £20. Dama. & 6d Cos__. Appeal prayed by Defendt. Elexander Stewart & Wm. Slade Securities. Bond £200.

245 – No. 33. Thomas Hyman vs. James Brinson} Refered to Abner Neale, Levi Dawson and James Carney who returned their award in favor of the Defendant Plantiff for the sum of £25.1.6 due from James Brinson Executor of Peter Hyman Decd. to the Heir Peter Hyman Decd. award filed & Judgment Pursuant to award.

No. 24. Commissrs. Of Newbern vs. James McCafferty} Debt. The following Jury empanelled vzt. No. 1. Thomas Webber 2. William McCoy 3. Cason Amery
4. Aaron Ernull 5. Andw. Richardson 6. Thos. G. Fonvielle 7. John Good
8. John Kennedy 9. John Moore   10. William Hawley 11. Joseph Clark
12. William Good Juror withdrawn & cause Canld.

No. 27. William Tisdale assignee Wm. Slade vs. The Admrs of John Starkey} Case
The same Jury as in the last Cause empanelled find the Defendts Intestate did assume & assess £70.10/ Damages and 6d Costs and no sett offs &c.

The Referees appointed to Audit the Accounts of John Bedscott jr. Guardian of the Orphans of David Purify Decd. made a return of the Accounts which were approved of by the Court and Ordered to be filed.

246 – The Referees appointed to Audit the Account of Charles Williams Executor of Stephen Wright decd. made a return of the Accounts Settled and Ordered to be filed.

No. 33. William M. Herritage Assignee &c. vs. William Henry} Case. The same Jury as in the last Cause except William Mitchell in the room of Wm. Hawley empanelled &c find the Defendant did assume & Assess the Plantiff's Damage to £10.9.10 & 6d Cos__ no further Payments of Sett off.

No. 32. William Mitchell vs. Wm. Hawley} Case. The following Jury empanelled viz.
1. Thomas Webber 2. William McCoy 3. Cason Amery 4. Andw. Richardson 5. John Good 6. John Kennedy 7. John Moore 8. Joseph Clark jr. 9. William Good 10. Thomas Parsons 11. Thomas Dunn 12. Aaron Ernull
find the Defendant did assume and assess £53.18.0 Da___ & 6d Costs.

Ordered that Elizabeth Taylor aged 13 years the 2d March la__ past be Bound to Alexander Duguid to learn to be _ Spinster. (Inds. made out.)

Adjourned till 4 oClock.

247 – Met Pursuant to adjournment.
Present the Worshipfull John Tillman, John Daly, Henry Tillman} Esqrs.

No. 37. William Good vs. Francois X. Martin} Debt in Act of Assembly. The following Jury empanelled &c. Viz. 1. John Clark 2. Charles Saunders 3. William Mitchell

4. Thomas Oliver 5. Thomas Webber 6. William McCoy 7. Cason Amary 8. Aaron Ernull 9. Andrew Richardson 10. Thos. G. Fonvielle 11. John Kennedy 12. Charles Williams one failing to Answer — mistrial.

A Division of Negroes belonging to the Estate of Thomas Delamar Decd. was returned by the persons appointed to Divide the same and ordered to be Recorded.

Then was the Grand Jury discharged.

No. 42. John Dixon vs. Francis Lowthorp} Case. The same Jury as in the last Cause empanelled. Judgment Confessed for £22.17.0. Dama. & 6d Costs.

No. 43. Richard Hunley vs. Jas. Davis & Wm. Davis} Case. The same Jury as in the last Cause except William Good in the room of Charles Williams empanelled find the Defendant did assume for the Plantiff in all the issues & assess £31.19.11 ½ Dama. & 6d Costs.

248 — Adjourned till 9 oClock.

Thursday June 12th 1794. Met Pursuant to adjournment.

Present the Worshipful John Tillman, Henry Tillman, William Tisdale} Esqrs.

An Inventory & account Sales of the Estate of Michal Hym__ decd. was returned & filed.

44. John Sheffield by Wm. Slade [illegible] vs. Thos. Webber Admr. Ann Webber decd.} Replevin

No. 44. Thos. Webber Admr. Ann Webber decd. vs. John
Sheffield} Replevin. The following Jury empanelled & Sworn
Viz. No. 1. John Clark 2. Charles Saunders
3. Thomas Oliver 4. George Lane 5. James McCafferty 6.
William McCoy 7. Cason Amory 8. Aaron Ernull 9. Andrew
Richardson 10. Thomas G. Fonvielle 11. John Kennedy 12.
Robert Hunt find for the Plantiff £43.10.4 Dams. & 6d Cost.

Evan Jones renewed his Bond for Inspector and offered for
Security John Bragg & Thomas Oliver.

The last Will and Testament of Francis Houston decd. was
produced in Court & proved by the Oath of Southy Rew ___ &
Ordered to be Recorded.

Ezekiel Delastatius renewed his Tavern license.

Ordered that Francis Lowthorp, John Fonvielle & Jno.
Gooding be appointed to audit the Accounts of the
Administrators of Silas S. Stevenson decd. & report thereon to
this Court.

249 — No. 45. Daniel Dishon vs. Thomas Turner admr. Wright
Stanly} Case.
The same Jury as in the last Cause except Thomas Webber in
the room of Robert Hunt empanelled &c. one failing to
answer. Mistrial.

Adjourned till 3 oClock.

Met Pursuant to Adjournment. Present the Worshipful John
Tillman, James Gatlin, John Bragg} Esqrs.

Ordered that Edmund Perkins Guardian of the Orphans of James Perkins decd. be allowed for two thousand Acres of Land out of his Taxes for the year 1793 being so much Charged to him in the List for 1792 thro Mistake.

Ordered that Richard Nixon, John Daly and John Allen Esqrs. be appointed to Audit the Accounts of James Gatlin Guardiand of Winifred and Sarah Kemp Orphans of James Kemp decd. and report thereon to next Court.

No. 47. Burwell Mooring vs. James McCafferty} Case. The following Jury empanelled vzl. No. 1 John Clark 2. Charles Saunders 3. Thomas Oliver 4. William McCoy 5. Cason Amery 6. Andw. Richardson 7. John Kennedy 8. Thomas Webber ([illegible]) 9. Thos. G. Fonvielle 10. James Wilson 11. John Gooding (J. McCafferty) 12. William Mitchell find the Defendant did not assume. Appeal prayed by Plff. and allowed. John Goulding & William Slade Securities. Bond £50.

250 — Ordered that George Ellis, Isaac Guion & Saml. Chapman assessors of Town property for the year 1793 be allowed Forty shillings each for their Services. (Issd.)

An Acct. Sale of a Negro Boy belonging to the Estae of Thos. Gatlin Decd. was returned & filed.

Read the Petition of Lucas Jacob Benners setting forth that he owns Land upon both sides of Mill Creek on the North side of Neuse River and praying Leave to Build a Public W___ Grist Mill thereon. Ordered that the Prayer of said Petition be Granted.

No. 52. Thomas Webb Admr Amos Webber decd vs. Levi
Dawson} Case. The same Jury as in the last Cause except
James McCafferty in the room of Thos. Webber [?] empanelled
find the Defendant did assume & assess £40.1.9 Dams. & 6d
Cost. Appeal prayed and allowed the Defend. upon Entering
into Bond with William Speight & William M. Herritage &
~~Levi~~ Francis Lowthorp Securities.

No. 53. James Pearce vs. Levi Dawson} Case. The same Jury as
in the last Cause empanelled find the Defendant did assume
and assess £30.19.4 Dams. & 6d Costs. Appeal prayed upon
entering into Bond with Wm. Speight & Wm. M. Herritage &
Frans. Lowthorp Securities.

No. 55. Richard D. Spaight vs. Wm. Henry & Geo. Ellis} Case.
The same Jury as in the last Cause empanelled find the
Defendants did assume and assess £38.8.7 Dams. & 6d Costs.

251 – No. 56. Richard Nixon & Wm. Slade vs. John Pearson &
John Gooding &} The same Jury as in No. 47 except James
McCafferty in the Room of John Gooding empanelled &c. find
the Defendants did assume & that they assumed within 3
years and assess the Plantiffs Damages to £42.10/ & 6d Costs.

Adjourned till 9 oClock.

Friday, June 13th, 1794. Met Pursuant to adjournment.

Present the Worshipfull John Tillman, William M. Herritage,
John Bragg, William Tisdale} Esqrs.

Account Sales of the Estate of Margaret Rew, Orphan was
returned and Ordered to be Recorded.

Ordered. Francis Lowthorp, John F. Smith & James Carney be appointed to audit the Accounts of William Johnston Guardian to Margaret Rew Orphan of Beverly Rew Decd. and make report thence to the next Court.

William Henry Esqr. Sheriff of Craven County Produced his Commission signed by his Excellency the Governor and Qualified agreeable to Law and entered into Bond in the sum of £5000 with John Tillman, Henry Tillman, John Allen, Aaron Ernull, John Daly & John Gooding his Securities.

252 – (Dr.) Ordered that William Johnston, James Carney & James Da___ are appointed to audit the accounts of Thomas Thomlinson Executor of Sarah Saunders decd.

(Dr.) John Sears Esqr. renewed his Inspector Bond and offered for Security Francis Lowthorp & William Sears.

Ordered that William Sears be appointed Guardian to George Sears upon his entering into Bond in the sum of £200 with John Sears & John Gatlin Securities.

(Dr.) Ordered that Francis Lowthorp, Isaac Guion & Saml. Chapman be appointed to Audit the Accounts of Farnifold Green & Richard Nixon Exrs. of Francis McIlwean decd. & Mary McIlwean Decd.

No. 84. John Gooding vs. Martha Sealey} Appeal by Plantiff. The following Jury empanelled & sworn.
No. 1 John Clark 2. Charles Saunders 3. William Mitchell 4. Thomas Webber 5. William McCoy 6. Cason Armory 7. Andrew Richardson 8. Cason Armory Aaron Ernull 9. Andrew Richardson 10. Thomas G. Fonvielle 11. John Kennedy 12. Mathew Brinson find the Defendant did not assume.

Ordered that William Moore be appointed Coroner for Craven County upon Qualifying and entering into Bond in £1000 with William M. Herritage & ~~Wm. M. Herritage~~ Abner Neale [?] his Securities.

Ordered that John Gooding be appointed Coroner for Craven County upon his Qualifying and entering into Bond in £1000 with John Daly and ~~John Allen~~ [?] William M. Herritage Se___. (Dr. Charged [Changed?])

253 – Ordered that Richard Nixon Esqr. be appointed Guardian to Silas S. Stevenson Orphan upon his entering into Bond in the Sum of £1000 with John Gooding & Thos. G. Fonvielle.

No. 49. ~~James Wilson vs.~~ John Tilman vs. James Wilson} Case. The following Jury empanelled & Sworn Viz. No. 1. John Clark 2. Charles Saunders 3. William Mitchell 4. Thomas Webber [?]   5. William McCoy 6. Cason Amery 7. Andrew Richardson 8. Thomas G. Fonvielle
9. John Kennedy 10. ~~Thomas G. Fonvielle~~ Mathew Brinson
11. Jno. Arnold 12. Charles Williams   Mistrial.

Ordered that Thomas A. Green, John Daly and John Gooding be appointed to Divide the Estate of John Green decd. and also to Audit the Accounts of the Executor of said Deceased and report thereon to the next Court.

Ordered that John Gooding be appointed Guardian to John Green (Minor) upon his entering into Bond in the sum of £1000 with John B. Herritage & Richard Nixon Esqrs. his Securities

Adjourned till 4 oClock.

Met Pursuant to adjournment. Present the Worshipful Levi Dawson, Wm. M. Herritage, John Bragg}

Ordered that Francis Lowthorp, James Carney, John Craddock, Edward Pasteur & Abner Neale be appointed to Divide the [illegible] personal Estate of Charles Johnston decd. between his Widow & Child and that they or any three of them Report thereon to the next Court.

254 — Then was the following Jurors appointed to attend at the next Superior Court. Viz.   1. Lucas J. Benners 2. William Smyth 3. Southy Rew   4. Levi Dawson 5. William Mitchell 6. John Sears 7. John Tillman
8. Isaac Guion   9. John F. Smith. (issd.)

Then were the following Jurors appointed to attend the next County Court.
1. Frederick Johnson 2. John Nelson   3. Edward Nelson 4. Jarvis Fillingim 5. William B. Fonville 6. Joseph West 7. Thomas Yorke 8. John Foster   9. Mathew Neale 10. John S. Nelson 11. Willis McCoy 12. James Whitfield 13. Jonathan Perkins 14. William Cox 15. John Jones (Clubft. Ck) 16. Wm. Lovick 17. Edward Pritchard 18. John Cummins 19. George Lovick 20. Frederick Turner 21. Benja. Mason 22. ~~William Clark~~ Joseph Shute 23. Frederick Lane 24. Philip Neale 25. Richard Hickman 26. ~~William Gatling~~ [?] Thomas Cox 27. James Little 28. James Stewart 29. Lewis Jones 30. Robert Young
31. William Lawrence   32. Roger Handcock 33. William Davis 34. Francis Webber 35. Charles Saunders Sen. 36. Frederick Foy

Wm. Slade & Rd. Nixon vs. John Pearson & John Gooding}
The Defendants in this Cause pray an Appeal to the Supr.
Court. Granted upon their entering into Bond with Wm. W.
Herritage & Levi Dawson S____.

255 — No. 110. John Lovett vs. Nathan Smith} Appeal. The
same Jury as in the last Cause empanelled find the Defendant
did assume & assess £12.8.4. Dams. & 6d Costs.

No. 111. Isaac Barrington vs. Peter F. Palatin} Appeal. The
same Jury as in the last Cause empanelled find the Defend.
did assume & assess £13.2.6 Dams. & 6d Costs.

John Biggs & Thomas Sparrow are appointed Inspectors of the
Poll of Election at Smiths Creek in August next.

Richard Nixon & John Daly are appointed Inspectors of the
Poll of Election in Newbern in August next.

Adjourned till 9 oClock.

Saturday, June 14, 1794.
Met Pursuant to Adjournment. Present the Worshipfull John
Tillman, Levi Dawson, John Bragg, John Sears} Esqrs.

The Referees appointed to Audit the Accounts of Thomas
Thomlinson Exr. of Sarah Saunders made a return of the
Accounts Settled by them which was approved of by the
Court & Ordered to be filed.

William Slade & William Mitchell Guardians of the Orphans of Yelverton Probart Decd. resigned their Guardianship. Whereupon Ordered that John Dewey be appointed Guardian to Polly & Robert Betsy & James Probart upon his entering into Bond in the sum of £250 for each orphan with William Mitchell and William Slade is Securities.

256 — No. 7. State vs. William Arthur} Indt. P. Larceny. The following Jury empanelled & Sworn. Viz. No. 1. John Clark 2. Charles Saunders 3. William Mitchell 4. James McCafferty 5. Thomas Webber 6. Cason Amery
7. Andrew Richardson 8. Thomas G. Fonvielle 9. John Kennedy 10. John Gooding 11. William Sears 12. Joseph Willis find the defendant Guilty, upon which the Court proceeded to pass Sentence that the said William Arthur reveive twenty stripes upon his bare back during this day.

Then was the following Justices appointed to take the List of Taxable Property in Craven County for the year 1794. Viz.
John Sears Esqr.   Captain Philips District
William M. Herritage   ---   Cox   Do.
Thomas A. Green   ---   Green   do.
John Fonvielle   ---   Lewis   do.
Francis Lowthorp   Town District
Spyers Singleton   formerly Capt. Dun's do.
John Bragg   Masters Do.
Hardy Gatlin   Bryan   Do
James Gatlin   Ernulls   Do
Henry Tillman's   Tillman Do.
Levi Dawson   Danl. Wests Do.
Joshua Fulsher   Delamar Do.
John Allen   Jones   Do.
John Dawson   Jas. Wests Do.
(issued)

Ordered that John Gooding be appointed Guardian to Dorothy Stevenson & John Stevenson Orphans of Silas S. Stevenson Decd. upon his entering into Bond in the sum of £600 for each Orphan with William Slade & Andrew Richardson Secys. (Dr. 16/ Charged)

257—Ordered that William Henry Sheriff of Craven County be [illegible] in the sum of £50 for making an improper return upon a Writ of Vinditerori Exponas issd. at March Term last at the Instance of Thos. Turner Exr. Jno. W. Stanly decd. against George Duffy and James Ellis unless Cause shewn &c. at the next Term agreeable to Act of Assembly in such Case made & Provided.

The Referees appointed at June Term 1791 to Audit the Accounts of John Benners Herritage Admr. of Henry [?] Herritage Decd. and with the Heir at Law of said Decd made a return of their proceeding which was Ordered to be Recorded.

Ordered that Spyers Singleton & Jno. Knox be appointed to Audit the Accounts of Peter Smith Guardian to Sarah Smith (Minor) and make a return to the next Court also to Divide the Estate of Jesse Smith Decd. between the Widow & Child.

Ordered that a Commission issue directed to Jno. Daly to take the private examination of a Deed of Elizabeth Henry Wife of Wm. Henry respecting the Execution of a Deed or Mortgage granted to Joseph Taggert returnable to the next Court.

An Inventory and three accounts of sales of the Estate of Jesse Bryan Decd was returned & filed.

Ordered that Mrs. Ann Ellis have letters of Administration on the Estate of her decd. husband James Ellis upon her entering into bond of £2000 with William Henry and John Fonville Esqrs her Securities upon which she qualified accordingly.

258 – An Acct Sales and postea division of the estate of S.S. _____ deceased and also a Settlement of the Accounts of William Slade and Richard Nixon the administrators of said deceased was returned by the referees appointed to settle the same, and was approved of by the Court & ordered to be recorded. (Dr. 8/ Charged Slade)

Adjourned till 3 oClock.
Met Pursuant to Adjournment. Present the Worshipful John Tillman, Levi Dawson, John Bragg} Esqrs.

The Petition of John Sears, Admr. of the Estate of James Sears, being heard, and the facts alledged therein being pro__d it is ordered that the prayer of said Petition be granted & that Execution issue against the Lands and other real Estate of said James Sears, decd. in the possession of his heirs, the defendts in sd Petition, for the sum of seventy Pounds. (Fi. Fa. issd.)

Nancy Wright vs. Exr. Stephen Wright & Nancy Wright by her Guardian Chs. Williams} Petition for Dower & distributive Share of Decd. Estate.
On Petition being read Ordered and Devised that the Sheriff of Craven County Summon a Jury to lay off the Dower to the Petitioner and to Allot to her one third part of all the Personal Estate of which Stephen Wright did possess. (issd.)

John McGraw & Wm. Ross renewed their Tavern License.

259 — State vs. Lewis White} Petit Larceny. The same Jury as in the last Cause empanelled and Sworn find the Defendant Guilty. Judgment that he receive fifteen Lashes upon his bare Back.

Ordered that Edmund Perkins be appointed Keeper of the Standard Weights & Measures in Craven County upon his entering into Bond in the sum of £50 with Joseph Clark & Thomas Webber Securities.

Ordered that John Latham Constable be allowed two pounds eight shillings for his Services attending this Court at this Term. (issd.)

Ordered that Thomas C___ [smeared ink] Constable be allowed three Pounds twelve shillings for his attendance upon this Court at this Term. (issd)

___ ___ Docket. William Bush vs. Abner Nash} Silas W. Arnett & Edward Harris appeared in Court and acknowledged themselves Special Bail for the Defendant in this Cause.

Lewis White a prisoner in Goal was Discharged by taking the Oath of an Insolvency.

Ordered that William Johnston, James Carney & Francis Lowthorp be appointed to Audit the Accts of Wm. Slade & Wm. Mitchell Guardians to the Orphans of Yelverton Probart Decd. and make return thereon to the next Court.

260 — J. Tillman
William Tisdale
John Bragg

[September 1794]

261 – At a County Court of Pleas & Quarter Sessions begun & held for the County of Craven at the Court House in Newbern on the second Monday in September being the 8th day of the Month A.D. 1794 and in the 19th year of American Independence.

Present the Worshipful
Isaac Guion, Richd. Nixon, John Fonvielle, Richard Nixon}
Esqrs.

The last Will & Testament of Mason Lewis decd. was proved by the Oath of William Ives, one of the Subscribing Witnesses thereunto agreeable and at the same time Polly Lewis the Executrix therein named appeared in Court and Qualified agreeable to Law.

Ordered that John Horsends aged five years the 2d day of May next be bound to Avery Bowden to learn the Shoemakers Trade.

Ordered that Ephraim Willis be bound to Joshua Willis to learn the Coopers Trade aged 14 years last June.

Read the Petition of James Willis praying for the alteration of a Patent granted to him in the year 1763. Ordered that a Summons issue to Thomas Smyth & William Smyth & Samuel Willis proprietors of the lands adjoining to appear at the next Court & shew Cause &c.

262 – The following Gentlemen Sworn as Grand Jurors. Viz. 1. Frederick Foy, Foreman 2. Frederick Johnston 3. Jarvis Fillingham 4. Philip Neale 5. Frederick Lane 6. Thomas Cox 7. James Whitfield 8. Jonathan Perkins 9. James Stewart 10. Wm.B. Fonvielle 11. Frederick Turner 12. Benja. Mason 13. Mathew Neale   Edmd. Perkins, Constable.

An account of Sales of the Estate of Jesse Willis Decd. was
returned & ordered to be filed.

Ordered that ~~Joseph~~ William Heartly aged 19 years in August
last be bound to Joseph Palmer to learn the Trade of a House
Carpenter & Joiner. Dr.

Adjourned till ½ past 3 oClock.

Met Pursuant to adjournment. Present the Worshipful John
Fonvielle, Isaac Guion, Francis Lowthorp}

Ordered that Mrs. Mary Heath be appointed Guardian to
Nancy Fordham upon her entering into Bond in the sum of
£200 with Wm. Slade & Thos. Badger securities.

Ordered that Edward Harris, Benja. Woods & Thos. Badger be
appointed to audit the Accounts of Alice Williams Admx. to
the Estate of Abram Fordham Decd. also to Divide the Estate
of said Decd. between the Widow and Heir of said Decd.

263 — Ordered that Thomas Willis be appointed Guardian to
Joseph Willis a Minor Orphan upon his entering into Bond in
the sum of £100 with James Gatlin & Joseph Willis Securities.

Ordered that Joshua Willis be appointed Guardian to Ephraim
Willis upon his entering into Bond in the sum of £100 with
James Gatlin & Joseph Willis his Securities.

Ordered that Ephraim Willis be appointed Guardian to Jesse
Willis upon his entering into Bond in the sum of £100 with
James Gatlin & Joseph Willis his Securities.

An Inventory of the Estate of Danl. Daughety was returned by the Executor & ordered to be Recorded.

Ordered that James Gatlin & Ephraim Willis be appointed to Audit the Accounts of Thomas Willis Admr. to the Estate of James Ives decd. and make return thereof to the next County Court.

On the Petition of William Phipps & David King Ordered that Jacob Johnston Esqr., Joseph Palmer, Charles Roach, Frederick Johnston & Steven Harris Commissioners be appointed to lay off and Divide the Real Estate of Jeremiah King decd. between the Heirs of said Deceased and make return of their Proceedings to the next County Court. Dr. issd.

Ordered that Thomas Hunter be appointed Administrator to the Estate of Katherine Hunter decd. upon his Qualifg. & entering into Bond in the sum of £500 with James Whitfield & Richard Hunter his securities.

264 – Ordered that William Johnston, Philip Neale & Francis Lowthorp Esqs be appointed to Audit the Accounts of Charity James Admx. of Dunard James Decd. and report thereon as soon as possible.

Ordered that James Coor, Aaron Ernull & Moses Ernu__ be appointed to Audit the Accounts of Richard Whitf___ Executor in right of his Wife of the last Will & Testament of Jesse Willis Decd.

Ordered that Joseph Leech, Francis Lowthorp, James Daves, James Carney & Abner Neale be appointed to Audit the Accounts of David Witherspoon Admr. &c to the Estate of Abner Nash decd.

Ordered that Joseph Leech, Francis Lowthorp, James Daves, James Carney & Abner Neale be appointed to Audit the Accounts of David Witherspoon Guardn to the Orphans of Abner Nash decd.

Ordered that Joseph Norton aged 13 years be bound to William Adams to learn to be a Shoemaker. (Dr.)

Ordered that Negro Joe belonging to John Green be permitted to Carry a Gun when looking after his Master's Stock upon the said John Green's entering into Bond with Isaac Guion his Security — agreeable to Law.

Ordered that Josiah Hewkins aged thirteen years the 4th January last be bound to William Gatlin to learn the Coopers Trade. (Dr.)

John Bragg Esqr. made a return of the Taxable Property in Capt. Master's District for the year 1794.

265 — Adjournd till 9 oClock.

Tuesday, Sepr. 9 1794
Met Pursuant to adjournment.
Present the Worshipful Spyers Singleton, James Gatlin, Isaac Guion} Esqrs.

No. 4. Moorland on Demise of John Benners vs. Stiles & John Cox} Eject. The following Jury empanelled & Sworn. Viz. 1. Willis McCoy 2. Thomas Smith 3. Joseph Shute 4. Richd. Hickman 5. James Little   6. Robert Young

7. William Davis 8. Francis Webber 9. Charles Saunders Sen.
10. Hardy Huskins 11. George Lane 12. William Good Juror
withdrawn & Cause Continued. Geo. Lane Surveyor Thos. A.
Green & Frederick Lane Jurors of Vineri [?] upon the premises
in dispute Vineri to appear [?]

An Inventory & Account of Sales of the Estate of Briscoe Davis
decd. was returned & filed.

No. 7 James McCafferty vs. Jeremiah Redding} Tr[???]. The
following Jury empanelled Viz. No. 1. Willis McCoy 2.
William Cox 3. Joseph Shute 4. Richard Hickman 5. James
Little   6. Robert Young 7. William Davis
8. Francis Webber 9. Charles Saunders Senr. 10. John Jones
11. Geo. Lovick 12. Wm. Good   Juror withdrawn. Cause
Contd.

266 – Ordered that John Clark Admr of John Clark decd have
leave to sell the perishable Estate of said Decd. agreeable to
Law.

No. 10. William M. Herritage vs. George Lovick & Thos.
Lovick} Debt. The same Jury as in the last Cause except
Thomas Austin in the room of Geo. Lovick empanelled find
the Writing Obligatory to be the Act & Deed of the Defendants
and assess the Plantiffs Damages £39.17.7 & 6d Cost and they
further find all the issues in favr. of the plantiff. Appeal
prayed. Wm. Cox & John Jones Secys.

Ordered that William Cox & John Cox & Fredk. Lane be
appointed to Audit the Accounts of Lawson Davis Exr. of
Briscoe Davis decd.

The auditors appointed to Settle the Accounts of Charity James Admx. of the Estate of Dernard James decd. made a return of the Acct. Settld. by them, and find a Balance due the Admx. £42.10. — Ordered that the same be Recorded.

No. 11. Executors of William Murphy vs. Samuel Jackson}
Case. The same Jury as in No. 7 impanelled & Sworn — find the Defendant did assume and asses the Plantiffs Damages to £1.10 & 6d Costs.

The last Will & Testament of Thomas Loftin decd. was produced in Court and proved by the Oath of Lawson Davis one of the Subscribing Witnesses thereto and Ordered to be Recorded and at the same time Joseph Loftin one of the Executors therein named, appeared in Court & Qualified, agreeable to Law. Ordered that Letters issue &c.

267 — Whereas the last Will & Testament of Francis Houston decd was proved at the last Term and the Executors therein named having refused to Qualify. Ordered that Letters of Administration Cum Testamento Annex__ be granted to James Houston only son of the Deceasd. upon his Qualifying and entering into Bond in the sum of £1000 — with Joseph Burney & William Gardner his Securities. Whereupon the said James Houston Qualified & entered into Bond and returned an Inventory of said Decd. Estate.

Adjourned till ½ past 3 oClock.
Met Pursuant to adjournment, Present the Worshipful Richard Nixon, James Gatlin, Francis Lowthorp} Esqrs.

Ordered that Moses Ernull, Charles Williams & Thomas Willis be appointed to Divide the personal Estate of Edward Pearce Decd. between the Widow & Children of said Decd.

Edward Simpson vs. William Vendrick} Judgement upon a Warrant & Execution issued by John F. Smith Esqr. for the sum of £5.3.6 and four shillings Costs & returned by Cason Emery Constable that he had levied the same upon one hundred Acres of Land on the Et. Side of Bury Creek in Craven County. No Goods & Chattels to be found. Ordered that a Writ of Vende. Exponas issue directed to the Sheriff of Craven County agreeable to Law. (Vende. Exp. Issd.)

Levi Dawson Esqr. Inspector at Broad & Goose Creeks entered into Bond in the sum of £500 with James Gatlin & Francis Lowthorp Securities.

268 – No. 18. Commissrs. Of Newbern vs. James McCafferty} Debt. The same Jury as in No. 7 empanelled except John Moore in the room of William Good empanelled find the Writing Obligatory to be the Act & Deed of he Defendant & assess 6d Dams. & 6d Costs and that he has not performed the Condition of the Bond. Appeal prayed & allowed. James Gatlin & Levi Dawson Security.

Ordered that Isaac Guion, Levi Dawson & Francis Lowthorp be appointed to Audit the Accounts of Isaac Barrington Guardian to Nancy Hill Wright.

Spyers Singleton Esqr. returned the list of Taxable property in the District formerly Capt. Dunn's in Craven County for 1794.

Ajourned till 9 oClock.
Wednesday Sepr. 10, 1794
Met Pursuant to adjournment. Present the Worshipful Levi Dawson, Isaac Guion, Francis Lowthorp} Esqrs.

No. 26. William Good vs. Francis X. Martin} Debt. ~~The same Jury as in the last Cause~~. The following Jury empanelled & Sworn. Viz. 1. William Cox 2. John Jones 3. Geo. Lovick 4. Richard Hickman 5. James Little 6. Robert Young 7. William Davis 8. Francis Webber
9. Josh. Shute 10. Josiah Fisher 11. Sampson Morris 12. James Nelson Find the Defendant owes nothing. Plantiff prayed

269 – an appeal to the Superior Court which was granted upon his entering into Bond in the sum of £100 with Wm. Slade & Thos. Badger his securities.

Ordered that Joseph Nelson be appointed Guardian to John Delamar upon his entering into Bond in the sum of £600 ~~upon his entering into Bond~~ with James Wilson & Francis Nelson his securities.

Ordered that John Dawson, Thomas York & John Biggs be appointed to Audit the Accounts of Thomas Sparrow & Francis Delamar Executors Thomas Delamar Decd. returnable to next Court.

Ordered that Francis Nelson be appointed Guardian to John Nelson minor upon his entering into Bond in the sum of £1000 with James Nelson & Joseph Nelson is securities.

Hardy Gatlin Esqr. returned the list of Taxable property in Capt. Bryan's District for the year 1794.

Ordered that Joseph Nelson be appointed Guardian to Smith Delamar minor upon his entering into Bond in the sum of £600 with James Nelson & Francis Nelson his securities.

No. 30. Daniel Dishon vs. Thos. Turner Admr. of Wright Stanly decd.} Case. The same Jury as in the last Cause empanelled &Sworn – find the Defendants Intestate did assume and assess the Plantiffs Damages to £41.5.8 and they further find all the issues in favor of the Plantiff.

No. 157. Farnifold Green Guardn Ann Greaves vs. Wm. Davis Exr of James Davis decd & [?? Page cut off at bottom in copy] }Sci Fa [??illegible] the Heirs of James Davis decd for sale of the lands of the Decd.
Judgement against the Lands of James Davis Decd to Satisfy the Plantiffs Demand.

270 – No. 31. Francis Harper vs. Francis X. Martin Exr. De St Leger decd.} Trover The same Jury as in the last Cause empanelled & Sworn find the Defends. Testator Guilty of the Trover & Conversion &c and assess £8 Dam[ages??] & 6d Costs. Appeal allowed the Defends. Jno. C. Bryan & John W. Arnoll [?? Word in gutter]

Ordered that Benjamin Mason be appointed Guardian to Asa Nelson (minor) upon his entering into Bond in the sum of £1000 with Joshua Fulsher & Jonathan Perkins his securities.

No. 32. John Tillman vs. James Wilson} Case. The same Jury as in No. 26 except Willis McCoy in the room of George Lovick empanelled & Sworn find the Defendant did assume, as assess the Plantiffs Damages to £30 & 6d Cost and they further find all the issues in favour of the Plantiff. Appeal prayed by the Defends. & allowed. Wm. Moore & Geo. Lovick Securities.

Adjourned till 4 oClock. Met Pursuant to adjournment. Present the Worshipful John Tillman, Levi Dawson, James Gatlen}Esqrs.

No. 33. John Smallwood vs. Philip Knowis} Case, plea in
Abatement. The following Jury empanelled & Sworn Viz. No.
1. Willis McCoy 2. John Jones 3. George Lovick
4. Wm. Cox 5. Richd. Hickman 6. James Little   7. Robert
Young 8. Wm. Davis 9. Josiah Fisher 10. Sampson Morris 11.
Francis Webber 12. Thomas Austin One failing to Answer.
Mistrial.

John Dawson Esqr. made return of the Taxable Property in
Capt. Joseph West's District for the year 1794.

271 — Then was the Grand Jury discharged.

Joseph Fulsher Esqr. made a return of the Taxable Property in
Capt. F. Delamar's District for the year 1794.

Adjourned till 9 oClock.

Thursday Sept. 11th 1794. Met Pursuant to adjournment.
Present the Worshipful John Tillman, Levi Dawson, Hardy
Gatlin}Esqrs.

[No. ??]7. Elizabeth Bell vs. Benja. Borden} Tres. A&B The
following Jury empanelled & Sworn. No. 1. Willis McCoy 2.
George Lovick 2. William Good 3. William Cox 4. Richard
Hickman 5. James Little   6. Joseph Shute
7. Francis Webber 8. Charles Saunders Senr 9. Josiah Fisher
10. David Pearce 11. William Physioc 12. W.John Moore find
the Defendant Guilty and assess £100
Damages & sixpence Cost. Appeal prayed by the Defendant &
Granted upon his entering into Bond in the sum of £200 with
David Wallace & Robert Wallace his Securities.

No. 35. John Bedscott Jr. vs. Abner Neale} Replevin. The
following Jury empanelled & Sworn Viz. No. 1. Willis McCoy
2. Geo. Lovick 3. William Cox 4. John Jones 5. Richard
Hickman 6. James Little 7. Joseph Shute
8. Francis Webber 9. Charles Saunders Senr. 10. Josiah Fisher
11. David Pearce 12. William Physioc find the Defendant
John Bedscott.

270 [i.e. 272] — Ordered that William Tignor have
Administration De Bonis non upon the Estate of James Tignor
Decd upon his Qualifying and entering into Bond in the Sum
of £1000 with James Carney & Charles Williams Security.

Ordered that Eleonora Pearce have Administration upon the
Estate of William R. Pearce Decd. upon her Qualifying and
entering into Bond in the sum of £600 with John Tillman &
Saml. Sparrow Securities.

An Account Sales of the Estate of Isaac Blanchard Decd. was
returned & filed. Dr.

No. 59. Saml. Sparrow Admr. Samuel Sparrow decd. vs. John
Smallwood & Benjamin Brinson} Case. Default. The same
Jury as in the last Cause empanelled & Sworn find for the
Plantiff £176.16.8 and 6d Cost. Appeal prayed & allowed Deft.
Richd. Hunley & William Henry Securities.

John Fonvielle Esqr returned a List of Taxable Property in
Capt D. Lewis' District for 1794.

Adjourned til ½ past 3 oClock.
Met Pursuant to adjournment. Present the Worshipful John
Fonvielle, Levi Dawson, ~~Wm. McClure~~ Richd. Nixon}Esqrs.

Ordered that Gilbert Collins aged 14 years be bound to John Burt to learn the art and mystery of a Mariner. Capt. Burt engages to teach him to Read, Write and [?? Page cut off at bottom]

273 – Tobias Cobb vs. Jno. C. Bryan Bail [??] for Henry P. Haines} Sci. Fa. The following Jury empanelled & Sworn Viz. No. 1. Willis McCoy 2. Geo. Lovick 3. Wm. Cox 4. John Jones 5. Richard Hickman 6. James Little 7. Francis Webber 8. Charles Saunders Senr 9. William Good 10. John Moore 11. David Pearce 12. Hardy Bush find the Service of Sciri Facias was duly Executed.

The Referees appointed to Audit the Accounts of Alice Williams Admx. to the Estate of Abraham Fordham Decd and also to Divide the Estate between the Widow & Heir of said Decd. made a return of their proceedings which was Ordered to be Recorded.

No. 40. John Moore vs. Wm. Lovick} Case. The following Jury empanelled & sworn – 1. Willis McCoy 2. Josiah Fisher 3. William Cox 4. John Jones 5. Richd. Hickman 6. James Little 7. Francis Webber 8. Charles Saunders Senr 9. William Good 10. William Tignor 11. David Pearce 12. Hardy Bush find the Defendant did assume and assess the plantiffs damages to £55.18.10 & six pence costs, and they also find for the Plantiff in all the issues. Appeal prayed.

Ordered that Beverly Wallace aged 16 years in Decr. next be Bound to William Tignor to learn the Blackmakers Trade (Inds. End.)

No. 41. Joseph Crispin Indorsee Wm. Gardner junr. vs. William M. Herritage & William Lovick} Debt. The same Jury as in the last Cause empanelled find the Writing Obligatory is the Act & Deed of the Defendt. and assess £17.6.8 Dam & 6d Costs and further find all the issues in favr. of the Plantiff — appeal prayed.

274 — No. 42. John Sheffield vs. Charles Roach} Case, Default & Enquiry. The same Jury as in the last Cause empanelled — assess the Plantiffs Damages to £50 & 6d Cost — appeal prayed by Deft. John Tillman & Joseph West Securities — appeal withdrawn. New Trial granted.

No. 141. Ambrose Jones vs. William Lovick} Case Default. The same Jury as in the last Cause empanelled assess the Plantiffs Damages to £25.16.6 & 6d Costs.

The Auditors appointed to Settle the Accounts of David Witherspoon Adminisr &c to the Estate of Abner Nash also to Audit the Accounts of David Witherspoon Guardian to the Orphans of Abner Nash decd. made a return of the Accounts Settled by them, which was Ordered to be Recorded. Adjourned till 3 oClock.

Friday, Sepr. 12, 1794.
Met Pursuant to adjournment. Present the Worshipful Levi Dawson, Isaac Guion, Hardy Gatlen} Esqrs.

No. 40. John Moore vs. Wm. Lovick} Appeal by Defendt. John B. Herritage & William M. Herritage Security.

Ordered that Evan Evans aged 17 years be bound to Hardy Bush to learn the Taylors Trade (Inds. made out)

275 — Ordered that William Shine, John Dawson, ~~Lucas J. Benners~~, John Biggs, Joshua Fulsher & James Oliver Commissioners be appointed to Divide the Real Estate of John Green Decd. between the Widow and Heir of said Decd. and make a return of their proceedings to the next Court.

No. 106 — James McMains vs. Thomas Davis} Appeal by Defendt. The following Jury empanelled & Sworn.   No. 1. Willis McCoy   2. William Cox 3. John Jones   4. Richard Hickman 5. James Little   6. Francis Webber 7. George Lovick 8. Joseph West 9. Charles Saunders Senr. 10. Joseph Shute 11. Wm. Whitford 12. John Whitford Nonsuit.

No. 107. Peter Guro vs. Silas Jernagan} Appeal by Deft. The same Jury as in the last Cause empanelled & sworn. Nonsuit.

On a return of Joseph Clark, Wm. Conner, and Benajai Boagie, Searchers for Capt. Lewis District, that they have found three guns on the plantation of Doct. McClure in possession of James Emmery, it is Ordered that notice issue to James Emmery to appear and shew cause why said Guns should not be appropriated to the use of the County, agreeably to Law.

Ordered, That Isaac Guion, Francis Lowthorp and James Carney, audit the accounts of William McClure Treasurer of Craven County.

276 — 110. Stephen Williams vs. Chs. Saunders Adr. Of Jas. Saunders.} Appeal by Defendt. The same Jury as in the last cause except Thomas Spikes in the room of Charles Saunders Senr. find for the Plantiff five pounds, ten shillings & Costs.

Dr. 12/ The auditors appointed to Settle and examine the accounts of Richard Nixon, acting Executor to the estate of Francis, and Mary McIlwean, made return thereof.

145. Christopher L. Lente vs. James Potter} Appeal by Defendt. Same Jury as in No. 106. except Mathew Brinson in the room of Wm. Whitford — empanelled find for the Plantiff £5.0.11 & 6d Costs.

Ordered that John Bedscott have leave to keep Public House in Newbern. Charles Williams & John ~~Bedscott~~ Latham, Securities.

Adjourned till 3 oClock.
Met Pursuant to Adjournment. Present the Worshipful John Fonville, Levi Dawson, Hardy Gatlin} Esqr.

On Petition of Benjamin Williams Esqr setting forth that he is Security for David Witherspoon Esqr Administrator Debonis non upon the Estate of Abner Nash decd. also Security for the said David Witherspoon as Guardian to Anna, Elizabeth, Frederick, Francis & Maria Nash, Orphans of Abner Nash Decd. and praying to be released from his Bonds. Ordered that he be released and that the said David find other Security. Whereupon the said David offered Doctor Wm. McClure as Security in the room of the sd.

277 — Benjamin Williams ~~which~~ who was approved of by the Court upon his entering into Bonds in the same sums as then signed by sd. Benjamin Williams.

Ordered that Burwell Bryan aged fifteen years last June the 10th day be bound to David Clark to learn the Trade of a Carpenter.

No. 82. James McGraw & Wife vs. James Clark & Wm. Ross}
Appeal by Plantiff. The following Jury empanelled & Sworn.
Viz. No. 1. Willis McCoy
2. James Little   3. William Cox 4. John Jones   5. Richard
Hickman 6. Francis Webber 7. Joseph West 8. Charles
Saunders Senr 9. Mathew Brinson 10. Benja. Brinson 11. John
Whitford 12. Wm. Gaskins find for the Plantiff Seven
Pounds, and 6d Costs. Motion for Writ of Error.

James Gatlin Esqr returned his List of Taxable Property in
Capt. Moses Ernull's Company for the year 1794.

Ordered that Thomas Turner be appointed Guardian to the
orphans of Wright Stanly, viz. Wright Cogdell Stanly, Lydia
Duncan Stanly and John Wright Stanly, upon entering into
bond with Joseph Shute and William M. Herritage, ~~John
Gooding~~ his Securities in the sum of two thousand Pounds.

No. 146. Thomas Williams vs. Charles Saunders} Appeal by
Deft. The same Jury as in the last Cause except Joseph Shute in
the room of Chas. Saunders Senr. empanelled & Sworn assess
the Plantiffs Damages to £2.17.6 & 6d Cost.

Adjourned till 9 oClock.

278 — Saturday, September 13, 1794. Met Pursuant to
adjournment.
Present the Worshipful John Tillman, Levi Dawson, Isaac
Guion, Francis Lawthorp} Esqrs.

The was the following Jury appointed to be summoned to
attend the next County Court.

1. William Adams 2. Joseph Carter 3. Benja. Brinson 4.
Francis Carraway 5. Alexander Carruthers 6. John S. Nelson
7. Southy J. Rew 8. William Clark 9. William Gaskins 10.
John Arthur 11. Charles Johnston
12. Thomas Smith 13. Joseph Heartley 14. John Nelson 15.
John Ernull 16. William Dixon 17. Samuel Sparrow 18.
Joseph Brinson 19. Jeremiah Warren 20. John Fell   21. Caleb
Willis 22. Weeks Chapman 23. Thomas Fornes
24 Jacob Johnston jr 25. Edward Pritchard 26. Michael
Mitchell 27. Jeremiah James 28. Lewis Jones 29. John Potter
30. Mathew Stevens 31. James Hyman
32. James Clark 33. Thomas Pryor 34. Joseph Loftin 35.
Spencer Murphy 36. William Bryan 37. Lewis Bryan 38.
James McCafferty S. Creek.

Ordered that Joshua Forbes & Stephen Quincy be appointed
Patrollers in Capt. Masters District. Issd.

Read the Petition of Elizabeth Vail and George M. Leech
setting forth that Jeremiah Vail late of Craven County Died
intestate and that they are each of them entitled to one third
part of the Real Estate of said Decd. and praying that
Commissioners may be appointed to lay off and appropriate
their part of the Real Estate of said Decd. as aforesaid
agreeable to Law. Ordered that Francis Lowthorp, John F.
Smith, William Good, James Coor & James Carney be
appointed Commissioners for that purpose. Issd.

279—On application of Mrs. A. Caroline Biggleston setting
forth that Sundry Persons are in possession of her property
illegally, Ordered that the Sheriff of Craven County be
directed to put her in possession of the property Which hath
been illegally taken from her by Wilson Blount, Wm. McClure
& others.

Ordered that Francis Lowthorp & Edward Harris & Stephen Camberling be appointed to Audit the Accounts of Bela Badger & Wife late Guardians to the Orphans of Wright Stanly decd. and any two of them make report thereon to the next Court. Dr.

The Referees appointed to Audit the Accounts of William Johnston Guardian to the Orphans of Beverly Rew decd. and made a return of their proceedings & Accounts which were ordered to be Recorded.

State vs. Lewis White} Indt. Misdeameanor. The following Jury empanelled & Sworn viz. 1. Willis McCoy 2. William Cox 3. John Jones 4. Joseph Shute 5. Joseph West 6. James Little 7. Charles Saunders Senr. 8. Francis Webber 9. William Wayne 10. William Whitford 11. Archibald McCalep 12. Josiah Fisher find the Defendant Guilty of the Misdemeanor as he stands Charged in the Bill of Indictment.

McClure & Green vs. James Ellis} Judgement ~~& Execution~~ upon a Warrant tried before John Tillman Esqr & Execution issd by Wm. Tisdale, Esqr. directed to any Lawful Officer; which was returned to Court by Edmund Perkins Const. that he had levied upon a House & Lot No. 12 whereon the Defendt. formerly lived ~~no property~~ no personal property to be found. Judgement £10.10 & Cost. Ordered that a Writ of Vendo. Exponas issue directed to the Sheriff of Craven County agreeable to Law. Issued.

280 — An Inventory of the Estate of Abner Nash decd. was returned by David Witherspoon Adm. Debonis non.

Jarvis Buxton is appointed Coroner for Craven County, Francis Lowthorp & Isaac Guion Securities.

Ordered that Isaac Guion, Francis Lowthorp, William McClure, William Tisdale & William Johnston be appointed (or any three of them) to lay off and Allot such part of the Personal Estate of Abner Nash decd. as is given to his Widow in his last Will & Testament.

Wm. Moore resigned his Office of Coroner which was accepted by the Court.

James McMains & Thos. Creu Constables to attend at next Term. Issd.

John Daly Esqr renewed his Entry Takers Bond & Offered [blank]   his Securities.

Adjourned till 3 oClock.
Met Pursuant to adjournment. Present the Worshipful Levi Dawson, Isaac Guion} Esqrs.

An Inventory and Account Sales of the Estate of James Ellis Decd. was returned by the Admr.

Lewis White, a prisoner Confined in Goal for a Misdemeanor was discharged upon his taking the Benefit of the Insovent Act.

The Referees appointed to Audit the Accounts of Isaac Barrington Guardn. of Ann H. Wright made a return of their proceedings & Accounts which were ordered to be Recorded.

281 – No. 31 Francis Harper vs. Francis X. Martin Exr. De St Leger} Motion in arrest of Judgment on argument, Judgment arrested. Appeal prayed by Plantiff.

No. 12. Peter Harper vs. Winston Caswell Exr. Richard Caswell decd.} Case. Plea in Abatement that there is a suit defending in Dobbs County for the same Cause of Action — on argument Ordered that the Defendant answer over.

Ordered that James Gatlen, Thomas Webber and John Latham be appointed to Audit the Accounts of Jonathan Perkins Guardian to the Orphans of James Perkins decd. Dr.

Levi Dawson, J.P.
Is. Guion, J.P.
Jas. Gatlin, J.P.
F. Lowthorp, J.P.

283 — State of North Carolina, Craven County Court of Pleas & Quarter Sessions September Term 1794.
Then were the following Deeds, Bills of Sale &c. proved or acknowledged in Open Court and Ordered to be Registered, Viz.:
A Bill Sale from Elizabeth Brook & Wm Wharton to Eliza. Fulsher was proved by the oath of Joshua Fulsher Esqr.
A Deed from John Allen to Benjamin Fillingin was proved by the Oath of Frederick Lane.
A Deed from Simeon Moore to Frances Fonville was proved by the Oath of Lewis Fonville
A Mortgage Deed from Jonathan Fellows to Joseph Shute was proved by the Oath of Thomas Badger
A Deed from Bazell Smith & Wife to Frederick Ward was proved by the Oath of James McKinlay
A Deed from Frederick Ward to Jno. F. Smith was proved by the Oath of James McKinlay
A Deed from Elizabeth Potter to James McMains was proved by the Oath of Jno Howard.
A Lease from Joseph Burney to Jno Dewey was proved by the Oath of F X Martin

A Bill Sale from William Good to Edwd. Carraway was proved by the Oath of Philip Neale

A Deed from Jno Taylor to Michl. Arons was acknowledged by the Grantor

A Deed from Peter Physioc to Jno Bishop was proved by the Oath of Thomas Austin

284 – A Deed from Francis Willis to Charles Roach was proved by the Oath of Jacob Johnston Esqr.

A Deed from James W. Stanly to Silvanus Dixon was proved by the Oath of John Knowles

A Deed of Gift from John Hobday to Thomas Hobday, Mary Hobday, & Eliz. Hobday was acknowledged by the [illegible]

A Bill Sale from William Henry Sheriff to Wm. Gibbs was acknowledged by said Wm. Henry.

A Deed from William Henry Sheriff to Jno. G. Blount was proved by the Oath of Jno. F. Smith.

A Deed from James McMains to Nathan Smith was acknowledged by the the Grantor.

A Bill Sale from Wm. Henry Sheriff to David Wallace was proved by the Oath of Silas W. Arnett Esqr.

A Deed from Bazell Smith to Luke Foscue was proved by the Oath of James Potter

A Deed from John Civill to Francis Fonville was proved by the Oath of Lewis Fonvielle

A Deed from Cason Fulsher to Nathan Simmons was proved by the Oath of Nathl. Lewis

A Bill Sale from Abner Nash to David Witherspoon was proved by the Oath of Jos. Frelick.

A Bill Sale from Frederick Ward to Jno F. Smith was acknowledged by the said Frederick

A Deed from Jeremiah Warren to Benja. Fillingin was proved by the Oath of James Fillingim

A Deed from William Lovick to John Jones was acknowledged by the Grantor.

Two Deeds from John Lovick to John Jones was proved by the Oath of William ~~Lovick~~ Jones.

285 – A Deed from Nehemiah Cullen to George Spann & [illegible] was proved by the Oath of Abner Neale.

A Deed from Robert Hatfield to Jacob Cooke was proved by the Oath of William Moore.

A Deed from William Hayis to John Hayis was proved by the Oath of James Fillingim

A Deed from John Taylor to John Mills was proved by the Oath of Charles Roach

A Deed from Clayton Carruthers to William Clayton was proved by the Oath of Thomas Clayton.

A Deed from William Clayton to James Clayton was acknowledged by the Grantor.

A Deed from William Beasley to Willis McCoy Junr was proved by the Oath of John Mecoy.

A Deed from Thomas Parsons to Frederick Foy was proved by the Oath of William Dudley

A Deed from Isaac Reed to Alexander Stevens was proved by the Oath of Benjamin Brinson.

A Deed from William Adams to John Ipock was proved by the Oath of William Gatlen

Two Bills Sale from Bela Badger to Thomas Badger was proved by the Oath of Jno. Stanly. Dr. 12/

A Deed of Trust from Bela Badger to Thomas Turner and Thomas Badger was proved by the Oath of Jno. Stanly Dr. 6/

An Indenture of Covenants between Richard Blackledge, Chrisr. Neale & William Rumsey the parties being Dead the Hand writing of Richard Blackledge & Christopher Neale was proved by the Oath of Abner Neale and the hand writing of William Rumsey was proved by the Oath of John Fonville. Dr. 6/ [illegible] Sheets

286—A Deed from Francis Carraway & Patience Carraway to Thomas Casey was proved at June Term last by the Oath of Southy Rew and a Commission issued directed to Southy Rew & Jno. Carney Esqr to take the private Examination of Patience Carraway respecting her Voluntary Execution of the same— which was returned at this Term. Certified that the said Patience did Execute the same freely & Voluntaryly and with out any Caution. Ordered that the same be recorded. Dr. 12/4 A Mortgage Deed from James Ellis to George Ellis was proved by the Oath of F.X. Martin Esqr. Dr. 6/ A Deed from William Moore Coroner to George Ellis was acknowledged in Open Court by the Grantor Dr. 6/ A Deed from William Moore Coroner to Jno. C. Bryan was proved by the Oath of George Ellis. Dr. 6/ Received from S. Chapman Clerk of Craven County the aforegoing Deeds and payment for thirty seven, the eight last not paid for.   M.C. Stephens for James Bryan.

[December 1794]
287—State of North Carolina. At a County Court of Pleas & Quarter Sessions begun and held for the County of Craven at the Court House in Newbern, on the second Monday in December being the 8th day of the Month, in the 19th year of our Independence A.D. 1794.

Present the Worshipful Spyers Singleton, Joshua Fulsher, Henry Tillman} Esqrs.

William Henry, Esqr. returned the Writ of Vinire Facias [illegible] Jurors to this Court "Executed."

The last Will & Testament of John Fonvielle Decd. was proved in Open Court by the Oath of William Slade Esqr one of the subscribing Witnesses thereto and at the same time Thomas G. Fonvielle & Lewis Fonvielle the Executors therein names Qualified agreeable to Law. Ordered that Letters Testamentary issue.

Ordered that Lavinia Arentz have administration upon the Estate of Michael Arentz Decd. upon her Qualfying and entering into Bond in the sum of £100 with Harding Ives and John Taylor Jr. her securities. Whereupon she Quald. & entered into Bond & rendered an Inventory of said Decd. Estate.

Ordered that James Hoover have administration upon the Estate of Anna Hoover Decd. upon his Qualifying and entering into Bond in the sum of £100 with Charles William & John Taylor Junr. his Security's.

288 — The Referees appointed to Settle the Accounts of Thomas Willis, Administrator to the Estate of James Ives decd. made a return of the Proceedings, which were Ordered to be Recorded.

Ordered that William Tooley take into his Care George Carter a free mulattoe Boy until next County Court at which Term he is to bring the said Boy to Court that he may be bound to some Master rescended

Then were the Grand Jury impaneled and Sworn. Viz.
1. Lewis Bryan 2. Benja. Brinson 3. Charles Johnson 4. Thomas Smyth 5. John Nelson   6. John Ernull   7. William Dixon 8. John Fell 9. Caleb Willis 10. Thomas Fornes 11. Edward Pritchard 12. Mathew Stevens
13. Spencer Murphy

Ordered that John Bryan, Aaron Ernul, and John Harris be appointed to audit the accounts of Richard Whitford, Administrator (in right of his wife) of the Estate of Jessee Willis decd. and report to the next Court. Issd.

Ordered that Administration on the estate of Churchy Perkins be granted to Joseph West, upon his entering into bond with Charles William & Edward Griffith his Securities in the Sum of two hundred pounds.

Ordered that Administration on the estate of James Perkins, be granted to Jonathan Perkins, upon his entering into bond with Joshua Fulshire and William Smyth in the sum of £200.

289 — Ordered that Thomas Graves Fonville be appointed Guardian to Miss Elizabeth Franks upon his entering into bond ~~with~~ for the Sum of Three thousand Pounds with William Brice Fonville and Richard Fonville his Securities.

 Ordered that Thomas Graves Fonville be appointed Guardian to John ~~Whitlif~~ Wickliffe Franks, upon his entering into bond for the Sum of Three Thousand Pounds with William Brice Fonville and Richard Fonville his securities.

Ordered that Joshua Fulsher, John Biggs, & Jno. Dawson be appointed to Settle the Estate of James & Churchy Perkins Decd with their Guardians Jonathan & Edmd. Perkins.

Ordered that Joseph West, Admr. of Church Perkins Decd. have leave to sell the perishable Estate of said Deceased and Divide the same between the Heirs of sd. Decd.

Ordered that Jonathan Perkins Admr. of James Perkins Decd have leave to sell the perishable Estate of James Perkins Decd and Divide the same between sd. Heirs.

Ordered that Daniel West who superintended the Building of So.West Bridge in Craven County be allowed his Accounts Amounting to twelve pounds, nine shillings & six pence. Ordered that the County Treasurer pay the same out of the County Tax.

Ordered that John Humphrey Blyth aged 12 years the 31 Jany next be allowed Bound to William Tooley to learn the Coopers Trade.

290 — Ordered that George Carter, aged 17 years next [illegible] be bound to Harding Ives to learn the Turner's [?] Trade. Inds. Exd. 8/ pd.

Adjounred till 10 oClock tomorrow morning.

Tuesday, Decr. 9, 1794. Met Pursuant to adjournment. Present the Worshipful John Daly, Levi Dawson, Henry Tillman } Esqrs.

Ordered James Silburn aged 17 years of age last February be bound to Robert Young to learn the Trade of a Ship Carpenter. Dr.

Ordered that Administration on the Estate of James Winn Stanly decd. be granted to John Fox and James McConnell, upon their entering into bond in the sum of £200 with John Devereaux and George Ellis their Securities.

The last Will and testament of Bryan Edmundson was produced & proved by the oath of William Shine, one of the Subscribing Witnesses, Whereupon Joshua Fulshire, the Executor therein named appeared and Qualified accordingly.

Ordered that John Fish have Administration on the Estate of Thomas Fish decd. upon entering into bond in the Sum of Two thousand Pounds, with Danl. Witherington and Samuel Smith his Securities.

Ordered that the said Administrator have permission to sell the perishable part of the said Decd. Estate.

291 — Ordered that Francis Lowthorp, Thomas Badger & William Slade be appointed to Audit the accounts of Samuel Chapman, Guardian to William G. Berry (Minor) returnable to the next County Court.

James McMains renewed his appointment of Standard Keeper. Samuel Chapman & Francis Lowthorp, Secys.

No. 15. William Henry vs. William M. Herritage} Slander. The following Jury empanelled & Sworn. Viz. 1. William Adams 2. Southy J. Rew 3. William Clark 4. Thomas Pryor 5. Joseph Loften 6. William Bryan 7. David Pearce 8. Harman Gaskins 9. Charles Roach 10. Josiah Fisher 11. John Morgan 12. Danl. West find the Defendant not Guilty. Appeal prayed.

Ordered that Ambrose Jones have Administration upon the Estate of his Decd. Brother William Jones upon his Qualifying and entering into Bond in the sum of £1000 with William M. Herritage & Arthur Daw his Securities. Whereupon the said Ambrose Jones Qualified, entered into Bond & returned an Inventory of said Estate.

On Motion of Thomas Tyre, Heir of Thomas Tyre decd., Ordered that an Order of this Court Obtained in Decr. Term 1791 in favr. of Elizabeth West Widow of James West decd. for Dower in her late Husband's Lands and the proceedings thereon be rescinded and made void it having appeared to this Court that the said Order was illegally obtained.

Acct. Sales of the Estate of John Ignatius Bailey decd was returned & ordered to be filed.

292—Ordered that Administration upon the Estate of Francis Delamar Decd be Granted to Joseph Burney upon his Qualifying and entering into Bond in the sum of £400 with Joshua Fulshire & Henry Tillman Esqrs his Securities. Whereupon the said Jos. Burney Quald. Entered into Bond and returned and Inventory of said Decd. Estate.

No. 26 Richard Nixon & William Slade vs. Thomas Custis & Frederick Fonvielle} Case
The same Jury as in the last Cause except Charles Stevenson & Joseph Hall in the room of Josiah Fisher and John Morgan empanelled find the Defendants did assume & assess £21.17.0 Damages and 6d Cost.

No. 28. James McKinlay vs. James Sandy} Case. The same Jury as in No. 26 empanelled & Sworn find the Defendant did assume and assess the Plaintiff's Damages to £46.2.5 & 8d Cost.

No. 34. John Brown vs. Abner Nash} Case. The same Jury as in the last Cause empanelled and Sworn find the Defendant did assume and that he assumed within 3 years and Assess the Plantiff's Damages to £36.8.0 & 6d Cost.

Adjourned till tomorrow morng. 10 oClock.

293 — Wednesday, Decr. 10, 1794
Met Pursuant to Adjournment. Present the Worshipful John
Daly, Levi Dawson, Francis Lowthorp}Esqrs.

The last Will & Testament of Mary Oliver Decd. was proved in
Open Court by the Oath of James Bryan. Evidence thereto and
at the same time the said James Bryan Qualified as Executor
thereunto. Ordered that Letters issue.

Ordered that William Cox, Wm. Henry & George Lane be
appointed to Audit the Accounts of the Exrs. of William Bryan
Decd. who was executor of Hardy Bryan and report thereon to
the next Court.

Peter Harper vs. Winston Caswell Exr. of Richard Caswell
decd.} Case. The following Jury empanelled & Sworn Vz. No.
1. Daniel Lane 2. Lewis Jones 3. William Graves 4. Frederick
Lane 5. John West 6. Danl. West 7. Wm. Smyth 8. Longfield
Loften 9. William Adams 10. Thomas Pryor
11. Joseph Loften 12. Wm. Clark origl. Panell.
find the Defendant's Testator did assume, and that he
assumed within three years and assess the Plantiff's Damages
to £68.0.0 & 6d Cost. Bill of Exception filed and Writ of Error
Prayed. D. Caswell and John Caswell Securities (Bond taken)

An Account Sales of the Estate of Levi Hill decd was produced
in Court and ordered to be filed.

294 — The Commissioners who were appointed to divide the
estate of Jeremiah Vail decd. between the Heirs of said decd.
made return thereof which was ordered to be registered.

No. 27. James Parrott & Wife vs. Isaac Guion} Case. The same Jury as in the last Cause empanelled find the Defendant did assume & that he assumed within three years, no set off, and Assess the Plantiff's Damages to £31.7.11 & 6d Cost.

No. 29. Francis Conner vs. Joseph Loften} Case. The following Jury empanelled & Sworn. Viz. 1. William Adams 2. Thomas Pryor 3. William Clark
4. Daniel Lane   5. Lewis Jones   6. William Grover 7. Frederick Lane 8. John West   9. Daniel West   10. Thomas Clements 11. Thomas G. Fonvielle 12. David Pearce find no cause of Action.

Ordered that Thomas G. Fonvielle be appointed Guardian to Ann Fonvielle upon his entering into Bond in the sum of £1000 with John Daly & Thomas A. Green his securities.

No. 37. Charles Williams Exr. Stephen Wright vs. Jacob Ipock & Samuel Ipock} Case.
The following Jury empanelled & Sworn. No. 1. William Adams 2. Thomas Pryor 3. William Clark 4. Lewis Jones   5. William Grover 6. Thomas Clements 7. Thos. G. Fonvielle 8. David Pearce 9. Daniel West   10. Joseph Loften 11. Thomas Webber 12. Moses Lambert find the Defends. did assume and assess £27.12. Dam & 6d Cost.

295 — Ordered that Daniel Bryan Admr. of Mary Ann Brown be [??] to appear before Hardy Gatlin, Wm. Bryan & Joseph Palmer and settle his account of said Administration.

No. 125. Admr of Thomas Collier decd vs. Jacob Cooke} Default & Enq. The same Jury as in the last Cause empanelled assess the Plantiff's Damages to £35/5 and 6d Costs.

Thomas Sparrow Senr and John Biggs are appointed Inspectors of the Poll to be opened at Smiths Creek ~~to be held~~ in February next for the election of a Representative of this District in Congress of the U.S. Issd.
And John Green and John Craddock, Inspectors of the Poll to be opened for said purpose in New Bern.

Ordered that William Henry Esquire High Sheriff of this County be allowed the sum of Twenty five Ponds for his Extra services this Year. And that the Sum of Twenty Pounds for extra Services and Five pounds for Stationary be allowed Samuel Chapman, Clerk of this Court.

Ordered that John McGraw, Crier of this Court be allowed the Sum of Twenty five Pounds, for his Services and keeping Court House &c.

Ordered that Counsil Lambert aged 14 years next March be bound to Moses Lambert to learn the Trade of a Cooper (Inds. Exd.)

296 — Thursday, December 11th, 1794 — Met Pursuant to Adjournment. Present the Worshipful John Daly, Spyers Singleton, Thomas A. Green} Esqrs.

Ordered that William Burney aged 14 years the 26 Nov. last be bound to William Grover to learn the Trade of a House Carpenter. Exd.

Ordered that John Shannon have leave to keep a Tavern in Newbern upon his entering into Bond with Francis Lowthorp & Henry Bettner his Securities.

The Court having reconsidered the Petition of John Bryan for leave to Build a Public Water Grist Mill upon Poplar Branch in Craven County. And the persons appointed to lay off and Value one Acre of Land upon both sides of said Stream, and also to enquire respecting the Title of said Bryan in the premises which was disputed by Jno. S. West having returned under their Hands that they find the said John Bryan is the proprietor of the Lands upon both sides of the Stream — Whereupon Ordered that the said John Bryan have permission to Build the said Mill agreeable to Law.

Adjourned till tomorrow morng. 10 oClock.

Friday, Decr. 12, 1794
Met Pursuant to adjournment. Present the Worshipful John Daly, Henry Tillman, Thomas A. Green} Esqrs.

297 — Thomas A. Green Esqr. returned the list of Taxable property in his District for the year 1794.

Henry Tillman Esqr. also returned his list.

A Division of the Estate of Hannah Gaskins Decd was returned by the Referees appointed for that purpose & ordered to be Recorded.

William M. Herritage returned the list of Taxable property in his District for the year 1794.

Ordered that Benjamin Beasly the reputed father of a Bastard Child sworn to him by Elizabeth Heath pay unto the said Elizabeth Heath the sum of ten pounds for Expences during her Lying in &c.

Ordered that a Commission issue to Chrisr. Dudley & Josiah Howard of Onslow County to take the Examination of Mary Thomlinson Wife of Wm. Thomlinson Respecting her Execution of a Deed for her right of Dower &c in a House & Lot in Newbern.

The last Will & Testament of Sarah Burney Decd. was proved in Open Court by the Oath of Mary Cannon and at the same time Francis Lowthorp Esqr the Executor therein named, appeared in Court & Qualified agreeable to Law. Ordered that letters Testamentary issue.

Ordered that Francis Lowthorp have Letters of Administration Cum Testamento annexo upon the Estate of William Burney Decd. upon his Qualifying and entering into Bond in the sum of £600 with Levi Dawson & Charles Williams his Securities.

298 — Ordered that Levi Dawson Esqr. have administration upon the estate of Churchy Carraway Dawson Decd. upon his Qualifying and entering into Bond in the sum of £200 with Francis Lowthorp & Thomas A. Green his Securities. Dr.

Adjourned till tomorrow morning 10 oClock.

Saturday, Decr. 13th, 1794. Met Pursuant to Adjournment. Present the Worshipful John Daly, Levi Dawson, Henry Tillman} Esqrs.

An Inventory and account Sales of the Estate of Katherine Hunter Decd. was returned & filed.

Matzurin Offre has permission to keep Tavern in Newbern, Monsr. Chaponall Security.

Ordered that Administration be Granted to John Curman upon the Estate of Michael Curman Decd upon his Qualifying and entering into Bond in the sum of £3000 with Moses Ernull & Levi Reel his Securities.

Ordered that Moses Ernull be appointed Guardian to Henry Curman upon his entering into ~~Judgment~~ Bond in the sum of £1000 with John Curman & Charles Williams his Security.

An Inventory of the Estate of James Tignor Decd. was returned by the Admr.

The Referees appointed to settle & Divide the Estate of Charles Johnston Decd. ~~was~~ Between the Widow & Son made a return of their proceedings which was ~~returned &~~ ordered to be filed. WS 10/

299 — The Referees appointed to settles the Accounts of John B. Herritage Executor in the right of his Wife of the Estate of John Green Decd. made a return of said Accounts which were ordered to be filed.

Motion of Francis X. Martin to set aside an Execution issue against Nathan Smith by the Clerk of this Court for his fees in a suit instituted by Nathan Smith against Rachel Hackburn on argument Ordered that the Execution issued remain in force; Appeal prayed and not allowed.

Ordered that John Curman be appointed Guardian to Ann Curman upon his entering into Bond of £1000 with Moses Ernull & Levi Reel his securities.

On Motion of Thomas Badger Esqr. Atto. for Swan[??] &c that Willian Henry Esqr Sheriff of Craven County be summoned agreeable to Act of Assembly for neglecting to make return of Sundry Writs of Attachment put into his Hands which were returnable to this Court unless Cause shown be at the next Court and that Sci Fa issue. (Rescinded)

Then were the following Gentlement appointed to attend at the next Superior Court as Jurors. Vzl:
1. Levy Dawson 2. Aaron Ernull 3. John Gooding 4. James Gatlin 5. John Dawson 6. Isaac Guion 7. Charles Williams 8. Francis Delamar jr. 9. John Tillman.

300—Then were the following Gentlemen appointed to attend as Jurors at the next County Court. Viz:
1. William Dudley 2. Michael Mitchell 3. Jeremiah James 4. James McCafferty (S. Creek) 5. Joseph Carter 6. William Gaskins 7. John Arthur 8. Joseph Heartly 9. Jeremiah Warren 10. Weeks Chapman 11. Alex. Carruthers 12. Francis Fonvielle Junr 13. Shadrick Swann
14. Thomas G. Fonvielle 15. Charles Stevenson 16. John Physioc 17. William Brooks 18. Clayton Carruthers 19. James Clayton 20. Joseph Tingle 21. Nathan Carraway 22. Duren Hall 23. Joseph Nelson 24. John Spikes 25. John West 26. James Brinson, Jr. 27. James Nelson 28. Joseph Carraway 29. Malachi Russell 30. Hardy Hewkins
31. Thomas Parsons 32. John Biggs 33. Gideon McCoy 34. Joseph Hall jr. 35. John Bedscott 36. Worry Kilpatrick

Hardy Gatlin is appointed to take the list of Taxables in Capt. Jones District for the year 1794—Colo. Allen being so indisposed that hath failed to make return. issd.

On Motion of Edward Harris Attorney for Ann Wright
Widow of Stephen Wright decd. Ordered that the Sheriff put
her in possession of One Negro Boy name Cudge, and one
Negro girl named Rose divided and layed off to her by a Jury
for her Division of her late Husband's Estate; upon her
entering into Bond with Security to the Executor to refund in
Case of Debts, agreeable to the Act of Assembly &c.

Adjourned to Court in Course.

[March 1795]
301 — At a County Court of Pleas & Quarter Sessions, begun &
held for the County of Craven at the Court House in Newbern
on the second Monday in March being the 9th day of the
month in the 19th year of our Independence AD 1795
Present the Worshipful Isaac Guion, Jno. F. Smith, F.
Lowthorp, Henry Tillman} Esqrs.

Wm. Henry Esq. Sheriff of Craven County returned the Writ
of Venire Facias for Jurors to attend this Court in these words
"Executed."

The last Will & Testament of Stephen Tinker decd. was
produced in open Court and proved by the Oath of William
Mitchell one of the Subscribing Witnesses thereto and ordered
to be Recorded at the same time. Judith Tinker & William
Johnston the Executors therein named appeared & Qualified
as such agreeable to Law. Ordered that Letters Testamentary
issue.

Benjamin Wood Esqr. resigned his appointment of States
Attorney for the County, and at the same time Thomas Badger
Esqr was unanimously appointed to said office.

Ordered that Mrs. Ann Seamore [?] have permission to keep Public House in Newbern upon her entering into Bond with F. Lowthorp & Jno. Devereux securities.

An Inventory of the Estate of Michael Curmon was returned & filed.
302 — Ordered that Howell Keale aged 14 years be bound to Edward Nelson to learn the Trade of a Cooper. Dr. 9/

Ordered that William Mitchell aged twelve years be bound to Joel King to learn the Coopers Trade. Inds. Exd.

Ordered that James McDowell, an orphan Lad aged nine years — be bound to Richd. D. Spaight Esq. to learn Surveying &c.

Then were the following Grand Jurors empanelled & Sworn, Viz.
1. William Dudley, foreman 2. Michael Mitchell 3. Joseph Carter 4. William Gaskins 5. John Arthur   6. Weeks Chapman 7. Shad. Swann 8. Thomas G. Fonveille 9. Joseph Tingle 10. Gideon McCoy 11. John Bedscot 12. Joseph Heartly 13. Malachi Russell Jas. McMains, Cons.

The last Will & Testament of Humphry Wilks decd. was produced in Court & proved by the Oath of Emanuel Simmons Evidence thereto and at the same time Sarah Wilks the Executrix appeared in Court & Qualified as such agreeable to Law and also rendered an Inventory & Account of Sales of said Decd. Estate.

Ordered that Edward Nelson have Administration upon the Estate of William Nelson decd, upon his Qualifying and entering into Bond in the sum of £200 with Joseph Heartley & Weeks Chapman securities.

303 — The Referees appointed to Audit the Accounts of
Richard Whitford Admr. in right of his Wife of the Estate of
Jesse Willis Decd. made a return of their proceedings which
were approved of by the Court & Ordered to be Recorded.

The last Will & Testament of Nehemiah Cullon Decd was
proved in Open Court by the Oath of Joseph Masters one of
the subscribing Witnesses thereto and at the same time George
Sparrow the Executor therein named appeared in Court &
Qualified agreeable to Law.

An Inventory of the Estate of Ann Hoover decd. was returned
& filed.

Read the Petition of John Curmon praying that
Commissioners be appointed to Divide the Real Estate &
Negroes of Michael Curmon Decd. between the Heirs.
Ordered that Aaron Ernull, Joseph Willis, John Hanes,
Abraham Warren & James Gatlen be appointed
Commissioners to lay off & appropriate said Estate between
the Heirs agreeable to Law.

Ordered that John Mason be appointed Admr. of the Estate of
Joseph Mason decd. upon his Qualifying and entering into
Bond in the sum of £400 with Joseph Masters & George
Sparrow securities.
Whereupon the said Admr. Qualified & returned an Inventory
of said Decd. Estate.

Ordered that Charles Williams, Aaron Ernull & James Gatlin
audit the Accs. of the Executor of James Pearce decd. and
make return to next Court.

304 — Ordered that John Mason Admr. of the Estate of Joseph Mason decd. sell the perishable part of said Decd. Estate at six months Credit. issd.

Jonathan Fellows renewed his Tavern License.

Ordered that John Curmon Adm. Michael Curmon Decd. have leave to sell the perishable part of said Decd. Estate agreeable to Law. Dr. Issd.

Ordered that Abraham Harper have administration upon the Estate of Thomas Harper Decd. upon his entering into Bond in the sum of £100 with Charles Williams & Edmund Perkins his securities.

Ordered that Isaac Read a Wounded Soldier at the Battle of Alamance be allowed the sum of Twenty Pounds for his support to be paid him out of the County ~~Court~~ Taxes.

Adjourned till 9 cClock.

Tuesday, March 10, 1795.
Met Pursuant to Adjournment. Present the Worshipfull
Levi Dawson, Jno. F. Smith, Henry Tillman} Esqrs.

An Inventory of the Estate of James W. Stanly decd. was returned by Jno. Fox the Adminr. & filed.

Account of Sales of the Estate of Edmund Pearce decd. was returned & filed.

305 – No. 118. Robert Sage junr. vs. James Houston & Joseph Wallace} Case. Default & Enquiry. The following Jury empanelled & Sworn Assess the plantiffs Damages to £37.3.10 & 6d Costs. Viz.: 1. Abm. Carruthers 2. William Brooks 3. Clayton Carruthers 4. Jno. Moore 5. Thomas York 6. Wm. Tyre 7. John Ipock 8. Wm. Wadsworth 9. Jona. Perkins 10. Joseph West 11. Jno. Blanks 12. Thomas Pearce.

161. Edward Hean vs. Winston Caswell} Case. Default & Enqy. The same Jury as in the last Cause empanelled & Sworn assess the plantiffs Dama. to £31.12.4-1/4 & 6d Cost.

The last Will & Testament of Joseph Good decd. was produced in Open Court & proved by the Oath of John Carruthers one of the subscribing Witnesses thereto agreeable to Law & ordered to be Recorded.

An Account of Sales of the Estate of Wm. R. Pearce decd. was returned by the admx. & filed.

No. 25. Exr. of Richard Grist vs. Samuel Simpson} The same Jury as in the last case empanelled & Sworn find the Writing Obligatory not the [stricken words illegible] there has no payment been made and assess the Damages of the Plantiff to £32.1.5-1/4 & 6d Costs.

Mrs. Heath renewed her Tavern License.
Joseph Oliver renewed his Tavern License.

306 – No. 27. Francis X. Martin vs. Joseph Leach} Case. The same Jury as in the last cause empanelled & sworn find the Defendant did assume & assess £28.7.6 Damages & 6d Cost.

No. 29. John Goulding Indorsee &c. vs. Abner Nash} Case. The same Jury as in the last Cause empanelled & Sworn find the Defends. did assume and assess the Damages of the Plantiff to £34.6.0 3/4 and six pence Cost. and also find all the issues in favr of the Plantiff.

The last Will & Testament of Solomon Tingle decd. was proved in Open Court by the Oath of William Wain one of the subscribing Witnesses thereto and a Codicil thereunto annexed was proved by the oath of Jno. Blakey one of the subscribing Witnesses thereto, and at the same time Amos Cutrell & John Tingle the Executors therein named appeared in Court & Qualified agreeable to Law. Ordered that Letters Testamentary issue.

Ordered that Mary Peak & Edward Bowen have Administration upon the Estate of Jesse Peake decd. upon their Qualifying & entering into Bond in the sum of One Hundred Pounds with Thomas A Green and Frederick Lane their Securities.

307 — No. 30. Edward Kean vs. Jeremiah Redding} Case. Default & Enquiry. The same Jury as in the last Cause empanelled. Moses Griffen in the room of Jona. Perkins — assess the Damage of the Plantiff to £27.11.7 & 6d Cost.

Ordered that Letters of Administration be Granted to Spyers Singleton Esqr. upon the Estate of James McDowell decd. upon his Qualifying & entering into Bond in the sum of £100 with David Witherspoon & John Blanks securities.

Ordered that William Cox, John Gooding & William Henry be appointed to Audit the Accounts of Frederick Lane Executor of the last Will &c of William Bryan decd. and make return of the same to the next Court.

An Inventory & Acct. Sales of the Estate of Rebecca Taylor decd. was returned & filed.

An Account Sales of the Estate of Michael Arentz was returned & filed.

Adjourned till 3 oClock. Met Pursuant to Adjournment.
Present the Worshipfull
Joshua Fulsher, James Gatlin, Jno. F. Smith } Esqrs.

The Referees appointed to Audit the Accounts of James Gatlin Guardian to the Oprhans of James Kemp decd. made a return of the Account Settled by them, which were approved of by the Court and Ordered to be filed.

308 – No. 32. Nathan Smith vs. Richard Cogdell} Case. The following Jury empanelled & Sworn. Viz. 1. James McCafferty 2. Abm. Carruthers 3. William Bisok [?] 4. Clayton Carruthers 5. James Clayton 6. Nathan Carraway
7. Duran Hall 8. James Nelson 9. Jno. Biggs 10. Thomas York 11. Jno. Ipock 12. Jno. Moore find the Defendant did assume & assess the Plantiffs Damages to £81.12.0 & 6d Cost and find all the issues in favr. of the Plantiff.

The last Will & Testament of Nathanl. Carraway Decd. was produced in Court and proved by the Oath of Thomas Sparrow one of the Subscribing Witnesses thereto agreeable to Law and the same Nathan Carraway one of the Executors therein appeared & Qualified, and also rendered an Inventory of the said Decd. Estate Ordered that Letters Testamentary issue.

The Referees appointed to Audit the Account of Jno. Bedscott Senr. late Guardian to the Orphans of David Purify decd. made a return of the Accounts settled by them which was ordered to be filed.

John Bedscott Junr. [?] made a Return of his his having sold two leases of land, one of a half Lot in New bern to Other of a plantation upon Beards Creek belonging to Jno Purify, Orphan of David Purify decd.

The Referees appointed to Audit the Account of the Exr. of William Bryan decd. who was Executor of Hardy Bryan Decd. made a Return of the Accounts Settled by them which was ordered to be filed. On motion leave to Except &c Recd. [???] till next Court.

309 — On Motion at the instance of John Taylor, Ordered that Benjamin Tolston appear before this Court on Friday next and bring into Court Davis Taylor an orphan lad, whom it is suggested he detains without any authority. And that the said Lad may be bound out to an apprenticeship.

Ordered that Thomas Webber, William Lawrence and William Moore be appointed to audit the Accounts of Benja. Grenade admr. of Arthur Smith decd.

Abner Pasteur of age to choose a Guardian came into Court and made choice of William Johnston for his Guardian, upon his Qual Entering into Bond in the sum of £2000 with Francis Hawks & Thomas Hyman his securities.

Read a Commission from his Excellency the Govenor under the Great Seal of the State; directed to ~~George~~ Jos: Leech, John Tillman & Isaac Guion, Esquires, authorizing empowering and requiring them to qualify as Justices by administering the proper oaths, Charles Williams, George Lane, Lewis Bryan, Francis McIlwean, William Johnston and David Witherspoon Esquires.

Ordered that Francis Harper aged twelve years be bound to Jonathan Perkins to learn the Turners Trade.

Adjourned till tomorrow morng. 9 oClock.

Wednesday, March 11, 1795 Met Pursuant to adjournment. Present the Worshipful Joshua Fulsher, Jno. F. Smith, Jno. Dawson} Esqrs.

310—Charles Williams Esqr. appeared in Court and Qualified by taking the Oath of a Justice of the Peace & also the Oath of Allegiance to this State & the United States and took his Seat upon the Bench.

No. 37. Moses Griffin vs. Philip Turner} Case. The following Jury empanelled &Sworn Vzl. No. 1. James McCafferty 2. Alexr Carruthers 3. William Brooks
4. Clayton Carruthers 5. Nathan Carraway 6. Duren Hall 7. James Clayton 8. James Nelson 9. Jno. Biggs 10. Jno. West ~~Wm. Gardner~~ WG 11. Joseph Carraway 12. Jona. Perkins Wm. G. find the Defendant did assume and assess the Damages of the Plantiff to £29.14.4 1/4 & 6d Cost and they also find all the issues in favr. of Plantiff.

No. 38. Josias Jones vs. Joseph Clark} Case. The same Jury as in the last Cause empanelled & Sworn find the Defendant did assume & assess the Plantiffs Damages to £82.12.0 & 6d Cost and they also find all the issues in favr. of the Plantiff.

Ordered that William Cox have Administration upon the Estate of John Cox decd. upon his entering into Bond in the sum of £2000 with Thos. A. Green & Frederick Lane his securities.

Stephen Quincy his mark a Crop on the Right Ear and a Swallowfork in the left Ear.

311 — No. 40. Admr. of William Buxton decd. vs. John Fell & Benjamin Brinson} Debt. The same Jury as in the last Cause empanelled & Sworn find a payment of Forty Pounds has been made and they assess the Damages of the Plantiff to £6.1.0 Principal £41.19.0 & 6d Cost.

No. 45. John Fell vs. Daniel West} Case. The same Jury as in the last Cause except William Gardner in the room of Jno. West – empanelled & Sworn find the Defendant did assume and they assess the Plantiffs Damages to £82.2.2d and they all say there is no release on subsequent agreement.

No. 46. Charles Williams vs. Levi Dawson} Case. The same Jury as in No. 37 except William Gardner in the room of Jonathan Perkins — empanelled & Sworn find the Defendant did assume and assess the Plantiffs Damages to £38.3.6 & 6d Cost and they also find all the issues in favr. of the plantiff. Appeal prayed & allowed, Francis Stringer & James Hyman securities.

George Lane Esqr. appeared in Court & Qualified by takin the Oath of a Justice of Peace als the Oath of Allegiance to this State & the United States and took his seat upon the Bench.

No. 49. William Tyre vs. Thomas Oliver} Case. The same Jury as in No. 37 except William Gardner in the room of Jno. West empanelled & Sworn find no Cause of Action.

312 — Ordered that Jacob Rhem, George Lane & Worry Kilpatrick be appointed to Divide the Estate of John Cox Decd between the Widow & Children of said Deceased agreeable to Law — issd.

No. 50. Jno. McHenry Assignee Jno. Waite vs. William Hawley} Case. The same Jury as in the last Cause empanelled & Sworn find the Deft. did assume & assess £22.10 Dam. & 6d Cost.

No. 51. Jno. McHenry assignee Jno. Waite vs. William Hawley} Case. The same Jury as in the last Cause empanelled & Sworn find the Deft. did assume and assess £22.8.0 Dam. & 6d Cost.

Adjourned till 3 oClock
Met Pursuant to Adjournment. Present the Worshipful Joshua Fulsher, Jno. F. Smith, John Dawson} Esqrs.

On Motion of Benjamin Wallace. Ordered that John Sammons & Sophia his Wife, Admrs. Zachariah Merrett Decd. be called to appear before the next Court & Settle their accounts of said Administration. Issd.

Ordered that Jonathan Perkins & John West Defaulting Jurors be fined five shillings Each. Absloute.

313 — No. 55. Nathaniel Gooding vs. Ann Ellis Admx of James
Ellis Survg. Copartner of Rd. & James Ellis} Case. The
following Jury empanelled & Sworn Viz
No. 1. James McCafferty 2. Alexr. Carruthers 3. William
Brooks 4. Clayton Carruthers 5. Nathan Carraway 6. Duren
Hall 7. James Clayton 8. James Nelson (J. West) 9. John Biggs
10. Joseph Carraway 11. William Gardner
12. Moses Rountree Juror withdrawn & cause contd.

No. 54. Thomas Turner vs. Frederick Ward} Case. The same
Jury as in the last Cause empanelled & Sworn, find the
Defends. did assume and assess £60 Dams. & Cost and they
also find all the issues in favor of the Plantiff. Plantiff Releases
twenty four Pounds.

No. 58. Executors of Thomas Delamar vs. Thomas Hyman
Admr. } Debt. The same Jury as in the last Cause except John
West in the room of James Nelson empanelled & Sworn find
the Writing Obligatory to be the Act & Deed of the Defend.
and Assess £13.17.0 Dama. & 6d Cost and further find no
payment has been made.

314 — No. [blank] John Clements vs. Rachel Swann} Detinue.
The same Jury as in No. 55 empanelled & Sworn. Juror
withdrawn. Cause contd.

No. 73. Jno. Benners assignee John Simpson vs. Geo. Ellis
Admr Richd. Ellis, decd.} Case. The same Jury as in No 55
empanelled & Sworn find the Defends. Intestate did assume
and assess the Damages of the Plantiff to £48.11.8 they also
found all the issues in favour of the Plantiff and that the Deft.
hath not fully Adminr. Appeal prayed & allowed. Francis
Lowthorp & Levi Dawson Sey.

75. Saml. Chapman vs. Daniel Carthy, Elizabeth Hazlen, Edwd. Kean} Debt. The same Jury as in the last cause find the writing obligatory to be the act and deed of the defendants assess ~~three~~ Six pence damage & 6d Costs & find a Debt of £130.7.0 — Execution to be stayed twelve Months.

Samuel Chapman Guardn. of Wm. Graves Berry. vs. Wm. Hannis and Danl. Carthy} The same Jury as in the last cause find the writing obligatory to be the act & deed of the defendts. and assess the Pltfs damage £4.12. & 6d Costs & find the other issue in the Pltfs favor.

315 — No. 81. Hargett & Downs vs. Jno. B. Herritage} Case The same Jury as in No. 55 empanelled & Sworn find the Defendant Did assume and assess the Plantiffs Dams. to £33.2.9 & 6d Costs and also find all the issues in fav. of Plaintiff.

No. 82. Bryan Whitfield vs. Wm. M. Herritage & Jno. B. Herritage} Debt. The same Jury as in the last Cause empanelled & Sworn find there has been no payment made and the Assess the Plantiffs Damages to £2:16:7 & 6d Costs

No. 83. Rachel Bryan vs. David Witherspoon & James Carney} Debt. The same Jury as in the last Cause empanelled & Sworn find there has been no payment made and they assess the Plantiffs Damages to £1.14.0 and 6d Costs.

No. 84. Eleanor Gray vs. Wm. M. Herritage} Debt. The same Jury as in the last Cause empanelled & Sworn find the Writing Obligatory to be the Act & Deed of the Defendant and assess the Plantiffs Damages to bt £10.6.0 and 6d Costs.

316 — The last Will & Testament of Rachel Hyman Decd was proved in Open Court by the Oath of Samuel Lawson one of the subscribing Witnesses thereunto and at the same time Jonathan Perkins the Exr therein named appeared & Qualified agreeable to Law. Ordered that Letters Testamentary issue.

Adjourned till 9 oClock.
Thursday March 12, 1795
Met Pursuant to adjournment, Present the Worshipful
John F. Smith, John Dawson, Charles Williams} Esqrs.

Hardy Perkins of Age to Choose a Guardian appeared in Court and made Choice of Alexander Carruthers for his Guardian which was approved of by the Court upon his entering into Bond in the sum of £1000 with Clayton Carruthers & James Nelson his Securities.

No. 85. Rachel Bryan vs. Jno. B. Herritage} Debt. The following Jury empanelled & Sworn Viz: No. 1. James McCafferty   2. Alex [illegible ?] 3. William Brooks
4. Clayton Carruthers 5. Nathan Caraway 6. Duren Hall 7. James Clayton 8. James Nelson   9. Jno. Biggs   10. Joseph Carraway 11. Jno. Thomas 12. Jacob Johnston Jun find no payment has been made and assess the Plantiffs Dama. to £2.16.0 & 6d Cost.

317 — The last Will & Testament of John Allen decd was produced in Open and proved by the Oath of Stephen Harris one of the Subscribing Witnesses thereto agreeable to Law and at the same time Shadrach Allen One of the Executors therein names appeared in Court and Qualified agreeable to Law. Ordered that Letters Testamentary issue.

No. 88. Henry Selby vs. Henry Tillman} Case. The same Jury as in the last Cause empanelled & Sworn find the Defendant did assume & assess the Plantiffs Damages to £37.19.6 & 6d Costs.

No. 89. David Perkins vs. Philip Knowes & Charles Williams} Case. The same Jury as in the last Cause empanelled & Sworn find the Defendants did assume and assess the Plantiffs Damages to £37.14.0-1/4 & 6d Cost. Appeal prayed by Deft & Granted James Hyman & Thomas Speight Securitys.

No. 91. Rachell Bryan vs. Wm. M. Herritage & Jno. B. Herritage} Case. The same Jury as in the last Cause except Wm. Smyth in the Room of Duren Hall, empanelled & Sworn find the Defendeants did assume and Assess the plantiffs Damages to £44.6.5 & 6d Cost.

318 — No. 92. James Nelson vs. John Tillman & Henry Tillman} Case. The same Jury as in No. 85 except Wm. Smyth & Thomas Hyman in the room of Duren Hall & James Nelson empanelled & Sworn find the Defendants did assume & assess the Damages of the Plantiff to £135.14.10 & 6d Cost.

No. 94. John Benners vs. John Fox} Debt. The same Jury as in No 85 except William Smyth in the room of Duren Hall empanelled & sworn find the Writing obligatory to be the Act & Deed of the Defendt and assess the Plaintiffs Damages & Debt £37.12. & 6d Cost.

No. 93. Admrs. of Marquis De Breteginy Decd. vs Daniel Carthy} Accot. The same Jury as in the last Cause empanelled & Sworn. the Defendant was the Bailiff & Receiver of Plantiffs Intestate as stated in the Declaration of the Plffs. and that he hath not accounted. Joseph Taggert, James McKinlay & John Devereux Auditors assigned by the Court.

Jno. Sears Esq. made return of the List of Taxables in his District for 1794.

319—No. 95. Thomas Turner Adm Wright Stanly decd. vs. Thomas Crew & James McMains} Case. The same Jury as in the last Cause empanelled & Sworn find the Defendants did assume & assess the Plantiffs Damages to £26.0.0 & 6d Cost.

No. 96. William Bush vs. Abner Nash} The same Jury as in the last Cause empanelled & Sworn find the Defendant did assume and assess the Damages of the Plantiff to £49.9.0 & 6d Cost and they also find all the issues in favr. of the Plantiff.

No. 98. Moses Griffin vs. Thomas Parsons} Case. The same Jury as in the last Cause empanelled & Sworn find the Defendant did assume and assess the Damages of the Plantiff £29.4.10 1/2 & 6d Cost and also find all the issues in favor of the Plantiff.

Joseph Frelick renewed his Tavern License.

320—On hearing the petition of Alexander Steward and wife, setting forth that they have a Mulatto boy slave named John, alias John Stanly, who has from his infancy faithfully and meritoriously served the said Alexander and his wife and praying that they may have license of this Court to reward the faithful and meritorious Services of said boy by emancipating & setting him free. Ordered that they have license accordingly, reserving however the
rights of all persons, except the Petitioners, their heirs, assigns, & all claiming under them by conveyance from this day.

On hearing the petition of Amelia Green, a free woman of Colour, setting forth that she has purchased from the owners her two daughters Nancy, alias Nancy Handy, and ~~Charlotte~~ Princess, alias ~~Charlotte~~ Princess Green, and that from maternal affection & in consideration of the meritorious Services of said Nancy & ~~Charlotte~~ Princess, she is desirous to emancipate & sett free said Girls. Ordered that said Amelia have license accordingly, reserving the rights of all persons, except the petitioner, her heirs, assigns & all claiming under her by conveyance from this day.

David Witherspoon Esquire appeared in Court and Qualified as a Justice of the peace for this County by taking the oath ~~necessary~~ directed by act of Assembly, viz the oath of allegiance to this State & the United States.

Ordered that John Tillman Esq. have Administration on the estate of Thos. Burns, on entering into bond with Chs. Williams Esq. & Isaac Guion Esq. his Securities in the Sum of fifty Pounds.

321 — Then were the following Gentlemen appointed to serve as Jurors at the next term of this Court — 1. John Oliver 2. Francis Hawks 3. James McKinlay 4. Joseph Clark 5. Francis Webber 6. William Mitchell 7. James Stewart 8. Moses Griffin 9. James M. McCafferty 10. Thos. Cox 11. Wm. Hawley 12. John Good ~~Jno. Physioc~~

13. Wm. Good ~~Jno Physioc~~ 14. John Clark 15. Geo Lane 16. Jno. C. Bryan 17. Wm. Clark 18. John Green 19. Isaac Cole 20. Isaiah [Josiah?] Fisher 21. ~~John Frater~~ [?] Jas B_____ 22. Fred. Foy 23. Wilson Blount 24. John Devereux 25. [stricken name illegible] Thos. Parsons [?] 26. Enoch Alexander 27. ~~William Gibbs~~ Hardy Hawkins 28. Nathan Smith 29. ~~Wm. Tignor~~ Jos Brinson jr. 30. ~~James Coor~~ Worry Kilpatrick 31. John Stanly 32. Thomas Hyman 33. Thomas Oliver 34. Joseph Shute 35. Joseph Crispen 36. Richd. Hunly.

It appearing to the Court that William G. Berry is of Lawful age Whereupon Ordered that Jno. F. Smith, Thomas Badger & Silas W. Arnett be appointed to audit the accounts of Samuel Chapman his Guardian and report thereon to the next Court and it is further Ordered that the said Guardian Deliver up to the said William G. Berry his Estate both Real & Personal.

Ordered that John Physioc, James Brinson, Jr., Hardy Hawkins, Joseph Hall & Worry Kilpatrick & Thomas Parsons Defaulting Jurors to this Term be fined NiSi agreeable to Act of Assembly & that [illegible ??]

322 – No. 99. James McKinlay vs. John Dewey} Case. The same Jury as in the last Cause empaneled & Sworn find the Defendant did assume and assess £31.12.0 & 6d Cost and also find all the issues in favr. of Plantiff. Appeal prayed by Defend. Wm. McClure & William Hawley Secys.

No. 110. Ann Randall vs. Joseph Carter} Debt. The same Jury as in the last Cause empaneled & Sworn find the Writing Obligatory to be the Acct. and Deed of the Defendant and that August 16 1794 a payment was made of the sum of £26.17.0 that there is no Sett off and assess the Plantiffs Damages to eighteen shillings & three pence and 6d Cost.

No. 113. Richard Hunley vs Thomas Hyman Admr Peter Franklin} Case. The same Jury as in the last Cause empaneled & Sworn ~~find the Defendants Intestate did assume & assess~~ Mistrial.

A Deed of Conveyance from Stephen H. Dunn & Elizabeth his Wife to John Hobday for a piece of Ground in Newbern was produced in Open Court and was proved agreeable to Law at March Term 1793 and it being Represented that Mrs. Dunn cannot Conveniently come to Court to be prively Examined respecting her voluntary Execution of the same Ordered that Spyers Singleton & Jno. Knowis be appointed Commissr. to take said Examination.

323 – [No. xx] John Harvey vs. Francis Stringer} The defendant comes into Court in his proper person and confesses Judgt. For the Sum of £56.2.6 & Costs. Stay Execution three Months granted.

The following persons are appointed Patrolls in Capt. Greens district, viz Moses Lambart, Thomas Clements, & Thomas Wyse for the upper part and John Gooding, Joseph Hall and Shadrach Swann for the lower part.

Adjourned till 3 oClock.

Met Pursuant to adjournment.

Present the Worshipfull Joshua Fulsher, Jno. F. Smith, John Dawson, David Witherspoon, Charles Williams} Esqrs.

Pd. 5/ Ordered that John Thomas a Defaulting Juror be fined five ~~ten~~ shillings absolute.

Ordered that Shadk. Allen Executor &c of John Allen Decd sell the perishable part of said Deceased Estate.

No. 128. Executors of James Lipsey decd. vs. William Hawley} Debt. Default & Enquires. The following Jury empaneled & Sworn vzl. No. 1. James McCafferty 2. Alexr. Carruthers 3. William Brooks 4. Clayton Carruthers 5. Nathan Carraway 6. James Clayton 7. James Nelson 8. John Biggs 9. Joseph Carraway 10. Jacob Johnston jr. 11. Wm. Smith 12. James Hyman assess the Plantiff Damages to One pound four shillings & 6d Cost. Principal £30.2.0

324 – No. 164. John Pearson vs. James Pearson} Default & Enquiry. The same Jury as in the last Cause empaneled & Sworn Assess the Plantiffs Damages to One hundred Pounds & 6d Cost.

No. 117. William Styron vs. Hardy Hewkins} Case. The same Jury as in the last Cause empaneled & Sworn, find the Defendant did assume and assess the Plantiff Damages to £70.0.0 & 6d Cost and find the other issues in favr. of the plantiff.

No. 120. Jacob Cooke vs. Abner Nash} Case. The same Jury as in the last Cause empaneled & Sworn find all the issues for the plantiff and that there has been paid on the 8th Decr. 1791 Six pounds Eight shippings on the 27t August 1792 thirty seven pounds twelve shillings, on April 3 1793 One hundred and ten pounds sixteen shillings and assess Six pence Cost. Appeal prayed by Deft. Attorney Edward Kean & Levi Dawson Secy.

No. 126. Bazell Polincie vs. Hugh O Neil} Trespass, Assault & Battery, Default & Enquiry. The same Jury as in the last Cause empaneled & Sworn find for the plantiff 6d Damage & 6d Cost.

325 – No. 169. Edward Tinker vs. John Sitgreaves} Case. The same Jury as in the last Cause empaneled & Sworn find the Defendant did assume and assess the Plantiffs Damages to £101.13.9 & 6d Cost and they find no further payment or Sett off. Appeal prayed by Defends Attorney & Granted Jno Daves & George Ellis Securities.

No. 175. William McClure vs. Saml. Gerock} Case. The same Jury as in the last Cause empaneled & Sworn find the Defendant did assume and assess £54.0.5 Damages & 6d Cost also find the Defendt. did assume within three years.

No. 176. Joseph Masters vs. John Robenson} Debt. The same Jury as in the last Cause find the Writing Obligatory to be the Act & Deed of the Defendt. and assess the Plantiffs Damages to £1.1.3 & 6d Cost & no Sett off. Principal £25

Adjourned till 9 oClock.
Friday March 13, 1795. Met Pursuant to adjournment. Present the worshipful Henry Tillman, Jno. F. Smith, Jno. Dawson, Charles Williams} Esqrs.

326 – Mrs. Lydia Stewart, Wife of Alexander Stewart, appeared in Court and was privily Examined by Jno. F. Smith Esqr. Respecting her Voluntary signing a Petition to the Court for the Emancipation of John, alias John Stanly-a Mulatto servant belonging to the said Alexander Stewart & Wife-who reported to the Court that he had privily Examined the said Lydia and that she freely and Voluntarily renounced her Claim to the said John and requested he might be sett free &c.

Pd. Jno. Biggs a defaulting Juror is fined five shillings.

No. 124. William Gatlin vs. Levi Dawson} Appeal by Plantiff. The following Jury empaneled & Sworn 1. James McCafferty 2. Alexander Carruthers 3. William Brooks 4. Clayton Carruthers 5. Nathan Carraway 6. James Clayton 7. James Nelson 8. Jno. Biggs 9. Joseph Carraway 10. Herman Gaskins 11. Isaac Kemp 12. William Adams find for the Plantiff & assess Six Pounds Damage & 6d Cost.

Ordered that Betty Copes (a free Negro Girl) be bound to James Houston Senr. aged nine years the 2d May next to learn to be a Spinster (Inds. Exd)

The last Will & Testament of Eunice Halling Decased was proved in Open Court by the Oath of John Craddock one of the Subscribing Witnesses thereunto and at the same time James Bryan the Executor therein named appeared in Court & Qualified agreeable to Law. Ordered that Letters Testamentary issue.

327 — Ordered that John Carpenter Guardian to William Carpenter be Suited to appear before the next Court and settle his account of said Guardianship.

Ordered that a Negro Girl named Nancy Carter about eight years and a half old be bound to Sarah Godfrey to learn to be a Spinster.

No. 67. Richard Johnston vs. Henry H. Harris} Appeal. The same Jury as the last Cause empaneled & Sworn find the Defendant did assume & that he assumed within three years & has ratified his Contract since he came of Age and Assess the plantiff Damage to fifteen pounds & 6d Cost.

Read the Petition of Lewis Holland & Sarah his Wife praying that Commissioners may be appointed to lay off and Divide a Certain Tract of Land Devised to them & ~~Sarah~~ Mary [?] Davis by the last Will & Testament of Buscoe Davis decd. Ordered that Brittain King, Alexander Harper, Josiah Turnage, Richard Philips & Ambrose Jones be appointed Commissioners to lay off and Divide the said Lands agreeable to Law.

No. 68. Thomas Speight vs. John Fell} Appeal by Deft. The same Jury as in the last Cause empaneled & Sworn — find the note of Twenty Pounds was given by the Defendant to the Plantiff in Consideration of a Canoe Race won by the Plantiff against the Defendant. If the Law is for the Plantiff the aforesaid sum of Twenty Pounds if for the Defendant then they find for the Defendant.

328 — Saml. G. Barron of Lawful Age to Choose a Guardian appeared in Court and made Choice of Thomas G. Fonvielle for Guardian which was approved upon his entering into Bond in the sum of Five thousand Pounds with John Daves & Joshua Fulsher Esqrs his Securities.

Elizabeth Barron, of lawfull age to choose a Guardian appeared in Court & chose Thomas G. Fonville, who was approved upon his entering into bond of Five thousand Pounds with John Daves & Joshua Fulshire his Securities.

Adjourned till 3oClock.
Met Pursuant to Adjournment. Present the Worshipful Joshua Fulsher, Jno. F. Smith, John Dawson} Esqrs.

No. 103. Stephen Nunn vs. F.X. Martin} Appeal by Defendant. The following Jury empaneled & Sworn Vzl. 1. James McCafferty 2. Alexander Carruthers 3. William Brooks 4. Clayton Carruthers 5. Nathan Carraway 6. James Clayton 7. James Nelson 8. Jno. Biggs 9. Joseph Carraway 10. Herman Gaskins 11. Isaac Kemp 12. Joseph Lewis find the Defendant did assume, and assess £3.18.9 Damages & 6d Cost.

Ordered that William Tignor have administration upon the Estate of Tolson Wallace (the Widow having resigned her right to him) upon his Qualifying and entering into Bond in the sum of £300 — with Charles Williams and Joseph Brinson his Securities.

329 — Ordered that William Tignor admr. Tolson Wallace have leave to sell the perishable part of sd Decd Estate.

Ordered that John Hall, aged fifteen years be bound to Lewis Bynum to learn to Shoemaker Trade.

No. 23. Levi Dawson vs. Thomas Speight} Case. Non Pros on Motion of Defendant for want of Declaration.

Adjourned till 9 oClock.
Saturday March 14. 1795 Met Pursuant to Adjournment. Present the Worshipful Jno. F. Smith, Francis Lowthorp, Charles Williams} Esqrs.

Ordered that William Dawson Bryan, aged sixteen years be bound to William & Edward Kean to learn the Business of a Merchant. (Inds. made out)

Ordered that the County Tax for the year 1794 be collected as follows for every Hundred acres of land Sixpence for every Hundred pounds value of Town Property one shilling & for every Poll one shilling.

Ordered that the Sheriff enter into Bond for the Collection of the County Tax for the 1794 in the sume of Five hundred Pounds with Frederick Lane & John Gooding Securities.

330 — Mrs. Ann Allen Widow of John Allen Esqr. Decd. came into Court and Signified her dissent to her late Husbands Will.

The Referees appointed to Audit the Account of Wm. Phipps Executor of Charles Marshall decd. was returned & filed made a return of their proceedings which was Orderd to be filed.

Joseph West, Jonathan Perkins, William Gardner & Mathew Neale are appointed Patrollers in Capt. Joseph West's District.

Henry Tillman Esqr. Surveyor for the County offered for his securities Charles Williams & William Henry Esqr Ordered that they enter into Bond in the sum of £1000.

Ordered that William Derick aged 12 years be bound to Amos Wade to learn the Art & Mistery of a Seaman. (Inds. Exd.)

Ordered that Ned Lewis a free Negro Boy aged 10 years be bound to Amos Wade to learn the Art & Mistery of a Seaman. (Inds. Exd.)

No. 1. Admr. Sam Smyth vs. Levi Dawson}} Caveat. Trial De No Vo upon the Premises order to issue directed to the Sheriff & cause plats &c to be returned and the Verdict of the Jury to the next Court.

Inventory & Account of Sales of the Estate of Sarah Burney Decd. was returned & filed also an Acct. Sales of the Estate of William Burney Decd.

331 — Ordered that the Sheriff of Craven County be directed & empowered to summon a Jury to lay off the Dower of Ann Allen Widow of Jno. Allen Decd in the Estate of her Deceased Husband and make a return to the next Court.

Thomas Ellis vs. George Ellis} Petn. Ordered that Jno. F. Smith, Jno. Craddock, William Shepard & Francis Hawks or any three of them be appointed to audit & State the Accounts of Geo. Ellis Admr. of Richd. Ellis decd. and make report thereon to the next Court.

No. 7. John F. Smith vs. John C. Clark & Wife Jane [?] Admr. of Rumsey Wt. Outerbridge Decd. } Petn. The Defendants in the Cause having failed to Answer the Petition of the Complainant and on Reading the same, Ordered and Decree that Judgment be entered up Against the Defendants for the sum of One hundred and thirty two pounds eleven shillings & two pence together with Cost of suit.

Mr. E. Perkins & Francis Brown to attend at next Term as Constables.

332 — Christopher L. Lente vs. Bela Badger & Wife}
The Garnishment of Daniel West.
1 Interogatory. Had you any property of Bela Badger, or Bela Badger and Wife, or do you owe him, or him & her any Monies? Or had you any such property or owed any thing as above , at the time you was summoned as Garnishee?
Answer. I have not nor had not At that thime.

2 Intr. Do you know any person or persons who has or have any property of his or thiers? Or owe him or them any monies?

Answ. I do not know of any person who has any property of his or owes him any thing.

3 Intr. Did you not purchase a horse of Bela Badger?

Ansr. I did not. Nor have I any horse belonging to him.

(No fourth)

5 Intr. Did you make any Contract about a mare with said Bela, and what Contract?

Ansr. Yes there was a Contract by which I was to have one mare and two negroes from Bela Badger with a good bill of Sales. I was to send him a Stud horse. The mare I received conditionally viz. I was to be ready on or before the 1st day of October to deliver the horse, on delivery of the mare & two negroes payment to be made before the delivery of the horse & he was to receive a bill of Sale from me on my receiving a bill of Sale from him. If the horse was to die or any accident happened, it was to be no bargain.

6 Intr. What became of the mare?

Ansr. I sold my title to said Mare to Frederick Lane, and at the same time told Mr. Lane there would be a dispute about the mare & if my right and title was defective it would be his loss.

7 Intr. How much did you get for it?

Ansr. Fifty five Pounds in Notes, but was to have Sixty If I warranted her.

333 — Int. Have you any of these Notes in hand, and what have you received; any Cash or Property?

Ansr. I sold the £51 note for one Mare & a Cow and Calf which I value at £40. I have in hand a note of £4.

Intr. Did you give any thing to Mr. Badger, in consideration of said Mare?

Ansr. I gave up a debt of three Pounds which Badger owed me and conceived the mare as forfeited by Badger, as he had sold the two Negroes which he was to give me with the mare for my horse and by that means broke his Contract with me — forfeited the Mare as he afterwards told John S. West himself that he expected the mare was forfeited and lost & that he did not care anything about her, as this deponent was at all times ready to deliver her up to the said Badger his hourse on the said Badger's delivering up to me the said two Negroes with a bill of Sale conveying them to me.
Intr. Did you ever apply to Mr. Badger to deliver the Negroes?
Ansr. No because the said Badger was to bring the Negroes to my own house, and deliver them there to me and give a good bill of Sale.
Intr. Was there any time fixed for the delivery?
Ansr. Yes, the delivery was to be on or before the first of October next ensuing our agreement and at my own house.
Signed Daniel West.

Jno. Dyni renewed his Tavern license.

[End March 1795]

INDEX

Jno.	100	Lambert	5
Allway		Lambeth	80
John	125	Mason	130
Obadiah	125	Perkins	55
Allways		Randall	255
John	127	Seamore	239
Obadiah	33, 127	Webber	87, 107, 142, 191
Almand		Wright	238

Benjamin   29

Ambrose

David   71

Amelia

Green   254

Amery

Cason 187, 188, 189, 190, 193, 196, 199

Amory

Cason   173, 185, 192

Amy

Gatlin   92

Ann

Allen   262, 263
Biggleston   44
Butler   162
Curman   236
Dorsett   46
Durand   29
Ellis   201, 249
Fipps   79
Fonvielle   232
Greaves   7, 211
Hoover   240

Ann C.

Biggleston   28

Ann H.

Wright   221

Anna

Daw   122
Hoover   226
Mason   135
Nash   217
Perkins   32

Anner

Coleman   66

Anthony

William 13, 22, 24, 28, 30, 56, 64, 66, 71, 84, 96, 98, 100, 102, 106, 107, 109, 110, 113, 173, 176, 180

Wm.   28, 33, 34, 35, 89, 99, 101, 107, 114

Archer

John   149

Arentz

Lavinia   226
Michael   226, 244

Armory

212, 213, 214, 216, 218,
220, 231, 243, 247

Wm.   80, 168, 207, 212, 214

Wm., Capt.   42

Craddock

Jno.   263

John   197, 233, 259

Crawford

Charles   113, 166, 185

Creek

Adams   55

Adam's   84

Ads.   69, 153

Beards   245

Brices   40, 149

Broad   11, 209

Bury   209

Clubfoots   56

Clubfords   112

Core   178

Goose   136, 209

Little Swifts   2, 5

Mill   193

Mosely's   168

Mosley's   107

Otter   111

Slocumbs   123

Smith   106

Smiths   198, 233

Swifts   65, 97, 112

Upper Broad   17

Crespin

Joseph   14

Creu

Thos.   221

Crew

Thomas   72, 93, 158, 253

Thos.   94

Crispen

Joseph   31, 50, 255

Crispin

_ph   13

Joseph   41, 44, 47, 48, 51, 53,
66, 124, 215

Cudge   238

Cullen

Nehemiah   224

Cullon

Nehemiah   240

Cumming

Thos.   22

Cummings

James   182

Jno.   112

John   182

Cummins

John   197

Curman

Ann   236

Henry   236

John   236

Michael   236

Curmon

John   240, 241

Michael   239, 240, 241

Curtis

    Thomas 10, 12, 47, 48, 50, 53

    Thos.   31, 41, 44, 51, 53, 83

Custis

    Thomas   230

Cutrel

    Amos   8, 174

Cutrell

    Amos   8, 243

    John   48

Cutting

    Leonard   4, 8, 19

Cuyler

    John   149

Da___

    James   195

Daly

    Jno.   119, 143, 200

    John 58, 60, 62, 72, 73, 81, 95, 98, 114, 115, 125, 126, 127, 128, 133, 134, 148, 150, 159, 176, 185, 190, 193, 195, 196, 198, 221, 228, 231, 232, 233, 234, 235

Daniel   67

Darby

    John   91

Daugherty

    Daniel   182

    Richard   95, 188

Daughety

    Danl.   205

Daves

    James   117, 205, 206

    Jno   258

    John   117, 172, 177, 178, 260

David

    James   123

    Joseph   25

Davis

    Briscoe   5, 6, 207

    Buscoe   260

    James 4, 6, 7, 31, 67, 84, 112, 120, 141, 173, 180, 189, 211

    Jas.   191

    Lawson   5, 6, 44, 207, 208

    Mary [?]   260

    Sarah   260

    Thomas   28, 216

    William 7, 28, 30, 66, 67, 87, 151, 154, 174, 185, 189, 197, 207, 210

    Wm.   86, 171, 191, 211, 212

Daw

    Anna   122

    Arthur   229

    James   41, 117

    John   41, 82, 122, 123, 149

    Mrs.   123

Dawly

    John   74

Dawson

    Churchy Carraway   235

    Colo.   100

280

Delemar

    Francis   86

Derick

    William   262

Devereaux

    Jno.   92

    John   228

Devereux

    Jno.   22, 166, 171, 178, 239

    John 1, 13, 31, 47, 69, 74, 129, 159, 173, 180, 189, 252, 255

Devoux

    Frederick   27

Dewey

    Jno   222

    John   9, 72, 199, 255

Dickenson

    Levin   19, 20, 150, 152

Dickerson

    Levin   47, 136

Dickinson

    Levin   20, 152

Dickson

    William   153

Digner

    John   179

Digsin

    John   186

Dishon

    Daniel   192, 211

Dixon

John   191

Silvanus   223

William   13, 22, 31, 56, 138, 219, 226

Wm.   160

Doherty

    Rd.   160

Donnell

    Robert   101

Dorothy

    Stevenson   200

Dorsett

    Ann   46

Dove

    Wm.   107

Dubberly

    Sacker   31

    Zachah.   4

    Zacher   41

    Zacker44, 47, 49, 51, 153, 165

Duck Creek   20

Dudley

    Chrisr.   235

    William   66, 112, 119, 143, 178, 224, 237, 239

    Wm.   120, 121

Duffy

    Geo.   104, 105, 119

    George   113, 200

    William   119

    Wm.   119

Duguid

Henry	46, 200
Hollis	74
Holten	39
Marshall	18
Nash	217
Peters	57, 96
Potter	29, 139, 222
Saunders	82
Taylor	190
Vail	45, 219
West	14, 230
Willis	38
Wrenford	35

Ellis

Ann	201, 249
Geo.	21, 23, 24, 28, 33, 34, 50, 66, 94, 177, 194, 249, 263
George	1, 13, 19, 24, 30, 33, 34, 79, 82, 84, 134, 167, 193, 225, 228, 258, 263
James	19, 36, 49, 50, 51, 68, 82, 102, 104, 109, 200, 201, 220, 221, 225, 249
Richard	1, 19, 23, 33, 50, 51, 109
Richd.	249, 263
Thomas	263

Elsbree

Almand	53

Emery

James	75
James R.	95
Thomas James	95

Emmerson

\<no first name\>	93
Elizabeth	161
George	14, 80, 90

Emmery

James	216
Enoch	26

Ephemia

Snead	88
Tinker	88

Ernell

Moses	77

Ernu__

Moses	205

Ernul

Aaron	5, 56, 60, 61, 165, 174, 227
Capt.	47, 49
Moses	9, 49, 53, 165, 174

Ernull

Aaron	2, 112, 117, 122, 124, 153, 185, 186, 187, 188, 189, 190, 191, 192, 195, 205, 237, 240
Capt.	25, 37
Captain	137
John	138, 153, 219, 226
Moses	38, 57, 99, 122, 153, 180, 186, 208, 218, 236

Ernulls	199

Esther

Johnston	154
Yates	162

Eunice

Franklin	62
Halling	259
Neale	174
Evans	
Evan	215
Fab__	116
Fabre	24
Faircloth	
John	51
Fairfield	
Reuben	33, 50
Fell	
John	12, 13, 138, 142, 172, 174, 175, 176, 219, 226, 247, 260
Fellows	
Jno.	176
Jonathan	52, 163, 222, 241
Fen___	
John	47
Fenner	
Richard	170
Ferebe	
Carlton	61
Ferguson	
Adam	164, 185
John	123, 164
Ferrell	
Elizabeth	36, 56
Ferry	
Adams	118
Ferry on Trent	25

Ferry over Adam's Creek	84
Ferry ten miles from Newbern	78
Fields	
Edward	106
Fillingame	
Jesse	57
Fillingham	
Jarvis	138, 142, 167, 184, 203
Fillingim	
James	223, 224
Jarvis	197
Fillingin	
Benja.	223
Benjamin	222
Fipps	
Ann	79
Joseph	79
Fish	
John	229
Th.	6
Thomas	6, 7, 42, 43, 46, 47, 50, 64, 229
Thos.	7, 31, 41
Fisher	
Isaiah	255
Josiah	210, 212, 213, 214, 220, 229, 230
Josiah?	255
Fisk	
Thomas	66
Thos.	66
Flood	

Thomas	144, 166
Thos.	165, 193
William	92, 206, 259
Gatlin (?)	
Hardy	122
Gatling	
William	197
Geb_	
William	116
Gero__	
Peter	129
Gerock	
Saml.	258
Gerone	
Peter	35
Gibbs	
William	22, 67, 101, 182, 255
Wm.	223
Gill	
John	176
Gillies	
Malcolm	127, 146, 177
Gilstrap	
Benjamin	115
Glover	
Samuel	29
Godett	
John	121
Godfrey	
Sarah	259
Good	

John	188, 189, 190, 254
Joseph	149, 242
William	10, 12, 13, 14, 15, 23, 24, 50, 84, 94, 121, 153, 160, 189, 190, 191, 207, 209, 210, 212, 214, 219, 223
Wm.	22, 35, 100, 124, 125, 127, 207, 255
Gooding	
James	55
Jno.	41, 70, 133, 134, 174, 175, 192
John	43, 69, 71, 89, 90, 112, 115, 132, 134, 155, 163, 172, 173, 176, 179, 193, 194, 195, 196, 198, 199, 200, 218, 237, 243, 256, 262
John, Jr.	178
Mathew	115
Nathaniel	249
Saml.	82, 112
Sarah	164
Thomas	61
Thos.	61
Goose Creek	22
Gordon	168
Gordon & Kean	168
Goulding	
John	82, 87, 88, 193, 243
Graff	
Anthon	55
Graham	
Mary	82
Mr.	152

Holloway	
Jno	22
John	13, 59, 95
Holston	
Geo.	71
Holten	
Elizabeth	39
Harrell	39
Holton	
George	71
Jesse	153, 165
Merrill	56
Thomas	153, 160
Honey	
William	147
Hoover	
Ann	240
Anna	226
James	226
Samuel	38, 78
Wm.	82
Horesheens	
James	76
Horsends	
James	38, 39
John	203
Horshends	
Jesse	142
Houston	
Francis	192, 208
James	48, 208, 242, 259
Hover	
John	48
Samuel	38, 74
Howard	
Jno	222
Josiah	235
William	162, 187
Howell	
John	109
Huckins	
Hardy	170
Josiah	121
Hukins	
Hardy	80, 81, 83, 85, 87, 89, 91
Hung	
Robert	176
Hunley	
Richard	11, 24, 44, 54, 84, 90, 111, 117, 138, 191, 256
Richd.	24, 213
Hunly	
Richd.	255
Hunt	
Joseph	57
Rob.	84
Robert	10, 12, 13, 14, 16, 21, 23, 30, 35, 43, 87, 91, 92, 112, 125, 127, 129, 131, 132, 133, 168, 170, 175, 187, 192
Robt.	135, 139
Hunter	
Katherine	205, 235

Nancy Hill

  Wright   155

Nash

  Abner2, 14, 18, 27, 29, 32, 36,
    40, 48, 109, 111, 117, 142,
    175, 187, 202, 205, 206,
    215, 217, 220, 221, 223,
    230, 243, 253, 257

  Anna   217

  Elizabeth   217

  Francis   217

  Frederick   217

  Justina   85

  Maria   217

Neal

  Mathew   112

Neale

  Abner10, 63, 77, 98, 105, 119,
    189, 196, 197, 205, 206,
    213, 224

  Barre   3, 23

  Chrisr.   224

  Christopher   224

  Eunice   174

  Mathew   3, 10, 12, 123, 174,
    197, 203, 262

  Philip   13, 22, 31, 42, 43, 46,
    47, 49, 51, 54, 59, 197, 203,
    205, 223

  Philip, Jr.   54

  Philip, Junr.   54

  Philip, Senr.   54

  Richard   54

Neggle

John   151

Negro

  Ben   138

Nelson

  Asa   211

  Edward   183, 197, 239

  Francis   210

  James   56, 64, 66, 67, 69, 70,
    71, 87, 89, 91, 133, 135,
    154, 166, 210, 237, 244,
    246, 249, 251, 252, 257,
    259, 261

  Jno. S.   138, 160

  John   4, 17, 42, 69, 197, 210,
    219, 226

  John S. 55, 112, 153, 197, 219

  Joseph   56, 64, 66, 67, 69, 70,
    71, 81, 83, 85, 87, 88, 91,
    92, 210, 237

  Mary   96

  Thomas   31, 42, 45, 69

  William   183, 239

Nero   56

New Jersey

  Burlington   79

Newbern Academy   19

Newbern Accademy   8

Nixon

  Rd.   198

  Richard 3, 21, 43, 88, 95, 110,
    122, 126, 127, 128, 155,
    169, 176, 187, 193, 194,
    195, 196, 198, 201, 203,
    208, 217, 230

Thomas 13, 14, 15, 21, 23, 78, 84, 96, 98, 100, 101, 102, 105, 109, 110, 112, 113, 114, 150, 173, 174, 175, 185, 187, 188, 189, 191, 192, 193, 248, 255

Thos. 109

Ordinary Keepers's Rates 24

Osborn

Jno. C. 177

Outerbridge

John 24, 32, 33
Rumsey Wt. 263

Oxley

George 7

Palatin

Peter F. 198

Palaton

Peter F. 156

Palmer

Joseph 4, 94, 182, 204, 205, 232

Parrott

James 232

Parson

Captain 185

Parsons

Hillary 44
Jeremiah 15, 24, 31, 43, 44, 89, 91, 156
Josiah 132

Thomas 10, 12, 14, 44, 70, 132, 164, 170, 190, 224, 237, 253, 255

Thos. 69, 70, 131, 132, 255

Pasteur

Abner 245
Doct. 105
Doctor 105
Ed. 90
Edward 63, 73, 91, 98, 125, 197
Edwd. 184

Patience

Carraway 225

Patrick

Joel, Jr. 41

Patsey

Gainer 23

Paul

George 61

Paxton

William 71, 94
Wm. 84

Peak

Mary 243

Peake

Jesse 243

Pearce

David 49, 167, 212, 213, 214, 229, 232
Edmund 241
Edward 208
Eleonora 213

Captain	199
James	7
John	76
Richard	260
Thomas	76, 85
Phillip	
John	64
Phillips	
Capt.	25
Captain	117
Hannah	163
John	64
T.168	
Thomas	7, 57, 64, 96
Thos.	31
Phills	
Joseph	138
Phipps	
Joseph	8, 55, 57
William	17, 18, 34, 94, 115, 182, 205
Wm.	262
Physioc	
Jno.	254
John	132, 133, 237, 255
Peter	101, 128, 223
William	212, 213
Pittman	
Betsy	181
Jane	181
John	181
Obedience	181
Thomas	153, 165

Polincie	
Bazell	257
Poll	35
Brown	35
Pollock	
Cullen	48, 77
George	77
Thomas	79, 166
Polly	
Hurley	179
Lewis	203
Probart	199
Pondrill?	
Christiana	18
Pope	
Elijah	63
Porter	
John 31, 41, 42, 43, 46, 47, 49, 51, 53, 139, 143, 169	
Postlewaite	
James	172
Potter	
Edward	23, 29, 53
Edwd.	139
Edwd., Jr.	175
Elizabeth	29, 139, 222
George	175
James 125, 127, 168, 170, 171, 175, 217, 223	
John	138, 219
Joseph	175
Potts	

John	258	Southy Jordan	138
Roe		Southy Jourden	154
Avey	170	Ruff	
James 133, 135, 152, 154, 168, 170		James	152
		Rumley	
Thomas	4, 128, 178	Edward	57, 77
Thos.	4, 101	Mary	57, 77
William	4	Zadock	129
Rooke		Zadok	16
Barta.	22	Rumly	
Barth.	14	Zadock	17
Bartho.	12, 22	Rumsey	
Rose	83, 238	William	224
Mathias	150	Russell	
Ross	160	Malacha	80, 81
William 36, 91, 94, 121, 135, 172		Malachi 60, 61, 142, 237, 239	
Wm. 51, 84, 90, 173, 201, 218		Ruth	
Roundtree		Moore	66
Francis	74, 75	Ryal	
Moses	74, 75	James	27
Rountree		Ryan	
Francis	48	William	170
Moses	249	S.Leger	
William	5	Duryl. D.	111
Rouse		Sage	
Simon	161	Robert, Junr.	242
Rowe		Sailer	
James	31	George	55
Rue		Sally	
Southy	153	Bridghtm__	159
Southy J.	150	Salt	

Samuel   9, 36, 44, 49, 50, 53, 59, 107

Thomas   59, 138, 203, 226

Thos.   146, 148, 150

William   112, 131, 172, 176, 180, 197, 203, 227, 252

Wm.   129, 132, 133, 135, 231, 252

Snead

Ephemia   88

Leah   88

So.West Bridge   228

Sophia

Simmons   248

Spaight

Richard D.   6, 12, 27, 28, 29, 45, 67, 109, 125, 179, 194

Richard Dobbs   81

Richd. D.   1, 19, 46, 239

Richd. Dobbs   21

Thos.   28

Spann

George   224

Sparrow

Benja.   35

Elizabeth   3

George   183, 240

Henry   183

Joseph   3

Paul   84

Saml   2

Saml.   2, 138, 213

Samuel   2, 3, 213, 219

Sarah   2, 3

Thomas   96, 129, 153, 173, 198, 210, 233, 244

Speight

John   48

Thomas 12, 13, 122, 129, 137, 173, 176, 180, 252, 260, 261

Thos.   22, 24, 30, 174

William   11, 17, 39, 174, 194

William, Junr.   49

Wm.   49, 137, 194

Spelman

David   90

Spight

Thos.   28

Spikes

John   237

Thomas   176, 216

Spivey

Moses   5

Spyers

John   8

Squires

Amos   56, 69, 80, 81, 83, 85, 112, 123, 148, 150

St Leger

Duryvault D   104

St. Leger

Duryvault   47

Stanley

Jno. W.   98

Stanly

Edward 26, 44, 66, 71, 84, 91, 94, 171, 258
Edwd. 56, 67, 69, 70, 133, 134
Ephemia 88
Judith 238
Stephen 13, 21, 69, 84, 238

Tisdale
Nathan 31, 41, 94
William 3, 26, 62, 88, 92, 119, 189, 191, 194, 202, 221
Wm. 37, 162, 180, 187, 220

Toleson
Benja. 182

Tollman
Henry 141

Tolson
Benja. 143

Tolston
Benjamin 245

Tooley
Adam 25, 50, 98, 100, 101, 125, 126, 146, 187
William 226, 228
Wm. 15

Trewhitt
Levi 147
William 147

Trippe
William 164, 165, 171

Turnage
Josiah 260

Turner
[Tho]mas 98
Frederic 112
Frederick 197, 203
Philip 79, 146, 246
Tho. 91
Thomas 6, 21, 22, 42, 55, 72, 91, 102, 103, 104, 106, 113, 114, 120, 131, 136, 157, 192, 218, 224, 249, 253
Thos. 118, 156, 200, 211
Widow 6

Tutle
William 56

Tyre
Lewis 143
Thomas 42, 153, 230
William 51, 70, 146, 150, 154, 166, 248
Wm. 148, 242

Underhill
David 100

Utley
Jeptha 105

Vail
Elijah 148
Elisabeth 86
Elizabeth 45, 219
Jeremiah 219, 231
Sarah 45, 55, 86

Van Baerle
J.L.C. 22

Vance
Mary 76, 132

Thomas 56, 64, 66, 69, 71, 88,
    91, 92, 104, 109, 131, 142,
    156, 172, 176, 180, 185,
    187, 188, 189, 190, 191,
    192, 193, 195, 196, 199,
    202, 222, 232, 245
Thos.   35, 50, 59, 67, 70, 71,
    135, 148, 173, 191, 192, 194
West

Capt.	25
Dan'l	61
Daniel 17, 42, 48, 61, 63, 78, 80, 82, 90, 91, 117, 131, 144, 158, 228, 232, 247, 263, 265	
Danl. 25, 107, 137, 143, 174, 199, 229, 231	
Danl., Capt.	64
David 48, 114, 115, 116, 117	
Elizabeth	14, 230
J. 249	
James	14, 42, 62, 230
Jno.	7, 106, 246, 247, 248
Jno. S.	184, 234
John 8, 23, 55, 62, 81, 85, 86, 100, 107, 112, 116, 117, 125, 142, 143, 182, 231, 232, 237, 248, 249	
John S. 35, 57, 78, 79, 84, 91, 95, 161, 265	
John Spence	85
John, Sen.	76
Jos.	44, 145
Joseph 13, 15, 17, 32, 34, 48, 50, 55, 106, 124, 125, 127, 134, 140, 146, 147, 148,	

152, 154, 156, 176, 178,
    197, 212, 215, 216, 218,
    220, 227, 242, 262

Stephen	23, 51, 80
William	136
West's Ferry	97
Wests	
Jas.	199
Wetherington	
Nathn.	82
Robert	144
William	144
Wetherspoon	
David	86
Whaley	
William	185
Wharton	
Chrisr.	56, 69
David	56, 69, 74
Jas.	67
Wm	222
Wheadon	
John	69
Wheeding	
John	123
Whiding	
John	112
White	
Agatha	74
Agness	97
Lewis	202, 220, 221
Mary	115, 134

www.ingramcontent.com/pod-product-compliance
Lightning Source LLC
Chambersburg PA
CBHW052120270326
41930CB00012B/2703